The People of STRATHMORE

1600 - 1799

By
David Dobson

CLEARFIELD

Copyright © 2017
by David Dobson
All Rights Reserved

Printed for Clearfield Company by
Genealogical Publishing Company
Baltimore, Maryland
2017

ISBN 978-0-8063-5853-6

INTRODUCTION

The place-name Strathmore is derived from the Gaelic words *An Srath Mor*, signifying the broad or big valley. Strathmore lies in eastern Scotland, between the Grampian Mountains and the Sidlaw Hills, and runs in a north-east direction from Perth through eastern Perthshire, toward the Mearns alias Kincardineshire. Strathmore is a fertile valley containing several small towns and many farming communities.

The emphasis of this new book is on that part of Strathmore lying within the county of Angus (formerly known as Forfarshire), inasmuch as the western part of Strathmore, which lies in Perthshire, has been covered in my volume, *The People of Lowland Perthshire* [Baltimore, 2014]. *The People of Strathmore* identifies people living in the small towns,or burghs, of Kirriemuir, Forfar, and Brechin, as well as all the parishes in the area.

The major land-owning families of Strathmore were the Lyons based at Glamis, the Ogilvies at Cortachy, the Lindsays at Edzell, the Guthries at Guthrie, and the Carnegies (antecedents of the famous Andrew) at Farnell and at Kinnaird. These families were generally Royalist and, together with their followers, gave substantial support to the Jacobite Cause in the eighteenth century. [See *The Jacobites of Angus, 1689-1746* (Baltimore, 1997).] The Davidsons--of Harley-Davidson fame, the founder of the firm was born in Aberlemno—were also from Strathmore, and this book contains one of that name there, obviously of an earlier generation.

David Dobson, Dundee, Scotland, 2017

THE PEOPLE OF STRATHMORE, 1600-1799

ABBOTT, FREDERICK, in Glamis, 1681. [NRS.E69.11.1]

ABBOTT, JANET, in Glamis, 1681. [NRS.E69.11.1]

ABBOTT, WILLIAM, in Kinnetles, 1691. [NRS.E69.11.1]

ABBOTT, WILLIAM, in Glamis, 1681. [NRS.E69.11.1]

ABERCROMBIE, Mrs, in Forfar, 1759. [NRS.E326.1.169]

ADAM, AGNES, in Kingoldrum, testament, 1634, Comm. Brechin. [NRS]

ADAM, AGNES, spouse of William Leuchars a merchant citizen of Brechin, testament, 1634, Comm. Brechin. [NRS]

ADAM, ALEXANDER, a merchant in Brechin, testament, 1714, Comm. Brechin. [NRS]

ADAM, ALEXANDER, in Oathlaw, 1691. [NRS.E69.11.1]

ADAM, ALEXANDER, a mason in Forfar 1690s. [AA.F1.1.2] [NRS.E69.11.1]

ADAM. ALEXANDER, in Kinnetles, 1691. [NRS.E69.11.1]

ADAM, ALEXANDER, a merchant in Brechin, testament, 1714, Comm. Brechin. [NRS]

ADAM, ALEXANDER, in Forfar, 1753, 1759. [NRS.E326.1.169]

ADAM, ALEXANDER, 1768. [NRS.CH2.1302.2/31]

ADAM, ANDREW, servant of John Traill in Forfar, 1609. [RPCS.VIII.704]

ADAM, CHARLES, a mason in Forfar, husband of Elizabeth Wishart, daughter of Thomas Wishart at Milne of Glamis, sasine, 1680, 1686; deed, 1687. [AA.F5.103] [NRS.RS35.S3.VIII.280; RD4.61.974]

ADAM, CHARLES, servant to Thomas Keill in Inverarity, testament, 1657, Comm. Brechin. [NRS]

ADAM, CHARLES, a plasterer in Forfar before 1720. [AA.F5.97]

ADAM, DAVID, in Benshie, Kirriemuir, husband of Isobel Guthrie, testament, 24 October 1685, Comm. St Andrews. [NRS]

THE PEOPLE OF STRATHMORE, 1600-1799

ADAM, DAVID, in Forfar, 1759. [NRS.E326.1.169]

ADAM, DAVID, versus Torn and Ogilvie, Forfar Burgh Court, 2 June 1784, 5 November 1784; in Forfar, 1785, 1791. [NRS.E326.3.19][AA.F1.8.1]

ADAM, JAMES, and his spouse Margaret Walker, in Keithok, Brechin, testament, 1630, Comm. Brechin. [NRS]

ADAM, JAMES, in Guthrie, 1691. [NRS.E69.11.1]

ADAM, JAMES, minister at Cortachy, and his spouse Christian Straton, testament, 1695, Comm. Brechin. [NRS]

ADAM, JAMES, a plasterer in Forfar, was served heir to his father Charles Adam, a plasterer there, 1720. [AA.F5.97]

ADAM, JOHN, a tailor burgess of Brechin, testament, 1622, Comm. Brechin. [NRS]

ADAM, JOHN, in Kirriemuir, May 1686. [NRS.RH11.70.1/3]

ADAM, JOHN, a cordiner in Brechin, 1691. [RPCS.XVI.605]

ADAM, MARY, 1787. [NRS.CH2.1302.2/125]

ADAM, PATRICK, a baxter and councillor of Forfar, 1690s. [AA.F1.1.2] [NRS.E69.11.1]

ADAM, PATRICK, a baxter in Forfar, relict Agnes Adam, and children Elizabeth, John, and Patrick, a deed, 1705. [NRS.RD2.90/2.813]

ADAM, ROBERT, a cordiner in Brechin, 1621. [RPCS.XII.427]

ADAM, ROBERT, versus Henry and Adamson, Forfar Burgh Court, 17 November 1784. [AA.F1.8.1]

ADAM, THOMAS, in Cotton of Keithock, testament, 1634, his spouse Katherine Baillie, testament, 1628, Comm. Brechin. [NRS]

ADAM, THOMAS, son of William Adam a mason burgess, was admitted as a burgess and freeman of Forfar, 1690; a deed, 1697. [AA.F1.1.2][NRS.RD4.80.239; NRS.E69.11.1]

ADAM, WILLIAM, a mason and councillor of Forfar, 1687. [AA.F1.1.2]

THE PEOPLE OF STRATHMORE, 1600-1799

ADAMSON, ALEXANDER, a notary in Kirriemuir, father of Bessie and John, sasine, 1639. [NRS.RS35.S2.I.525, etc]

ADAMSON, ALEXANDER, in Kirriemuir, sasine, 1679. [NRS.RS35.S3.VII.45]

ADAMSON, ALEXANDER, a cordiner in Kirriemuir, sasine, 1694. [NRS.RS35.S3.IX.551]

ADAMSON, DAVID, a cordiner in Kirriemuir, husband of Isobel Nicoll, sasine, 1637. [NRS.RS35.S2.I.38]

ADAMSON, DAVID, son of David Adamson, a cordiner in West Roods of Kirriemuir, 1686, husband of (1) Isobel Cuthbert, (2) Agnes Mitchell, sasine, 1694. [NRS.RH11.70.1/4; RS35.S3.IX.389, etc]

ADAMSON, DAVID, in Kirriemuir, 1722. [NRS.CH2.1302.131]

ADAMSON, DAVID, a cordiner in Kirriemuir, husband of Isobel Cuthbert, sasines, 1704; dead by 1732. [NRS.RS35.11/74; GD7.2.151]

ADAMSON, DAVID, a brewer and vintner in Kirriemuir, sasines, 1770. [NRS.RS35.22/309, etc]

ADAMSON, DAVID, at the Denmilne of Glaswell, 1742, 1744. [NRS.RH11.70.7]

ADAMSON, DAVID, a chapman in Kirriemuir, 1745, son of Thomas Adamson a merchant there. [NRS.RH11.70.7]

ADAMSON, DAVID, versus D. Mauds, jr., Forfar Burgh Court, 16 June 1784, 25 June 1784; versus ... Malloch, 31 December1784; versus Patrick Neish, Forfar Burgh Court, 23 February1785; versus William Mitchell, Forfar Burgh Court, 4 November 1785. [AA.F1.8.1]

ADAMSON, GEORGE, in Kirriemuir, father of Thomas there, sasine, 1644. [NRS.RS35.S2.II.557]

ADAMSON, HELEN, spouse of William Doig in Kirriemuir, sasine, 1676. [NRS.RS35.S3.VI.93]

ADAMSON, ISABEL, a shopkeeper in Kirriemuir, 1741, 1745. [NRS.RH11.70.7]

ADAMSON, JAMES, in Balmadie, Rescobie, 1691. [NRS.E69.11.1]

THE PEOPLE OF STRATHMORE, 1600-1799

ADAMSON, JAMES, in Herdhill, 1730. [NRS.CH2.1302.179]

ADAMSON, JAMES, in Kirriemuir, 1732. [NRS.CH2.1302.189]

ADAMSON, JAMES, in the Kirkton of Kingoldrum, testament, 1738, Comm. Brechin. [NRS]

ADAMSON, JANE, an unmarried woman, 1783. [NRS.CH2.1302.2/97]

ADAMSON, JANET, the Countess Dowager of Southesk, testaments, 1683/1687, Comm. Brechin. [NRS]

ADAMSON, JOHN, in Kirriemuir, husband of Euphame Milne, sasine, 1639. [NRS.RS35.S2.I.471]

ADAMSON, JOHN, born 1622, a cordiner in Kirriemuir, died on 26 March 1674, father of Margaret. [Kirriemuir gravestone] [NRS.RS35.S3.IX.389]

ADAMSON, JOHN, a maltman in Kirriemuir, 1741. [NRS.RH11.70.7]

ADAMSON, JOHN, a flesher in Kirriemuir, 1745. [NRS.RH11.70.7]

ADAMSON, JOHN, a maltman in Kirriemuir, with a brewery at Kirkton of Airlie, 1774. [NRS.GD16.28.374]

ADAMSON, JOHN, born 1760, died 1819, spouse Elisabeth Bennet, born 1762, died 1799. [Kirriemuir gravestone]

ADAMSON, MARGARET, spouse of Thomas Mitchell a merchant in Kirriemuir, testaments, 1705, Comm. St Andrews. [NRS]

ADAMSON, PATRICK, in Glamis, 1681. [NRS.E69.11.1]

ADAMSON, ROBERT, tenant in Sheil Hill, 1731. [NRS.CH2.1302.181]

ADAMSON, ROBERT, 1743. [NRS.RH11.70.7]

ADAMSON, THOMAS, an elder in Kirriemuir, 1720, 1724, parish treasurer, 1728. [NRS.CH2.1302.1.121/145/169]

ADAMSON, THOMAS, a merchant in Kirriemuir, 1722, 1745, 1746. [NRS.CH2.1302.127; RH11.70.7]

THE PEOPLE OF STRATHMORE, 1600-1799

ADDISON, JANET, 1716. [NRS.CH2.1302.1.105]

ADESON, WALTER, in Muir Persie, Kingldrum, spouse Isobel Duncan, testament, 1621, Comm. Brechin. [NRS]

AIKEN, JOHN, in Strathcathro, 1691. [NRS.E69.11.1]

AIR, CHARLES, was served heir to his father George Air in Eastertoun of Guthrie in 1609. [NRS.Forfar.Retours]

AIR, D. died 1803. [Dunnichen gravestone]

AIR, GILBERT, a burgess of Brechin, bailie to James Hood of Keithock, a sasine, 1667. [NRS.RS35

AIR, WILIAM, in Eastertoun of Guthrie, born 1568, died 12 November 1641, spouse Bessie Scrymgeour, [Guthrie gravestone][RGS 1598,1610]

AIRTH, ALEXANDER, in Forfar, 1691. [NRS.E69.11.1]

AIRTH, JOHN, versus Webster and Barry, Forfar Burgh Court, 11 August 1784. [AA.F1.8.1]

AITKEN, JAMES, born 1757, minister of the Congregational Original Seceders in Kirriemuir, died 1834, wife born 1762, died 1822. [Kirriemuir gravestone]

AITKEN, JOHN, in Westerton of Strathcathro, testament, 1738, Comm. Brechin. [NRS]

AITKEN, WILLIAM, versus William Allan, Forfar Burgh Court, 2 July 1784. [AA.F1.8.1]

ALDIE, WILLIAM, a young man in Kirriemuir, 1723. [NRS.CH2.1302.139]

ALEXANDER, ALEXANDER, in Capo, Strathcathro, and Isobel Fotheringham his spouse, testament, 1628, Comm. Brechin. [NRS]

ALEXANDER, ALEXANDER, in Strathcathrow, testament, 1661, Comm. Brechin. [NRS]

ALEXANDER, ALEXANDER, in Methie Inverarity, 1691. [NRS.E69.11.1]

ALEXANDER, DAVID, in Herdhill, 1743. [NRS.RH11.70.7]

ALEXANDER, HELEN, an alleged witch imprisoned in Forfar, 1661, bond,1663. [AA.F5.35.3][RPCS.I.336]

THE PEOPLE OF STRATHMORE, 1600-1799

ALEXANDER, ISABEL, died 1768. [NRS.CH2.1302.2/29]

ALEXANDER, JAMES, a merchant burgess of Brechin, husband of Isobel Shepherd, testament, 1629, Comm. Brechin. [NRS]

ALEXANDER, JAMES, a maltman in Brechin, husband of Margaret Dall, a sasine, 1669. [NRS.RS35.83.IV.208]

ALEXANDER, JOHN, in Brechin, testament, 1612, Comm. Brechin. [NRS]

ALEXANDER, PATRICK, 1770; a church elder pre 1783. [NRS.CH2.1302.2/41/97]

ALEXANDER, WILLIAM, in Forfar, 1691. [NRS,E69.11.1]

ALEXANDER, WILLIAM, versus Rodger and Steel, Forfar Burgh Court, 25 June 1784. [AA.F1.8.1]

ALISON, COLIN, late servant to the Countess of Southesk, later in Farnell, testaments, 1754, 1760, Comm. Brechin. [NRS]

ALLAN, AGNES, in Kirriemuir, 1726. [NRS.CH2.1302.153]

ALLAN, ALEXANDER, in Forfar, 1691. [NRS.E69.11.1

ALLAN, ANDREW, in Kettins, testament, 1658, Comm. Brechin. [NRS]

ALLAN, ANDREW, bailie of Brechin, testament, 1676; relict Agnes Watson, testament, 1687, Comm. Brechin. [NRS]

ALLAN, DAVID, in Broomknowe, Farnell, spouse Isobel Dorward, born 1705, died 1762, children Robert, Thomas, John, Isobel, James, and George. [Kinnaird gravestone]

ALLAN, JAMES, a bailie and merchant in Brechin, a donor in 1689, husband of [1] Agnes Duncanson, testament, 1662, ans [2] Janet Coutts, sasine, 1673. [Brechin Cathedral] [NRS.RS35.S3.V.187]

ALLAN, JAMES, a cordiner in Kirriemuir, husband of Agnes Mylne, sasine, 1637. [NRS.RS35.S2.I.76]

ALLAN, JAMES, in Forfar, 1691. [NRS.E69.11.1]

ALLEN, JAMES, in Kinnetles, 1691. [NRS.E69.11.1]

THE PEOPLE OF STRATHMORE, 1600-1799

ALLAN, JOHN, in Cotton of Wester Futhie, Farnell, and spouse Katherine Jameson, testament, 1611, Comm. Brechin. [NRS]

ALLAN, JOHN, in Kirriemuir, sasine, 1654. [NRS.RS35.S2.IV.398]

ALLAN, JOHN, in Aberlemno, 1691. [NRS.E69.11.1]

ALLAN, ROBERT, a flesher in Brechin,1691.[RPCS.xvi.605]

ALLAN, THOMAS, a cadger burgess of Brechin, testament, 1614, Comm. Brechin. [NRS]

ALLAN, WILLIAM, versus Miller and Ramsay, Forfar Burgh Court, 11 August 1784. [AA.F1.8.1]

ALLARDYCE, DAVID, of Memus, a merchant in Brechin, testaments, 1792-1793, Comm. Brechin. [NRS]

ALLARDYCE, GEORGE, in Farnell, 1691. [NRS.E69.11.1]

ALLARDYCE, JAMES, a weaver in Brechin, his relict Jean, testament, 1792, Comm. Brechin. [NRS]

ALLARDICE, PATRICK, in Glamis, 1691. [NRS.E69.11.1]

ALLARDYCE, ROBERT, of Memus, a merchant in Brechin, testament,1793, Comm. Brechin. [NRS]

ALLARDYCE, SYLVESTER, in Glamis, testament, 1718, Comm. St Andrews. [NRS]

ALLARDYCE, THOMAS, in Easter Drums, Brechin, spouse Christian Soutar, testament, 1637, Comm. Brechin. [NRS]

ANDERSON, ALEXANDER, a burgess of Forfar, an assizeman in 1600. [RGS.VI.1176]

ANDERSON, ALEXANDER, in the Haugh, a donor in 1664, [Brechin Cathedral]

ANDERSON, ANDREW, in Forfar, 1691. [NRS.E69.11.1]

ANDERSON, ANDREW, in Dunnichen, 1691. [NRS.E69.11.1]

ANDERSON, ARCHIBALD, a burgess of Forfar, spouse Helen Wood, testament, 1620, Comm. St Andrews. [NRS]

ANDERSON, ARCHIBALD, in Guthrie, 1691. [NRS.E69.11.1]

ANDERSON, COLIN, in Forfar, 1691. [NRS.E69.11.1]

THE PEOPLE OF STRATHMORE, 1600-1799

ANDERSON, DAVID, in Forfar, 1691. [NRS.E69.11.1]

ANDERSON, DAVID, son of David Anderson a cordiner, was admitted as a burgess and freeman of Forfar, 1686. [AA.F1.1.2], in Forfar, 1691. [NRS.E69.11.1]

ANDERSON, DAVID, in Rescobie, 1691. [NRS.E69.11.1]

ANDERSON, FRANCIS, born 1737, tenant in Broadfold, died 1802, spouse Ann Smith. [Rescobie gravestone]

ANDERSON, GEORGE, guild officer of Brechin, testament, 1688, Comm.Brechin. [NRS]

ANDERSON, GEORGE, versus Wilkie and Soutar, 9 June 1784; versus Thomas Wilkie, Forfar Burgh Court, 1 December 1784; versus .... Rodger, Forfar Burgh Court, 1December 1784. [AA.F1.8.1]

ANDERSON, ISOBEL, in Kinnordie, 1717. [NRS.CH2.1302.1.107]

ANDERSON, JAMES, a baxter burgess of Brechin, 1605. [RPCS.VII.616]

ANDERSON, JAMES, in Kinclune, Kingoldrum, testament, 1629, Comm. Brechin. [NRS],

ANDERSON, JAMES, in Burnside of Ballindarge, 1745. [NRS.RH11.70.7]

ANDERSON, JAMES, a tailor in Forfar, wife Katherine Tarbat, born 1758, died 1783. [Forfar gravestone]

ANDERSON, JAMES, versus Alexander Bower, 9 June 1784; versus ... Peter, Forfar Burgh Court, 11 August 1784; versus Alexander Bower, Forfar Burgh Court, 22 September 1784, 2 February 1785, 23 February 1785, 1 April 1785; versus David Robertson, 18 February 1785. [AA.F1.8.1]

ANDERSON, JOHN, a tanner in Kirriemuir, sasine, 1631. [NRS.RS35.S1.VIII.162]

ANDERSON, JOHN, a merchant in Kirriemuir, sasine, 1665. [NRS.RS35.S3.II.334]

ANDERSON, JOHN, son of Andrew Anderson, was admitted as a burgess and freeman of Forfar, 1688. [AA.F1.1.2], in Forfar,1691. [NRS.E69.11.1]

THE PEOPLE OF STRATHMORE, 1600-1799

ANDERSON, JOHN, in Glamis, 1734. [NRS.CH2.1302.201]

ANDERSON, JOHN, born 1718, overseer at Pitmouies, died 1782, wife Ann Lawson. [Guthrie gravestone]

ANDERSON, JOHN, versus .... Peter, Forfar Burgh Court, 11 August 1784. [AA.F1.8.1]

ANDERSON, MAGDALENE, in Brechin, testament, 1783, Comm. Brechin. [NRS]

ANDERSON, PATRICK, a cordiner in Kirriemuir, husband of Katherine MacNab, sasine, 1669. [NRS.RS35.S3.IV.382]

ANDERSON, THOMAS, a merchant in Kirriemuir, husband of Isabel Peddie, father of Beatrix, sasine, 1665. [NRS.RS35.S3.II.334]

ANDERSON, THOMAS, son of David Anderson a cordiner burgess, was admitted as a burgess and freeman of Forfar, 1689. [AA.F1.1.2]

ANDERSON, WALTER, in Kirriemuir, a tack, 1661. [NRS.RD4.2.659]

ANDERSON, WILLIAM, a burgess of Forfar, an assizeman in 1600; a bailie there in 1607, 1608. [RGS.VI.1176][RPCS.VII.408; VIII.647]

ANNAN, ARCHIBALD, in Cotton of Gardin, Idvie, testament, 1682, Comm. St Andrews. [NRS]

ANNAND, JOHN, in Kirriemuir, husband of Margaret Young, a sasine,1643. [NRS.RS35.S2.II.370]

ANNAND, THOMAS, in Kinquhirrie, Kirriemuir, husband of Margaret Lyell, testament, 27 March 1616, Comm. St Andrews. [NRS]

ARBUTHNOTT, WILLIAM, in Kirriemuir, sasine, 1712. [NRS.RS35.12/227]

ARCHER, JOHN, of Drumshade, the younger, 1783. [NRS.CH2.1302.2/93]

ARCHER, WILLIAM, in Kinnell, 1691. [NRS.E69.11.1]

THE PEOPLE OF STRATHMORE, 1600-1799

ARCHIBALD, JAMES, a wheelwright burgess of Brechin, testament, 1663, Comm. Brechin. [NRS]

ARCHIBALD, WILLIAM, in Pendriche, Brechin, testament, 1612, Comm. Brechin. [NRS]

ARCHIBALD, WILLIAM, an alleged thief imprisoned in Forfar, 1665. [RPCS.II.101]

ARCHIT, JOHN, in Kinnell, 1691. [NRS.E69.11.1]

ARNOT, ALEXANDER, versus William Simson, Forfar Burgh Court, 25 May 1785. [AA.F1.8.1]

ARNOT, ANDREW, a gardener in Guthrie, 1691. [NRS.E69.11.1]

ARNOT, JAMES, a merchant burgess of Brechin, testament, 1688, Comm. Brechin. [NRS]

ARNOTT, JAMES, in Tannadice, 1691. [NRS.E69.11.1]

ARNOTT, JAMES, in Glamis, 1681. [NRS.E69.11.1]

ARNOTT, ROBERT, in Kirkton of Kinnell, sasine, 1741. [AA.F1.4.3]

ARNOTT, THOMAS, in Achnacaret, Brechin, testament, 1622, Comm. Brechin. [NRS]

ARNOT, WILLIAM, in Forfar, 1691. [NRS.E69.11.1]

ARNOT, Mr, minister of Tannadice, 1691. [NRS.E69.11.1]

ARROT, ISOBEL, in Cotton of Arrot, testament, 1610, Comm. Brechin. [NRS]

ARROT, JOHN, the younger of Foffarty, 1719. [NRS.CH2.1302.1.119]

ARROT, THOMAS, MD, brother of John Arrot of Foffarty, 1745. [AA.F14.3/14]

ARROT, WILLIAM, and spouse Margaret Fullarton, in Grange of Airlie, testament, 1659, Comm. Brechin. [NRS]

ARTHUR, ALLEN, in Guthrie, 1691. [NRS.E69.11.1]

THE PEOPLE OF STRATHMORE, 1600-1799

AUCHTERLONIE, JOHN, servant of the Commissary of Brechin, 1615. [RGS.VII.1167]

AUCHTERLONIE, JOHN, Provost of Brechin, husband of Agnes Carnegie, sasine, 1637. [NRS.RS35.S2.1.2]

AUCHTERLONIE, JOHN, in Brechin, 1656. [RGS.X.550]

AUCHMUTHIE, Captain GEORGE, was admitted as a burgess of Forfar, 1661. [AA.F1.1.1]

AULD, GEORGE, in Forfar, 1604. [RPCS.VII.564]

AULD, GEORGE, a cordiner in Forfar, brother of James Auld, burgess of Forfar, sasine, 1686; dead by 1692. [NRS.RS35.S3.VIII.435; GD1.61.12]

AULD, JAMES, Deacon of the Tailors' Craft in Forfar, 1668, 1681; a burgess of Forfar, sasine, 1686, son of Margaret Thornton. [NRS.GD1.61.6] [AA.F1.1.1] [RBF#216] [NRS.RS35.S3.VIII.435] , in Forfar,1691. [NRS.E69.11.1]

AULD, JAMES, a maltman in Forfar, 1689. [AA.F1.1.2]

AULD, JOHN, in Forfar, 1608. [RPCS.VIII.647]

AULD, JOHN, bailie and treasurer of Forfar, 1660. [AA.F1.1.1]

AULDIE, JOHN, at the Mill of Logy, 1746. [NRS.RH11.70.7]

AUSTIN, DAVID, born 1660, weaver in Moss-side of Towk, died 1723. [Kirkden gravestone]

AUSTIN, JOHN, a merchant in Brechin, a deed, 1688. [NRS.RD4.62.390]

BADENOCH, JAMES, a merchant in Kirriemuir, 1741, 1744. [NRS.RH11.70.7]

BALFOUR, JANET, in Capo, Strathcathro, testament, 1692, Comm. Brechin. [NRS]

BAILLIE, ALEXANDER, burgess of Brechin, husband of Agnes Finlason, sasines, 1638. [NRS.RS35.S2.I.160/234/236]

BAILLIE, DAVID, a miller burgess of Brechin, testament, 1596, Comm. Brechin. [NRS]

BAILLIE, DAVID, and his spouse Janet Kinugmont, in Wester Balnabriche, testament, 1621, Comm. Brechin. [NRS]

BAILLIE, DAVID, merchant burgess of Brechin and his spouse Katherine Knox, testament, 1646, father of Barbara, testament, 1658, Comm. Brechin. [NRS]

BAILLIE, GEORGE, merchant in Brechin, 1691. [RPCS.XVI.605]

BAILLIE, JAMES, a burgess of Brechin, husband of Bessie Scott, parents of Elspeth and Isabel, sasine, 1675. [NRS.RS35.S3.VI.11]

BAILLIE, JOHN, father of Alexander Baillie, burgess of Brechin, sasine, 1638. [NRS.RS35.S2.I.236]

BAILLIE, JOHN, burgess of Brechin, late in Birkenbush, sasine, 1644. [NRS.RS35.S2.II.376]

BAILLIE, JOHN, a merchant in Brechin, husband of Margaret Watson, a sasine, 1669, a donor in 1673. [Brechin Cathedral] [NRS.RS35.S3.IV.275]

BAILLIE, THOMAS, sr., and jr. in Brechin, 1606. [RPCS.VII.643]

BAYLIE, THOMAS, in Kinnell, 1691. [NRS.E69.11.1]

BAILLIE, WILLIAM, in Finavon in Oathlaw, 1691. [NRS.E69.11.1]

BAILLIE, WILLIAM, a merchant in Brechin, a sasine, 1691. [RPCS.XVI.605][NRS.RS35.S3.VIII.428]

BAILLIE, ALEXANDER, of Whitewells, bailie of the Regality of Kirriemuir, 1741. [NRS.RH11.70.7]

BAIN, ALEXANDER, in Glamis, 1681. [NRS.E69.11.1]

BAIRES, JAMES, in Glamis, 1681. [NRS.E69.11.1]

BALL, ROBERT, a weaver in Wester Tarbine, 1733. [NRS.CH2.1302.199]

BALLENTYNE, ALEXANDER, brother of Andrew Ballentyne, a merchant in Kirriemuir, a sasine, 1768. [NRS.RS35.22.390]

THE PEOPLE OF STRATHMORE, 1600-1799

BALLENTYNE, ANDREW, a merchant in Kirriemuir, son of Andrew Ballentyne of Turfhaugh and his wife Isobel Winter, husband of Isobel Wilson, a sasine, 1750. [NRS.RS25.17/83]

BALLINGALL, JAMES, a merchant in Forfar, sasine witness, 1744. [AA.F1.4.3]

BALVAIRD, JOHN, minister, in Glamis, 1681. [NRS.E69.11.1]

BARCLAY, ANDREW, a prisoner in Brechin Tolbooth, 1691. [RPCS.XVI.632]

BARCLAY, ANNA, widow of David, Bishop of Brechin, a donor in 1682. [Brechin Cathedral]

BARCLAY, GEORGE, a weaver in Kirriemuir, 1745. [NRS.RH11.70.7]

BARCLAY, JAMES, in Woodside, a tack, 10 March 1690. [AA/F5/23]

BARCLAY, ROBERT, of Syde, Strathcathro, testament, 1635, Comm. Brechin. [NRS]

BARNETT, DAVID, in Overinch, Kirriemuir, husband of Margaret Adam, testament, 16 January 1618, Comm. St Andrews. [NRS]

BARNET, DAVID, a weaver in Kirriemuir, husband of Janet Young, sasine, 1631. [NRS.RS35.S1.VIII.234]

BARNETT, DAVID, in Hillockhead of Caldham, 1744. [NRS.RH11.70.7]

BARNETT, DAVID, son of Thomas Barnett, a merchant in Kirriemuir, and spouse Margaret Martin, sasines, 1776. [NRS.RS35.25/250, etc]

BARNETT, JAMES, son of Thomas Barnett, a merchant in Kirriemuir, and spouse Margaret Martin, a sasine, 1776. [NRS.RS35.25/250]

BARNETT, JOHN, son of Thomas Barnett, a merchant in Kirriemuir, and spouse Margaret Martin, a sasine,1776. [NRS.RS35.25/250]

BARNETT, THOMAS, in Tannadice, 1691. [NRS.E69.11.1]

THE PEOPLE OF STRATHMORE, 1600-1799

BARNEY, JOHN, servant to the laird of Logie, 1720. [NRS.CH2.1302.1.123]

BARRENT, JOHN, in Tannadice, 1691. [NRS.E69.11.1]

BARRIE, ANDREW, a tailor in Kirriemuir, husband of Isobel Sand, sasines,1763. [NRS.RS35.20/223, etc]

BARRY, CHARLES, versus ... Ramsay, Forfar Burgh Court, 5 November 1784. [AA.F1.8.1]

BARRIE, ELIZABETH, 1785. [NRS.CH2.1302.2/115]

BARRIE, JAMES, a cordiner burgess of Forfar, testament, 1608, Comm. Edinburgh. [NRS]

BARRIE, JAMES, in Forfar, 1691. [NRS.E69.11.1]

BARRY, JAMES, born 1687, died 9 November 1764, husband of Agnes Grahame, born 1693, died 20 April 1740, in Newtyle, parents of James and William Barry. [Nevay gravestone]

BARRIE, JAMES, versus Patrick Neish, Forfar Burgh Court, 15 December 1784; versus Webster Mitchell, Forfar Burgh Court, 13 April 1785; versus Burnet and Allenrick, Forfar Burgh Court, 4 November 1785. [AA.F1.8.1]

BARRY, JAMES, in Herdhill, 1736. [NRS.CH2.1302.211]

BARRY, JAMES, in Hillhead, 1766. [NRS.CH2.1302.2/23]

BARRY, JAMES, in Logy, 1745. [NRS.RH11.70.7]

BARRIE, JANE, 1785. [NRS.CH2.1302.2/115]

BARRIE, JOHN, a merchant and cess collector of Forfar, 1688. [AA.F1.1.2], in Forfar, 1691. [NRS.E60.11.1]

BARRIE, JOHN, in Oathlaw, 1691. [NRS.E69.11.1]

BARRIE, JOHN, versus Andrew Millar, Forfar Burgh Court, 29 December 1784. [AA.F1.8.1]

BARRIE, JOHN, and Robert Milne, versus John Roberts, Forfar Burgh Court, 30 March 1785. [AA.F1.8.1]

BARRY, PATRICK, versus ... Irons, Forfar Burgh Court, 1 December 1784. [AA.F1.8.1]

THE PEOPLE OF STRATHMORE, 1600-1799

BARRIE, WILLIAM, in Forfar, spouse Margaret Henderson, testament, 1614, Comm.St Andrews. [NRS]

BARRY, WILLIAM, weaver in Kirriemuir, 1745. [NRS.RH11.70.7]

BARRIE, WILLIAM, born 1752, died 1827, spouse Jean Stevenson, born 1748, died 1831. [Kirriemuir gravestone]

BARRON, DAVID, a merchant in Brechin, testament, 1686, Comm. Brechin. [NRS]

BARRON, DAVID, a writer in Kirriemuir, 1733, bailie depute of the Regality of Kirriemuir, spouse of Isobel Deuchar, 1742, 1743, 1746; testament, 1764, Comm. St Andrews. [NRS.CH2.1302.199; RH11.70.7; RS35.16/146]

BARRON, DAVID, a shoemaker in Mireside, husband of Jean Scott, parents of Alexander born 1711, died 4 June 1732, and Alexander born 1712, died 25 December 1726. [Nevay gravestone]

BARRON, EDWARD, a writer in Kirriemuir, son of David Barron a writer there, sasines,1776, testaments, 1786, 1788, Comm. St Andrews. [NRS.RS35.25/494, etc]

BARTIE, DAVID, in Aberlemno, 1691. [NRS.E69.11.1]

BARTIE, THOMAS, in Aberlemno, 1691. [NRS.E69.11.1]

BASSLOUR, JOHN, in Heughhead of Guthrie, testament, 1686.Comm. Brechin. [NRS]

BAUTIE, JOHN, in Haugh Muir of Brechin, testament, 1637, Comm. Brechin. [NRS]

BAXTER, JOHN, a baker in Kirriemuir, sasine, 1780. [NRS.RS35.28/237]

BAXTER, PATRICK, in Rescobie, 1691. [NRS.E69.11.1]

BAYELL, DAVID, in Forfar,1691. [NRS.E69.11.1]

BAYELL, WILLIAM, in Forfar, 1691. [NRS.E60.11.1]

BAYNE, ALEXANDER, a flesher in Brechin, 1691. [RPCS.XVI.605]

THE PEOPLE OF STRATHMORE, 1600-1799

BAINE, JOHN, and spouse Isobel Taylor, in Mains of Futhie, Farnell, testament, 1629, Comm. Brechin. [NRS]

BEAN, ROBERT, in Cotton of Tullose, Forfar, testament, 1777, Comm. St Andrews. [NRS]

BEARN, ANNA, in Roods of Kirriemuir, 1745. [NRS.RH11.70.7]

BEATON, ALEXANDER, in Forfar,1691. [NRS.E69.11.1]

BEATON, CHARLES, tacksman in Forfar, 1680s. [AA.F1.1.2]

BEATON, CHARLES, a flesher in Forfar, deeds, 1689, 1690. [NRS.RD3.70.13; RD4.65.1023]

BEATON, CHARLES, a flesher in Forfar, deeds, 1689, 1690. [NRS.RD3.70.13; RD4.65.1023]

BEATON, CHARLES, a burgess of Forfar, a deed, 1700. [NRS.RD2.83.826]

BEATON, DAVID, heir to Thomas Beaton, Forfar Burgh Court, 13 May 1784. [AA.F1.8.1]

BEATON, JEAN, in Dunnichen 1691. [NRS.E69.11.1]

BEATON, JOHN, in Kinnetles, 1691. [NRS.E69.11.1]

BEATON, THOMAS, in Tannadice, 1691. [NRS.E69.11.1]

BEATTIE, AGNES, spouse to Andrew Dugal a wright, died 1654. [Kirriemuir gravestone]

BEATTIE, WILLIAM, in Keithock, relict Isobel Praitt, testament, 1611, Comm. Brechin. [NRS]

BEDDY, THOMAS, in Cotton of Pitpullocks, Brechin, testament, 1627. [NRS]

BEG, ALEXANDER, in Kirkhill of Farnell, spouse of Margaret Wood, testament, 1625, Comm. Brechin. [NRS]

BEINE, MICHAEL, a messenger in Forfar, 1685. [RPCS.X.387]

BELL, ALEXANDER, born 1738 in Kirriemuir, a laborer who enlisted in Major James Clephane's Company of the 78th [Fraser's

Highlanders] Regiment in Dundee on 10 February 1757, probably fought in the French and Indian Wars in North America. [NRS.GD125.22.16/17]

BELL, ROBERT, and spouse Grissell Symmer in Dubton, testament, 1629, Comm. Brechin. [NRS]

BELL, ROBERT, and JOHN, versus Alexander Robertson, Forfar Burgh Court, 23 March 1785. [AA.F1.8.1]

BELLIE, ANDREW, in Tannadice, 1691. [NRS.E69.11.1]

BELLIE, GEORGE, a burgess of Forfar, spouse Margaret Hunter, testament, 1618, Comm. St Andrews. [NRS]

BELLIE, ISOBEL, in Forfar, 1691. [NRS.E60.11.1]

BELLIE, Mr JAMES, in Forfar, 1691. [NRS.E69.11.1]

BELLIE, PETER, in Forfar, 1691. [NRS.E69.11.1]

BENE, PATRICK, a burgess of Forfar, 1620. [RPCS.XII.189]

BENNY, AGNES, in Forfar, 1691. [NRS.E69.11.1]

BENNY, ALEXANDER, bailie of Forfar, 1660; councillor there 1680s [AA.F1.1.1/2]; a dyer in Forfar, 1691. [NRS.E69.11.1]

BENNIE, ANDREW, in Forfar, 1759. [NRS.E326.1.169]

BENNIE, DAVID, a cordiner in Forfar, 1691. [NRS.E69.11.1]

BENNIE, ELSPET, in Forfar, 1691. [NRS.E69.11.1]

BENNY, GEORGE, in Forfar, 1691. [NRS.E69.11.1]

BENNY, JAMES, a shoemaker burgess of Forfar, eldest son of the late John Benny a shoemaker burgess, an obligation to John Benny his brother in law and Isobel Benny spouse of John and sister of James, 1650. [AA.F5.37]; the elder, bailie of Forfar, 1660. [AA.F1.1.1]

BENNY, JAMES, the younger, bailie of Forfar, 1660. [AA.F1.1.1]

BENNY, JAMES, a cordiner in Forfar, husband of Margaret Dickison, sasine, 1676. [NRS.RS35.S3.VI.178]

BENNIE, JAMES, in Forfar, 1759. [NRS.E326.1.169]

BENNY, JOHN, a skinner in Forfar, a bond, 1661.
[NRS.RD4.2.356]

BENNY, JOHN, son of James Benny, a cordiner in Forfar, husband of Isobel Benny, sasine, 1662.
[NRS.RS35.S2.III.338,][AA.F5.38/48]

BENNY, JOHN, Deacon of the Tailors of Forfar, 1655.
[RBF#216]

BENNY, JOHN, a bailie and councillor of Forfar, deeds, 1683, 1688, 1689, 1687-1690, 1691. [NRS.RD3.55.317; RD4.63.874; RD4.64.619; E69.11.1] [AA.F1.1.2]

BENNY, JOHN, heir to his father John Benny a shoemaker burgess, and Agnes Hummell his apparent spouse, liferent of a tenement in Forfar and of a rig in Whythills, 1693, 1696. [AA.F5.42/43] in Forfar, 1691. [NRS.E60.11.1]

BENNEY, MITCHELL, in Forfar, 1691. [NRS.E69.11.1]

BENNY, PATRICK, a burgess of Forfar, spouse Bessie Hunter, testament, 1620, Comm. St Andrews. [NRS]

BENNY, PATRICK, a burgess of Forfar, sasine, 1653, disposition, 1667. [NRS.RS35.S2.IV.203][AA.F5.90]

BENNIE, THOMAS, son of David Bennie a cordiner, was admitted as a burgess and freeman of Forfar, 1686. [AA.F1.1.2]; 1691. [NRS.E69.11.1]

BENNIE, THOMAS, in Forfar, 1691. [NRS.E60.11.1]

BETTY, DAVID, versus William Watt, Forfar Burgh Court, 8 September 1784. [AA.F1.8.1]

BINNING, JAMES, in Kinnell, 1691. [NRS.E69.11.1]

BINNING, MICHAEL, a messenger in Forfar, a bond, 1676. [NRS.RD4.38.605]

BINNY, ALEXANDER, born 1626, died on 20 June 1665. [Forfar gravestone]

BINNY, ALEXANDER, a litster in Forfar, a deed, 1696. [NRS.RD3.86.108]

THE PEOPLE OF STRATHMORE, 1600-1799

BINNIE, ALEXANDER, a litster in Forfar, deed, 1701. [NRS.RD4.89.69]

BINNY, ALEXANDER, of Whytewell, bailie depute of the Regality of Kirriemuir, 1742. [NRS.RH11.70.7]

BINNY, ALEXANDER, of Whitehall, provost of Forfar, sasine,1744; father of Alexander Binny, 1745. [AA,F1.4.3][NRS.GD45.1.228]

BINNY, ANDREW, town clerk of Forfar, protocol book, 1741-1762; 1745; 1748.[AA.F1.4.3] [NRS.NRAS#124/4/1/77; GD16.25.121]

BINNY, ANDREW, a shoemaker in Forfar, husband of Christian Hunter, a sasine, 1759. [NRS.RS35.19.14]

BINNY, ANDREW, protocol book, 1761. [AA.F1.4.3]

BINNY, ANDREW, born 1740, stamp-master in Forfar, died 1832, husband of Catherine Binny, born 1770, died 1844. [Forfar gravestone][NRS.E326.1.169]

BINNY, ANDREW, an inn-keeper in Forfar, 1777. [NRS.NRAS#124/4/1/78]

BINNY, ANDREW, versus ..... Wood, Forfar Burgh Court, 16 June 1784, 25 June 1784; versus Patrick Neish, Forfar Burgh Court, 2 February 1785; versus ...Nicoll, Forfar Burgh Court, 18 February 1785; 23 February1785. [AA.F1.8.1]

BINNY, DAVID, a shoemaker in Forfar, and spouse Margaret Thornton, disposition,1784. [AA]

BINNY, GEORGE, the elder, a shoemaker in Forfar, decreet, 16.. [AA.F5.41]

BINNY, JAMES, a cordiner and bailie of Forfar, son of Alexander Binny, 1658. [AA.F1.4.1]

BINNY, JAMES, a bailie in Forfar, 1753. [NRS.E326.1.169]

BINNY, JOHN, a burgess of Forfar, 1675. [AA.F5.36]

BINNY, JOHN, the younger, a shoemaker in Forfar, 16... [AA.F5.41]

THE PEOPLE OF STRATHMORE, 1600-1799

BINNY, JOHN, a bailie of Forfar, deeds, 1696, 1701.
[NRS.RD3.86.108; RD4.89.69]

BINNIE, JOHN, an innkeeper in Forfar, 1745.
[NRS.NRAS#124/4/1/75]

BINNY, JOHN, shoemaker in Forfar, spouse of Margaret Rhind, eldest son of the late Thomas Binny, shoemaker in Forfar, sasine, 1792. [NRS.B26.2.6]

BINNY, WILLIAM, in Forfar, 1734. [NRS.GD24.3.351]

BINNY, WILLIAM, a bailie in Forfar, versus Thomas Mitchell, 1 April 1785. [NRS.E326.3.19][AA.F1.8.1]

BISSET, ALEXANDER, MA King's College, Aberdeen, 1605, master of Brechin Grammar School 1606, minister there 1608, died 29 January 1644. Husband of [1] Jean Ogilvie -testament 1628, [2] Margaret Fullerton, parents of Robert and Margaret, testament, 1644, Comm. Brechin. [NRS]

BLACK, ANDREW, in Oathlaw, 1691. [NRS.E69.11.1]

BLACK, ANDREW, a gardener in Kirriemuir, a sasine, 1760. [NRS.RS35.19/486]

BLACK, DAVID, in Hillhead of Stannoch, spouse Janet Watson, testament, 1630, Comm. Brechin. [NRS]

BLACK, DAVID, a wright in Brechin, 1691. [RPCS.XVI.605]

BLACK, DAVID, in Rescobie, 1691. [NRS.E69.11.1]

BLACK, DAVID, born 1688, farmer in Templeton, died 16 February 1751, father of William, David, Jean, and Mary Black. [Nevay gravestone]

BLACK, ELIZABETH, in Kingoldrum, 1743. [NRS.RH11.70.7]

BLACK, GEORGE, a cordiner burgess of Brechin, and his spouse Janet Bowack, testament, 1656, Comm. Brechin. [NRS]

BLACK, HELEN, born 1677, died 1705. [Aberlemno gravestone]

BLACK, JAMES, and his spouse Agnes Dalgetty, in Brechin, testament, 1674, Comm. Brechin. [NRS]

BLACK, JAMES, in Glamis, 1691. [NRS.E69.11.1]

THE PEOPLE OF STRATHMORE, 1600-1799

BLACK, JAMES, in Aberlemno, 1691. [NRS.E69.11.1]

BLACK, JAMES, in Tannadice, 1691. [NRS.E69.11.1]

BLACK, JAMES, son of late Andrew Black, in Hillhead of Careston, testament, 1704, Comm. Brechin. [NRS]

BLACK, JOHN, in Tannadice, 1691. [NRS.E69.11.1]

BLACK, JOHN, a tailor in Forfar, 1753. [NRS.E326.1.169]

BLACK, JOHN, a weaver in Kirriemuir, a sasine, 1775. [NRS.RS35.25/147]

BLACK, MARGARET, spouse of Andrew Duncan in Ground of Langbank, 1745. [NRS.CH2.1302.247]

BLACK, WILLIAM, born 1763, a weaver in Paddock Hall, died 15 January 1805, husband of Helen Mitchell. [Nevay gravestone]

BLACKHALL, THOMAS, in Unthank, Brechin, spouse Margaret White, testaments, 1627 and 1638, Comm. Brechin. [NRS]

BLAIR, DAVID, versus James Wood, Forfar Burgh Court, 16 June 1784, 25 June 1784. [AA.F1.8.1]

BLAIR, JOHN, in Glamis, 1681. [NRS.E69.11.1]

BLAIR, PATRICK, in Glamis, 1681. [NRS.E69.11.1]

BOATH, DAVID, in Forfar, 1691. [NRS.E60.11.1]

BOATH, DAVID, versus Baxter and Smith, Forfar Burgh Court, 5 November 1784. [AA.F1.8.1]

BLYTH, JAMES, cotter in Linlathen, Kirriemuir, husband of Janet Colzear, testament, 9 July 1616, Comm. St Andrews. [NRS]

BOATH, DAVID, in Cotton of Gardin, Idvie, spouse Janet Deuchars, testament, 1606, Comm. St Andrews. [NRS]

BOATH, JAMES, of Caldham, was admitted as a burgess of Forfar, 1661. [AA.F1.1.1]

BOATH, WILLIAM, born 1708, tenant in Weltoun, died 1773. [Forfar gravestone]

BOOKE, WALTER, a cordiner in Brechin, 1621. [RPCS.XII.427]

21

THE PEOPLE OF STRATHMORE, 1600-1799

BOOTH, THOMAS, in Kinnetles, 1691. [NRS.E69.11.1]

BOOTH, WILLIAM, in Forfar,1691. [NRS.E69.11.1]

BOUMAN, ALEXANDER, in Forfar,1691. [NRS.E69.11.1]

BOUMAN, JAMES, in Forfar,1691. [NRS.E69.11.1]

BOUMAN, JOHN, in Dunnichen, 1691. [NRS.E69.11.1]

BOWACK, ALEXANDER, in Kinnell, 1691. [NRS.E69.11.1]

BOWACK, DAVID, in Kinnell, 1691. [NRS.E69.11.1]

BOWACK, JOHN, in Rescobie, 1691. [NRS.E69.11.1]

BOWELL, WILLIAM, schoolmaster of Farnell, 1690. [SHS.4.2]

BOWAR, ALEXANDER, heir to his father Alexxander Bowar of Kincaldrum, 1680. [NRS.Retours.Forfar.477]

BOWER, ALEXANDER, of Kilcaldrum in Methie Inverarity, 1691. [NRS.E69.11.1]

BOWER, ALEXANDER, a factor in Methie Inverarity, 1691. [NRS.E69.11.1]

BOWER, ALEXANDER, of Kincaldrum, letters, 1766-1772. [NRS.GD503.144]

BOWER, ALEXANDER, versus Alexander Smith, Forfar Burgh Court, 27 October 1784; versus ...Low, Forfar Burgh Court, 29 December1784. [AA.F1.8.1]

BOWER, JAMES, and spouse Isobel Hunter in Balnabriche, testament, 1613, Comm. Brechin. [NRS]

BOWER, PATRICK, in Kinnetles, 1691. [NRS.E69.11.1]

BOWER, WILLIAM, of Kinnettles, heir to his grandfather Patrick Bower of Wester Methie after of Kinnettles, sasine, 1744. [AA.F1.4.3]

BOWIE, IAN, in Hatton of Glen Ogilvy, 1797. [NRS.E326.10.3.24]

BOWMAN, ALEXANDER, a burgess of Forfar, husband of Margaret Hutcheon, 1721, 1733. [AA.F5.135/137]

THE PEOPLE OF STRATHMORE, 1600-1799

BOWMAN, ANDREW, a reedmaker in Forfar, son of John Bowman, a weaver there, 1772. [AA.F5.148]

BOWMAN, JANET, daughter of John Bowman, and wife of Alexander Tarbat a weaver in Forfar, 1773. [AA.F5.149]

BOWMAN, JAMES, a weaver in Kirriemuir, lately in Caldham, sasine, 1744. [NRS.RS35.16/559, etc]

BOWMAN, JOHN, a weaver in Forfar, 1745. [AA.F5.44]

BOWMAN, MATTHEW, a merchant in Brechin, father of Margaret, sasines, 1653. [NRS.RS35.S2.IV.385, etc]

BOWMAN, PATRICK, relict Marjorie Dougall, in Kirriemuir, sasine, 1727. [NRS.RS35.14/271]

BOWMAN, Captain THOMAS, a burgess of Brechin, testament, 1595, Comm. Edinburgh. [NRS]

BOYACK, JAMES, and spouse Isobel Gray at the Haugh Mill of Brechin, testament, 1668, Comm. Brechin. [NRS]

BOYLE, GIDEON, in Rescobie, 1691. [NRS.E69.11.1]

BOYLE, JAMES, in Dunnichen, 1691. [NRS.E69.11.1]

BOYLE, JANET, in Kirriemuir, 1719.[NRS.CH2.1302.1.117]

BOYLE, JOHN, in Dunnichen, 1691. [NRS.E69.11.1]

BOYLE, MARGARET, in Kirriemuir, 1723. [NRS.CH2.1302.139/141]

BOYLE, WILLIAM, in Dunnichen, 1691. [NRS.E69.11.1]

BRANDON, DAVID, a councillor of Forfar, 1660. [AA.F1.1.1]

BRANDON, DAVID, in Kirriemuir, 1686. [NRS.RH11.70.1/3]

BRECHIN, ALEXANDER, in Farnell, 1691. [NRS.E69.11.1]

BRECHIN, DAVID, a brabiner in Kirriemuir, testament, 18 January 1621, Comm. St Andrews. [NRS]

BRECHIN, DAVID, a weaver in Kirriemuir, husband of Agnes Riccard, sasine,1638. [NRS.RS35.S2.I.505]

BRECHIN, THOMAS, a weaver in Kirriemuir, husband of

THE PEOPLE OF STRATHMORE, 1600-1799

Grisel Ostler the relict of William Young a weaver in Bakie, sasines, 1639. [NRS.RS35.S2.I.445, etc]

BRECHIN, THOMAS, in Kirriemuir, 1732. [NRS.GD7.2.151]

BRESSAK, JOHN, portioner of Inverarity, testament, 1779, Comm. Brechin. [NRS]

BREWHOUSE, GEORGE, in Pendriche, husband of Agnes Watt, testament, 1636, Comm. Brechin. [NRS]

BROCAS, JOHN, a flesher burgess of Brechin, and spouses [1] Christian Brown, testament, 1665, [2] Isobel Edward, testament, 1671, Comm. Brechin. [NRS]

BRODIE, WILLIAM, a merchant in Kirriemuir, and husband of Agnes Grub, later in the parish of Derachie, Ireland, sasine, 1660. [NRS.RS35.S3.I.116]

BROKAS, PATRICK, master of Brechin Grammar School, husband of Elizabeth Fenton, sasine, 1654. [NRS.RS35.S2.IV.324]

BRODIE, ARCHIBALD, in Forfar, 1785. [NRS.E326.3.19]

BRODIE, ..., versus Neave, Forfar Burgh Court, 11 November 1785. [AA.F1.8.1]

BROKHOUSE, DAVID, a baxter burgess of Brechin, 1605. [RPCS.VII.616]

BROKHOUSE, PATRICK, a baxter burgess of Brechin, 1605. [RPCS.VII.616]

BROKHOUSE, THOMAS, a baxter burgess of Brechin, spouse Elspet Neish, testament, 1638, Comm. Brechin. [NRS]

BROUSTER, ALEXANDER, in Rescobie, 1691. [NRS.E69.11.1]

BROUSTER, ALEXANDER, in Methie Inverarity, 1691. [NRS.E69.11.1]

BROUSTER, ALEXANDER, born 1684, in Grounds of Idvie, died 1755, wife Margaret Reid, died 1736. [Kirkden gravestone]

BROUSTER, DAVID, in Kinclune, Kingoldrum, testament, 1621, Comm. Brechin. [NRS]

THE PEOPLE OF STRATHMORE, 1600-1799

BROUSTER, DAVID, a councillor of Forfar, 1688. [AA.F1.1.2]; in Forfar,1691. [NRS.E69.11.1]

BROUSTER, MARGARET, in Forfar,1691. [NRS.E69.11.1]

BROWN, ALEXANDER, debtor in Forfar, cautioner William Drummond the younger, 1594. [WCB#42]

BROUN, ANDREW, in Strathcathro, 1691. [NRS.E69.11.1]

BROWN, ANDREW, of Glaswell, 1746. [NRS.RH11.70.7]

BROWN, DAVID, in Kirriemuir, 1722. [NRS.CH2.1302.131/133]

BROWN, DAVID, a wright in Kirriemuir, 1742. [NRS.RH11.70.7]

BROWN, DAVID, a glover in Kirriemuir, 1746. [NRS.RH11.70.7]

BROWN, DAVID, versus ...Watt, Forfar Burgh Court, 11 August 1784. [AA.F1.8.1]

BROWN, GEORGE, a flesher in Kirriemuir, 1741, 1745. [NRS.CH2.1302.233; RH11.70.7]

BROWN, GEORGE, a wright in Kirriemuir, 1723, 1724, 1742, 1745. [NRS.GD137.2828; CH2.1302/147; RH11.70.7]

BROWN, ISOBEL, 1718. [NRS.CH2.1302.1.115]

BROWN, JAMES, a bailie of Forfar, bonds, 1666, 1671, 1676. [NRS.RD2.17.840; RD4.28.522; RD4.38.605]

BROWN, JAMES, son of James Brown, in Forfar, sasine, 1661. [NRS.RS35.S3.I.225]

BROWN, JAMES, a glover in Kirriemuir, 1742. [NRS.RH11.70.7]

BROWN, JAMES, a messenger in Forfar, 1742. [NRS.RH11.70.7]

BROWN, JAMES, in Forfar, 1759. [NRS.E326.1.169]

BROWN, JANET, at the Bridge of Darsie, Kirriemuir, testament, 1624, Comm. St Andrews. [NRS]

THE PEOPLE OF STRATHMORE, 1600-1799

BROWN, JEAN, in Kirriemuir, 1729. [NRS.CH2.1302.173]

BROWN, JOHN, in Auchinaday, Oathlaw, testament, 1664, Comm. Brechin. [NRS]

BROWN, JOHN, in Forfar,1691. [NRS.E69.11.1]

BROUN, JOHN, in Kinnell, 1691. [NRS.E69.11.1]

BROWN, JOHN, at Milne of Balmakathy, an elder in Kirriemuir, 1720. [NRS.CH2.1302.1.121]

BROWN, JOHN, of Glaswell, 1742, 1745. [NRS.RH11.70.7]

BROWN, JOHN, a butcher in Kirriemuir, a sasine, 1777. [NRS.RS35.26.437]

BROUN, ROBERT, in Kinnell, 1691. [NRS.E69.11.1]

BROWN, ROBERT, in Kirriemuir, 1726. [NRS.CH2.1302/159]

BROWN, ROBERT, son of James Brown, a flesher in Kirriemuir, 1744, 1745. [NRS.RH11.70.7]

BROWN, ROBERT, a flesher in Kirriemuir, heir to his cousin James Brown a weaver there; also to his cousin David Brown a surgeon later a shipmaster in Bristol, 1773. [NRS.S/H]

BROWN, THOMAS, in Kinnetles, 1691. [NRS.E69.11.1]

BROWN, WILLIAM, in Aberlemno, 1691. [NRS.E69.11.1]

BROWN, WILLIAM, in the Mill of Syde, Strathcathro, testament, 1711, Comm. Brechin. [NRS]

BROWN, WILLIAM, a writer in Forfar, 1744, 1745; a magistrate of Forfar, 1748; provost of Forfar, 1753. [NRS.RH11.70.7; NRAS#124/4/1/75; CS271.75551; E326.1.169]

BRUCE, ALEXANDER, a merchant in Brechin, spouse Katherine Wood, a sasine, 1684. [NRS.RS35.S3.VIII.39]

BRUCE, ALEXANDER, in Tannadice, 1691. [NRS.E69.11.1]

BRUCE, ANDREW, in the Meikle Mylne of Brechin, spouse Janet Mylne, testament, 1594. [NRS]

BRUCE, DAVID, versus David Low, Forfar Burgh Court, 25 June 1784. [AA.F1.8.1]

THE PEOPLE OF STRATHMORE, 1600-1799

BRUCE, JAMES, in Tannadice, 1691. [NRS.E69.11.1]

BRUCE, JOHN, a brabiner burgess of Brechin, spouse Katherine Scott, testament, 1614, Comm. Brechin. [NRS]

BRUCE, JOHN, in Shepherd's Seat, Oathlaw, spouse Agnes Bearen, testament, 1663, Comm. Brechin. [NRS]

BRUCE, JOHN, born 1758, educated at Marischal College, Aberdeen, minister in Forfar, from 178- until his death in 1817, wife Mary Ferguson, born 1759, died 1844. [NRS.E326.3.19; TNA#7336][Forfar gravestone]

BRUCE, JOHN, schoolmaster in Brechin, spouse Helen Bissett, testament, 1785, Comm. Brechin. [NRS]

BRUCE, ROBERT, in Kinnell, 1691. [NRS.E69.11.1]

BRUCE, WILLIAM, a brabiner burgess of Brechin, spouse Elizabeth Wilson, testament, 1596, Comm. Brechin. [NRS]

BUCHAN, Captain DAVID, heir to his father William Buchan, in lands in the lordship of Glamis, 1654. [NRS.Retours. Forfar.331]

BUCHAN, MARGARET, in Forfar,1691. [NRS.E69.11.1]

BUCHANAN, ANDREW, a merchant in Forfar, a deed, 1702. [NRS.RD4.90.30]

BULL, JOHN, in Haugh of Finavon, testament, 1631, Comm. Brechin. [NRS]

BULL, JOHN, and spouse Janet Sturrock, in Guthrie, testament, 1638, Comm. Brechin. [NRS]

BULL. MARGARET, in Kirriemuir, 1721. [NRS.CH2.1302.127]

BUNYON, DAVID, servant to Lord Southesk in Kinnaird, testament, 1636, Comm. Brechin. [NRS]

BURMAN, ANDREW, in Forfar,1691. [NRS.E69.11.1]

BURMAN, ANDREW, in Rescobie, 1691. [NRS.E69.11.1]

BURN, ALEXANDER, a litster in Kirriemuir, spouse Margaret Marshall, parents of Thomas a baxter, sasine. 1773. [NRS.RS35.24/437]

THE PEOPLE OF STRATHMORE, 1600-1799

BURNS, DAVID, in Forfar, 1759. [NRS.E326.1.169]

BURN, JAMES, in West Dinoon, Glamis, 1681. [NRS.E69.11.1]

BURN, MARGARET, daughter of the late Alexander Burn a litster in Kirriemuir, 1745. [NRS.RH11.70.7]

BURN, MATTHEW, in Oathlaw, 1691. [NRS.E69.11.1]

BURN, PATRICK, in Oathlaw, 1691. [NRS.E69.11.1]

BURN, THOMAS, Deacon of the Baxters of Brechin, testament, 1688, Comm. Brechin. [NRS]

BURNS, THOMAS, 1742. [NRS.RH11.70.7]

BURNETT, ALEXANDER, in Bademuir of Glaswell, 1745. [NRS.RH11.70.7]

BURNET, JOHN, a burgess of Brechin, husband of Helen Bowack, testament, 1659, Comm. Brechin. [NRS]

BURNETT, MARY, in Glamis, 1681. [NRS.E69.11.1]

BURNETT, ROBERT, in Mains of Glaswell, 1744, 1745. [NRS.RH11.70.7]

BURNET, THOMAS, and spouse Elizabeth Erskin, in Newbigging, Brechin, testament, 1649, Comm. Brechin. [NRS]

BURSIE, THOMAS, son of Isobel Rodger, in Kirriemuir, husband of Christian Douglas, testament, 1621, Comm. St Andrews, [NRS]; father of Janet and Alexander, sasine, 1637. [NRS.RS35.S2.I.4/160]

BUTCHART, JAMES, born 1738, a mason in Gateside of Nevay, died 5 March 1793, husband of Agnes Farquharson, born 1743, died August 1797, parents of William, Robert, and Jean Butchart. [Nevay gravestone]

BUTCHART, JEAN, born 1768, wife of Robert Robertson, died at Ingliston on 30 May 1820. [Nevay gravestone]

BUTCHART, JOHN, in Forfar, 1691. [NRS.E60.11.1]

BUTCHART, JOHN, versus ... Rodgers, Forfar Burgh Court, 19 January 1785. [AA.F1.8.1]

BUTCHART, PATRICK, in Kinnell, 1691. [NRS.E69.11.1]

THE PEOPLE OF STRATHMORE, 1600-1799

BUTCHART, THOMAS, in Forfar,1691. [NRS.E69.11.1]

BUTCHART, WILLIAM, a merchant burgess of Brechin, spouse Margaret Watt, testament, 1624, Comm. Brechin. [NRS]

BUTCHART, WILLIAM, in Cotton of Craig, a tack, 13 August 1683. [AA.F5.23]

BUTCHART, WILLIAM, in Forfar, 1759. [NRS.E326.1.169]

BUTTER, THOMAS, in Kirriemuir, husband of Agnes Cromb, sasines, 1660, 1709. [NRS.RS35.S3.I.10; 12.59]

CABLE, AGNES, relict of Archibald Cay in Kirriemuir, and spouse of Archibald Cuthbert a cordiner there, a sasine, 1631. [NRS.RS35.S1.VIII.30]

CABLE, ALEXANDER, son of Patrick Cable, a notary in Kirriemuir, 1642, husband of Isobel Piggott. [NRS.RS35.S2.II.250]

CABLE, ALEXANDER, a notary in Kirriemuir, husband of Isobel Piggott, sasine, 1648. [NRS.RS35.III.318]

CABLE, ALEXANDER, a schoolmaster in Kirriemuir, relict Anna Ogilvie, and daughter Beatrix, a sasine, 1648. [NRS.RS35.S3.III.189]

CABLE, [Kabel], ALEXANDER, versus Winter and Masterton, Forfar Burgh Court, 11 August 1784; versus ..... Masterton, Forfar Burgh Court, 4 January 1785, 13 April 1785. [AA.F1.8.1]

CABLE, BEATRIX, daughter of Alexander Cable a notary in Kirriemuir, a sasine, 1675. [NRS.RS35.S3.VI.103]

CABLE, BEATRIX, relict of Thomas Fithie a merchant in Kirriemuir, and spouse of Alexander Ogilvie a merchant there and bailie-depute of the Regality of Kirriemuir, a sasine, 1639. [NRS.RS35.S2.I.346]

CABLE, BEATRIX, relict of James Symson, a writer in Kirriemuir, and of David Ogilvy, minister of Arbroath, 1698. [NRS.RS35.S3.X.257]

CABLE, CATHERINE, daughter of Patrick Cable in Kirriemuir, and spouse of William Fitchett there, a sasine, 1652. [NRS.RS35.S2.IV.125]

THE PEOPLE OF STRATHMORE, 1600-1799

CABELL, DAVID, in Forfar,1691. [NRS.E69.11.1]

CABLE, [Kebel], DAVID, born 1723, a brewer in Forfar, died 1783, wife Lilias Dick, born 1728, died 1780. [Forfar gravestone]

CABLE, GEORGE, in Kirrimuir, testament, 1619; husband of Janet Bursie, testament, 1615, Comm. St Andrews. [NRS]

CABLE, GEORGE, in Kirriemuir, a sasine, 1652. [NRS.RS35.S2.IV.375]

CABLE, JANET, daughter of Patrick Cable in Kirriemuir, and spouse of James Dall in Milldens, a sasine, 1652. [NRS.RS35.S2.IV.375]

CABLE, PATRICK, a schoolmaster in Kirriemuir, 1613. [CLC#1686]

CABLE, PATRICK, in Kirriemuir, son of George Cable there, a sasine, 1652. [NRS.RS35.S2.IV.375]

CABLE, PATRICK, a notary in Kirriemuir, husband of Catherine Ogilvy, a sasine, 1643. [NRS.RS35.S2.II.250]

CADDEN, ANDREW, in Rescobie, 1691. [NRS.E69.11.1]

CABLE, BEATRICE, daughter of Alexander Cable formerly a notary in Kirriemuir, a sasine, 1725. [NRS.RS35.14/11]

CABLE, GEORGE, a maltman in Kirriemuir, son of Patrick Cable, a sasine,1712. [NRS.RS35.12/321]

CADGER, DAVID, a cordiner in Kirriemuir, husband of Isobel Young, 1686, sasine, 1693. [NRS.RH11.70.1/1; RS35.S3.IX.408]

CADGER, DAVID, a shoemaker in Kirriemuir, spouse of Isobel Young, a deed, 1703. [NRS.RD35.10/423]

CADGER, JAMES, a cordiner in Kirriemuir, husband of Janet Mylne, a sasine, 1648. [NRS.RS35.S2.III.111]

CADGER, JAMES, son of David Cadger, cordiner in Kirriemuir, a sasine, 1699. [NRS.RS35.S3.X.134]

CADGER, MARGARET, in Kirriemuir.1734. [NRS.CH2.1302.209]

CADGER, THOMAS, a cordiner in Kirriemuir, husband of (1)

THE PEOPLE OF STRATHMORE, 1600-1799

Agnes Anderson, and (2) Margaret Milne, a sasine, 1668. [NRS.RS35.S3.IV.18]

CADGER, THOMAS, a cordiner in Kirriemuir, spouse Agnes Anderson, parents of Margaret, sasine, 1750. [NRS.RS35.17/105]

CADZOW, JAMES, in Forfar, 1614. [RGS.VII.1024]

CAMPBELL, JOHN, in Ballinshoe, 1740. [NRS.CH2.1302.229]

CAMPBELL, JOHN, stampmaster in Kirriemuir, 1745. [NRS.RH11.70.7]

CAIRNCROSS, ALEXANDER, Bishop of Brechin, 1684. [F.6.375]

CAIRNCROSS, ALEXANDER, 1785. [NRS.CH2.1302.2/115]

CAIRNCROSS, DAVID, of Balmashanner, a bond, 1666. [NRS.RD2.15.914]

CAIRNCROSS, ISABEL, spouse of John Cromb in Kirriemuir, a sasine, 1637. [NRS.RS35.S3.V.375]

CAIRNCROSS, MARGERY, 1783.[NRS.CH2.1302.2/97]

CAIRNCROSS, NICOLL, of Balmashanner, 1608. [RPCS.VIII.647]

CAIRNCROSS, PATRICK, of Balmashanner, heir to his brother David Cairncross of Balmashanner, 28 August 1657, [NRS.Retours]; 1660.[AA.F1.1.1]

CAIRNCROSS, WALTER, brother of Nicoll Cairncross, in Forfar, 1608. [RPCS.VIII.647]

CAIRNCROSS, WILLIAM, of Balmashanner, deceased, father of Patrick Cairncross, 1609. [RPCS.VIII.704]

CAMPBELL, ALEXANDER, in Aberlemno, 1691. [NRS.E69.11.1]

CAMPBELL, NICOLAS, daughter of the late Mr Dugall Campbell the Dean of Brechin, testament, 1636, Comm. Brechin. [NRS]

CAMPBELL, ROBERT, in Forfar, 1791. [NRS.E326.1.169]

CANDO, ROBERT, in Easter Hillend, 1743. [NRS.RH11.70.7]

THE PEOPLE OF STRATHMORE, 1600-1799

KANDOW, WILLIAM, born 1725, schoolmaster, died 1798, spouse Jean Brown, born 1731, died 1801. [Ruthven gravestone]

CANT, JOHN, in Aberlemno, 1691. [NRS.E69.11.1]

CANT, JOHN, in Kirriemuir, sasine, 1718. [NRS.RS35.13/494]

CANT, JOHN, an officer of the Regality of Kirriemuir, 1744. [NRS.RH11.70.7]

CANT, MARGARET, in Brechin, testament, 1665, Comm. Brechin. [NRS]

CANT, ROBERT, in Kirriemuir, son of Alexander Cant in Balnagarrow, and husband of Agnes Mackie, a sasine, 1639. [NRS.RS35.S2.I.555]

CANT, ROBERT, in Kirriemuir, a sasine, 1718. [NRS.RS35.13/494]

CANT, WILLIAM, in Tannadice, 1691. [NRS.E69.11.1]

CAR, DAVID, in Methie Inverarity, 1691. [NRS.E69.11.1]

CAR, HENRY, in Tannadice, 1691. [NRS.E69.11.1]

CARDEN, ARCHIBALD, and spouse Beatrix Simpson, in Kynneill, Kincaldrum, testament, 1610, Comm. Brechin. [NRS]

CARDEAN, JAMES, in Kirriemuir, testament, 1689, Comm. St Andrews. [NRS]

CARGILL, JAMES, a cordiner in Kirriemuir, husband of Margaret Milne, a sasine, 1684. [NRS.RS35.S3.VIII.187]

CARGILL, HELEN, in Kirriemuir, 1721. [NRS.CH2.1302.127]

CARGILL, JAMES, a shoemaker in Kirriemuir, 1718, 1741, 1744. [NRS. CH2.1302.1.115; RH11.70.7]

CARGILL, JAMES, 'a poor man', 1732. [NRS.CH2.1302.187]

CARGILL, JAMES, the beadle, 1741. [NRS.CH2.1302.237]

CARGILL, JAMES, 1785. [NRS.CH2.1302.2/117]

CARGILL, JEAN, 1762. [NRS.CH2.1302.2/7]

CARGILL, JOHN, a merchant in Brechin, 1620, father of

Margaret Cargill, a sasine, 1654. [RPCS.XII.215]
[NRS.RS35.S2.IV.364]

CARNEGIE, ALEXANDER, a mealdealer in Brechin, husband of (1) Catherine Nory, (2) Grisel Wilson, 1620; in Brechn, 1628. [RPCS.II.174] testament, 1638, Comm. Brechin; a sasine. [NRS.RS35.S1.I.153, etc]

CARNEGIE, ALEXANDER, a maltman in Brechin, husband of Catherine Norrie, a sasine, 1638. [NRS.RS35.S2.I.192]

CARNEGIE, Sir ALEXANDER, of Balnamoon, testaments, 1658 and 1672, Comm. Brechin. [NRS]

CARNEGIE, ANDREW, in Muirton, Tannadice, 1691. [NRS.E69.11.1]

CARNEGIE, ANN, daughter o the deceased James Carnegie of Cockston, testament, 1778, Comm. Brechin. [NRS]

CARNEGY, CHARLES, born 1595, died 1655. [Kinnaird gravestone]

CARNEGIE, CHARLES, in Farnell, 1691. [NRS.E69.11.1]

CARNEGIE, CHARLES, of Finavon, testament, 1714, Comm. Brechin. [NRS]

CARNEGIE, DAVID, a saddler in Brechin, 1608. [RPCS.VIII.664]; in Brechin, 1620. [RGS.VIII.17]

CARNEGIE, DAVID, MA, minister in Brechin, 1631-1632. [F.6.179]

CARNEGIE, DAVID, a burgess of Brechin, spouse of Margaret Gibson, father of Agnes, Catherine, Janet, Jean, and Margaret, sasines, 1670s. [NRS.RS35.S3.IV.417, etc]

CARNEGIE, JAMES, son of George Carnegie, a burgess of Brechin, a sasine, 1673. [NRS.RS35.S3.V.303]

CARNEGIE, JAMES, son of James Carnegie, a flesher in Brechin, a sasine, 1673. [NRS.RS35.S3.V.303]

CARNEGIE, JAMES, in Kinnell, 1691. [NRS.E69.11.1]

CARNEGIE, JEAN, a relict, in Forfar, 1691. [NRS.E69.11.1]

CARNEGIE, Sir JOHN, of Kinnaird, testament, 1598, Comm.Brechin. [NRS]

CARNEGIE, JOHN, glover and provost of Forfar, deeds, 1683, 1687; 1688, 1691; 1690, 1691. [NRS.RD3.55.317; RD4.61.896; RD4.63.61/73/874; E69.11.1; GD1.61.11; e69.11.1] [AA.F1.1.2]

CARNEGIE, JOHN, of Kinnell, heir to his brother James Carnegie of Kinnell, sons of John Carnehie of Boyack, 1695. [NRS.Retours,Forfar.534]

CARNEGIE, PATRICK, in Cotton of Glasswell, Kirriemuir, testament, 1615, Comm. St Andrews. [NRS]

CARNEGIE, PATRICK, of Lour, a deed, 1707. [NRS.RD3.113.79; RD4.100.1169]

CARNEGY, PATRICK, of Lour, born 1720, died 1799, wife Margaret Bower. [Forfar gravestone][NRS.E326.1.50]

CARNEGY, PATRICK, in Balmashanner, 1752. [AA.F1.4.3/17]

CARNEGIE, ROBERT, of Leuchland in the parish and lordship of Brechin, spouse to Marjorie Wedderburn, 1625. [RGS.VIII.824]

CARNEGY, Mr ROBERT, son of David Carnegy the Dean of Brechin, a donor in 1684. [Brechin Cathedral]

CARNEGIE, ROBERT, Earl of Southesk, spouse Ann Hamilton, parents of Charles Carnegie, Earl of Southesk, born London 1661, died in Leuchars Castle, Fife, 1699, spouse Mary Maitland. [Kinnaird gravestone]

CARNEGY, ROBERT, of Ballindarg, sasine, 1744. [AA.F1.4.3/12]

CARNEGIE, ROBERT, of Ballindarge, 1745, 1746. [NRS.RH11.70.7]

CARNOCHT, JOHN, gardener at Kinnaird, testament, 1601, Comm. Brechin. [NRS]

CARR, JOHN, and spouse Christian Dakers, in Pentoscalcall, Kinnaird, testament, 1631, Comm. Brechin. [NRS]

CARR, JOHN, in Kinnell, 1691. [NRS.E69.11.1]

CARR, THOMAS, in the Tenements of Caldhame, testament, 1667, Comm. Brechin. [NRS]

CARR, THOMAS, died 1670, wife Euphan Simpson. [Kinnaird gravestone]

CARSON, Dr JOHN, in Forfar, 1778. [NRS.E326.3.19]

CARUS, JOHN, in Dunnichen, 1691. [NRS.E69.11.1]

CATHRO, JAMES, in Kirriemuir and Wester Tarbirne, husband of Margaret Clark, a sasine, 1643. [NRS.RS35.S2.II.256]

CATHRO, JOHN, a tailor in Kirriemuir, husband of Janet Adamson, a sasine, 1656. [NRS.RS35.S2.V.382]

CATTHIE, DAVID, in Aberlemno, 1691. [NRS.E69.11.1]

CATHIE, JOHN, in Aberlemno, 1691. [NRS.E69.11.1]

CATHROW, JAMES, in Burnsieisland, 1745. [NRS.RH11.70.7]

CATHROW, JOHN, in Claypots, 1746. [NRS.RH11.70.7]

CAUTIE, ANDREW, Deacon of the Tailors of Forfar, 1647, and assessor of the craft in 1655; bailie of Forfar, 1660. [AA.F1.1.1/2] [RBF#215/216]

CAUTY, DAVID, a writer and former bailie of Forfar, 1746. [.NRAS#124/4/1/75]

CAUTIE, JAMES, son of William Cautie a merchant burgess, was admitted as a burgess and freeman of Forfar, 1686. [AA.F1.1.2]

CAUTIE, JAMES, a litster in Forfar, 1689. [AA.F1.1.2]

CAUTIE, WILLIAM, treasurer of Forfar, 1686. [AA.F1.1.2]

COUTTY, Mrs, in Forfar, 1753, 1759. [NRS.E326.1.169]

CAY, ANDREW, messenger and cess collector of Forfar, 1690. [AA.F1.1.2][NRS.69.11.1]

CAY, JOHN, in Kirriemuir, a sasine, 1771. [NRS.RS35.23/250]

CHAPLAIN, ALEXANDER, a writer in Forfar, was admitted a burgess there on 26 June 1660. [AA.F1.1.1]

CHALMERS, ANDREW, a weaver in Kirriemuir, spouse Agnes Stormont, a sasine, 1768. [NRS.RS35.22.508]

THE PEOPLE OF STRATHMORE, 1600-1799

CHAPLAIN, JOHN, in Glamis, 1681. [NRS.E69.11.1]

CHAPLAIN, Mr WILLIAM, and his spouse Christian Duncan, in the Mill of Careston, testaments, 1705, Comm. Brechin. [NRS]; in Careston, 1691. [NRS.E69.11.1]

CHAPMAN, RICHARD, a burgess of Brechin in 1609. [RPCS.VIII.704]

CHRISTIE, ALEXANDER, in Rescobie, 1691. [NRS.E69.11.1]

CHRISTIE, JAMES, in Dunnichen, 1691. [NRS.E69.11.1]

CHRISTIE, WILLIAM, in Knowhead, 1745. [NRS.RH11.70.7]

CLERK, ALEXANDER, born 1540, a burgess of Brechon, died there in February 1620. [RPCS.XII.215]

CLERK, ALEXANDER, a burgess of Brechin, spouse of Janet Murray, testament, 1612, Comm. Brechin, sasine, 1631. [NRS.RS35.S1.VIII.269]

CLARK, ALEXANDER, son of James Clark, a burgess of Brechin, a sasine, 1637. [NRS.RS15.S2.I.95]

CLARK, ANDREW, a brewer in Kirriemuir, a sasine,1770. [NRS.RS35.23/160]

CLERK, ARCHIBALD, in Aberlemno, 1691. [NRS.E69.11.1]

CLERK, CHARLES, in Forfar, 1791. [NRS.E326.1.169]

CLARK, DAVID, a merchant and a donor in Brechin, 1649. [Brechin Cathedral]

CLERK, DAVID, in Methie Inverarity, 1691. [NRS.E69.11.1]

CLARK, EUPHAN, in Kirriemuir,1745. [NRS.RH11.70.7]

CLARK, JAMES, a merchant burgess of Brechin, a sasine, 1620, spouse Christian Ramsay, testament, 1633, Comm. Brechin. [NRS][RPCS.XII.215]

CLARK, JAMES, a burgess of Brechin, spouse Jean Junkin, a sasine 1637, parents of Nicolas, Alexander, and James. [NRS.RS35.S2.I.95]

THE PEOPLE OF STRATHMORE, 1600-1799

CLERK, JAMES, in Kinnattie, Kirriemuir, testament, 1638, Comm.St Andrews. [NRS]

CLARK, JAMES, a weaver in Kirriemuir, son of John Clark a weaver in Roods of Kirriemuir, a sasine, 1744. [NRS.RS35.16/510]

CLERK, JOHN, in Bank, 1742. [NRS.RH11.70.7]

CLARK, THOMAS, a merchant burgess of Brechin, husband of Katherine Barrie, testament, 1610, Comm. Brechin. [NRS]

CLERK, THOMAS, his wife, 1727. [NRS.CH2.1302.163]

CLERK, WILLIAM, in Tannadice, 1691. [NRS.E69.11.1]

CLERK, WILLIAM, in Stron,1742. [NRS.RH11.70.7]

CLEPHANE, Mr THOMAS, minister at Kingoldrum, testament,1717, Comm.Brechin. [NRS]

COBB, ALEXANDER, a brewer in Brechin, 1691. [RPCS.XVI.605]

COBB, ANDREW, a quarrier in Kirriemuir, sasines, 1725, etc. [NRS.RS35.14/23, etc]

COBB, JOHN, a cottar in Middle Drums, Kinnaird, testament, 1754, Comm. Brechin. [NRS]

COBB, JOHN, a tailor in Forfar, husband of Babie Deuchars, born 1757, died 1781. [Forfar gravestone]

COBB, JOHN, versus ..... Dickson, Forfar Burgh Court, 15 October 1784. [AA.F1.8.1]

COBE, GEORGE, in Aberlemno, 1691. [NRS.E69.11.1]

COBIE, JAMES, in Aberlemno, 1691. [NRS.E69.11.1]

COCHRANE, ALEXANDER, in Kirriemuir, husband of Catharine Graham, a sasine, 1637. [NRS.RS35.S2.I.54]

COCKBURN, ALEXANDER, in Forfar, an assizeman in 1600. [RGS.VI.1176]

COCKBURN, Mr JOHN, in Brechin, 1620. [RPCS.VIII.17]

THE PEOPLE OF STRATHMORE, 1600-1799

COLLACE, Mr JOHN, servant to Andrew, Bishop of Brechin, 1613. [RGS.VII.890]

COLLACE, Mr PATRICK, an advocate in Balnabrech, testament, 1661, Comm. Brechin. [NRS]

COLLACE, ROBERT, in Brechin, father of Margaret Collace, a sasine, 1664. [NRS.RS35.S1.II.21]

COLLIE, ALEXANDER, a shoemaker in Brechin, a donor in 1633. [Brechin Cathedral]

COLVILLE, ALEXANDER, in Kirriemuir, 1716. [NRS.CH2.1302.1.105]

COLVILLE, DAVID, in Kinnell, 1691. [NRS.E69.11.1]

COLVILLE, SYLVESTER, a young, unmarried man, in Kirriemuir, son of Alexander Colvill, 1722. [NRS.CH2.1302.133]

CONSTABLE, JOHN, minister at Kingoldrum, and spouse Magdalen Oilvie, testaments, 1704 and 1707, Comm. Brechin. [NRS]

COOK, ALEXANDER, born 1655, a writer and councillor in Forfar, 1688. [AA.F1.1.2]; in Forfar,1691. [NRS.E69.11.1]

COOK, ALEXANDER, a messenger in Forfar, 1705. [NRS.GD137.508]

COOK, ANDREW, in Drumbarro, in Dunnichen, 1691. [NRS.E69.11.1]

COOK, DAVID, in Kirriemuir, husband of Elizabeth Scott, a sasine, 1650. [NRS.RS35.S2.III.377]

COOK, JAMES, versus ...Kebel, Forfar Burgh Court, 13 September 1784. [AA.F1.8.1][NRS.CH2.1302.2/97]

COOK, JEAN, in Kirriemuir, 1725. [NRS.CH2.1302.149]

COOK, JOHN, a councillor of Forfar, 1660; disposition, 1670. [AA.F1.1.1; F5.122]

COOK, JOHN, a merchant, in Forfar,1691. [NRS.E69.11.1]

COOK, JOHN, treasurer of Forfar, 1712-1713. [AA.F5.5]

COOPER, ALEXANDER, a feuar in Kirriemuir, husband of Elizabeth Malcolm, a sasine, 1769. [NRS.RS35.22/500]

THE PEOPLE OF STRATHMORE, 1600-1799

CUPAR, JOHN, in Glamis, 1681. [NRS.E69.11.1]

CORKER, WILLIAM, in Cotton Dod, in Rescobie, 1691. [NRS.E69.11.1]

CORSER, WILLIAM, in Auchterlonie, Dunnichen, spouse of Marion Barrie, testament, 1626, Comm. Brechin. [NRS]

COSSINS, DAVID, and his wife Margaret Rusell, in Kinclunie, Kingoldrum, testaments, 1654 and 1662, Comm. Brechin.[NRS]

COSSINS, JAMES, in Redburn, Kingoldrum, testament, 1664, Comm. Brechin. [NRS]

COSSINS, JOHN, a chapman in Kirriemuir, testament, 1738, Comm. St Andrews. [NRS]

COSSANS, ROBERT, in Kirriemuir, 1724. [NRS.CH2.1302.143]

COSSANS, ROBERT, a weaver in Kirriemuir, 1733. [NRS.CH2.1302.193]

COTHALL, HELEN, an alleged witch in Forfar, 1661. [RPCS.I.122]

COUDIE, JOHN, in Forfar, 1691. [NRS.E60.11.1]

COULL, JOHN, at the Meikle Mylne of Brechin, husband of Isobel Knox, father of Isobel the wife of Robert Greig, and Janet the wife of James Daw, both in Greenden, sasine, 1642. [NRS.RS35.S2.II.133]

COUPAR, JOHN, a wright in Brechin, spouse of Isobel, daughter of David Mitchell, a sasine, 1637. [NRS.RS35.S2.I.82]

COUPAR, JOHN, a wheel-wright in Brechin, husband of Catherine Mathers, a sasine, 1666. [NRS.RS35.S3.III.24]

COUPAR, THOMAS, a donor in 1617. [Brechin Cathedral]

COUPAR, WALTER, in Cotton of Balnamoon, testament, 1598, Comm.Brechin. [NRS]

COUTIE, DAVID, a weaver in Kirriemuir, sasine, 1775.]NRS.RS35.25/147, etc]

COUTIE, JOHN, in Forfar,1691. [NRS.E69.11.1]

COUTIE, JOHN, a dyer, in Forfar,1691. [NRS.E69.11.1]

THE PEOPLE OF STRATHMORE, 1600-1799

COUTRIE, JAMES, in Tannadice, 1691. [NRS.E69.11.1]

COUTTS, ALEXANDER, minister at Strathcathro, spouse Elizabeth Burnet, testaments, 1695, 1696, Comm. Brechin. [NRS]; in Strathcathro, 1691. [NRS.E69.11.1]

COUTTS, JOHN, in Strathcathro, 1691. [NRS.E69.11.1]

COWIE, JAMES, a merchant in Brechin, spouse C. Young, a sasine, 1680, [NRS.RS35.S3.VII.453]

COWIE, ROBERT, a burgess of Brechin, spouse Isobel Muirton, a sasine, 1620. [NRS.RS35.S1.I.156]

CRABB, ANDREW, in Cotton Dod, Rescobie, 1691. [NRS.E69.11.1]

CRAB, JOHN, in Oathlaw, 1691. [NRS.E69.11.1]

CRABB, JOHN, in Loan then in Cotton of Balmaskelly, 1746. [NRS.RH70.11.7]

CRABB, JOHN, a wheelwright in Kirriemuir, 1769. [NRS.RS35/22/498]

CRABB, THOMAS, a cordiner in Kirriemuir, husband of Margaret Anderson, a sasine,1698. [NRS.RS35.S3.X.161]

CRABB, THOMAS, a shoemaker in Kirriemuir, sasine, 1704. [NRS.RS35.11/33]

CRAB, WILLIAM, in Blackbeard, 1745. [NRS.RH11.70.7]

CRAFTS, JAMES, in Tannadice, 1691. [NRS.E69.11.1]

CRAIG, AGNES, spouse to John Incheak ploughman to James Haliburton of Kirkton of Eassie, testament, 1600, Comm. Edinburgh. [NRS]

CRAIG, ANDREW, in Oathlaw, 1691. [NRS.E69.11.1]

CRAIG, DAVID, 1746. [NRS.RH11.70.7]

CRAIG, JAMES, a mason in Kirriemuir, 1733. [NRS.CH2.1302.193]

CRAIG, ELIZABETH, spouse of David Dickson, in Nether Migvie, parish of Kirriemuir, testament, 1745, Comm. St Andrews. [NRS]

CRAIG, JOHN, charter, 1681; sasine, 1682. [AA.F5.126/127]; a cordiner in Forfar, 1691, [NRS.E69.11.1]

CRAIG, JOHN, in Kincreiff in Methie Inverarity, 1691. [NRS.E69.11.1]

CRAIG, JOHN, was served heir to his father John Craig a merchant in Forfar, 1710. [AA.F5.130]

CRAIG, ..., in Breckhillock, Glamis, 1797. [NRS.E326.10.3.24]

CRAIGHEAD, JOHN, schoolmaster in Kirriemuir, 1717, 1742, 1743, 1746. [NRS.RH11.70.7; RS35.13/277, etc; CH2.1302.1.109]

CRAIGIE, JOHN, a merchant, 1681. [AA.F5.125]

CRAIK, ALEXANDER, in Oathlaw, 1691. [NRS.E69.11.1]

CRAIK, CATHERINE, in Aberlemno, 1691. [NRS.E69.11.1]

CRAIK, DAVID, in Forfar,1691. [NRS.E69.11.1]

CRAIK, DAVID, in Aberlemno, 1691. [NRS.E69.11.1]

CRAIK, JAMES, in Dunnichen, 1691. [NRS.E69.11.1]

CRAIK, JOHN, in Muir Mills, Farnell, testament, 1602, Comm. Brechin. [NRS]

CRAIK, JOHN, in Rescobie, 1691. [NRS.E69.11.1]

CRAIK, JOHN, in Aberlemno, 1691. [NRS.E69.11.1]

CRAIK, WILLIAM, in Whinnydrum, Kirriemuir, testament, 1650, Comm. St Andrews. [NRS]

CRAIK, WILLIAM, in Aberlemno, 1691. [NRS.E69.11.1]

CRAMOND, JAMES, in Tannadice, 1691. [NRS.E69.11.1]

CRAMOND, JAMES, heir to his father Patrick Cramond of Brathinch, Menmuir, 1699. [NRS.Retours.Forfar.554]

CRAMOND, JOHN, a cordiner in Kirriemuir, a sasine,1695. [NRS.RS35.S3.IX.405]

CRAMOND, JOHN, a cordiner in Kirriemuir, sasine, 1711. [NRS.RS35.12/247]

THE PEOPLE OF STRATHMORE, 1600-1799

CRAWFORD, JAMES, a brewer in Kirriemuir, spouse Elizabeth Donaldson, sasine, 1777. [NRS.RS35.26/226]

CRAWFORD, MATTHEW, an excise officer, 1729. [NRS.CH2.1302.173]

CRIGHTON, ALEXANDER, in Forfar,1691. [NRS.E69.11.1]

CRICHTON, ANDREW, in Kirriemuir, 1686. [NRS.RH11.70.1/4]

CRICHTON, DAVID, a shoemaker in Kirriemuir, sasine, 1777. [NRS.RS35.26/410]

CRICHTON, ELIZABETH, daughter of Thomas Crichton formerly clerk of the Regality of Kirriemuir, wife of William Mathie, sasine, 1757. [NRS.RS35.18/476]

CRICHTON, JAMES, born 1626, in Hatton of Eassie, died 1683, wife Euphane Broun. [Eassie gravestone]

CRIGHTON, PATRICK, in Glamis, 1681. [NRS.E69.11.1]

CRICHTON, THOMAS, clerk of Kirriemuir, husband of Janet Raitt, a sasine, 1698. [NRS.RS35.S3.X.56]

CRISSNIEL, ANDREW, in Forfar,1691. [NRS.E69.11.1]

CROCKATT, JOHN, in Tannadice, 1691. [NRS.E69.11.1]

CROCKETT, MARY, deceased, 1717. [NRS.CH2.1302.1.107]

CROCKATT, PATRICK, in Kinnetles, 1691. [NRS.E69.11.1]

CROFTS, JOHN, in Tannadice, 1691. [NRS.E69.11.1]

CROLL, ANDREW, a bonnet-maker in Brechin, 1606. [RPCS.VII.643]

CROLL, JOHN, a bonnet-maker in Brechin, 1606. [RPCS.VII.643]

CROLL, JOHN, and spouse Elspet Bell, in Keithok, Brechin, testament, 1625, Comm. Brechin. [NRS]

CROLL, JOHN, in Kirriemuir, 1722. [NRS.CH2.1302.135]

CROMB, DAVID, brewer in Kirriemuir, father of Agnes, sasines, 1706. [NRS.RS35.12/3]

THE PEOPLE OF STRATHMORE, 1600-1799

CROMBE, JAMES, royal messenger in Kirriemuir, 1607. [NRS.GD68/1/129]

CROMB, MARGARET, daughter of the late John Cromb, a brabiner weaver of Forfar, a sasine,1676. [NRS.GD.16.76]

CROMBIE, DAVID, in Kirriemuir, husband of Janet Palmer, a sasine, 1648.. [NRS.RS35.S2.III.26, etc]

CROMBIE, JOHN, in Kirriemuir, 1732. [NRS.GD7.2.151]

CROOKSHANK, WILLIAM, dead by 1787. [NRS.CH2.1302.2/125]

CROSS, DAVID, in Kinnell, 1691. [NRS.E69.11.1]

CROW, ALEXANDER, a mason in Glamis, 1691.[NRS.E69.11.1]

CROWDEN, PATRICK, in Frankfrie, Kirriemuir, testament, 1675, Comm. St Andrews. [NRS]

CUTHBERT, JAMES, a wright in Kirriemuir, testament, 29 July 1696, Comm. St Andrews. [NRS]

CUTHILL, DAVID, in Kinnell, 1691. [NRS.E69.11.1]

CRUICK, JANET, in Forfar,1691. [NRS.E69.11.1]

CUBLEN, ALEXANDER, in Tannadice, 1691. [NRS.E69.11.1]

CURR, JOHN, a weaver in Kirriemuir,a sasine, 1726. [NRS.RS35.14/138]

CUTHBEARD, JOHN, in Oathlaw, 1691. [NRS.E69.11.1]

CUTHBERT, ALEXANDER, born 1614, a cordiner in Garlobank, died on 26 March 1674, husband of Janet Samson. [Kirriemuir gravestone]

CUTHBERT, ALEXANDER, in Kinnetles, 1691. [NRS.E69.11.1]

CUTHBERT, ALEXANDER, in Herdhill, formerly in Kirriemuir, sasine,1757. [NRS.RS35.18/314]

CUTHBERT, ARCHIBALD, in Kirriemuir, husband of Margaret Hutcheon, a sasine,1643. [NRS.RS35.S2.II.412]

THE PEOPLE OF STRATHMORE, 1600-1799

CUTHBERT, ARCHIBALD, in Kinnetles, 1691. [NRS.E69.11.1]

CUTHBERT, DAVID, in Drumglay, a shoemaker in Forfar, a deed, 1694. [NRS.RD3.83.114]

CUTHBERT, GEORGE, in Tannadice, 1691. [NRS.E69.11.1]

CUTHBERT, JAMES, a wright in Kirriemuir, testament, 29 July 1696, Comm. St Andrews. [NRS]

CUTHBERT, JAMES, in Dunnichen, 1691. [NRS.E69.11.1]

CUTHBERT, JOHN, in Garlabank, Kirriemuir, testament, 1618, Comm. St Andrews. [NRS]

CUTHBERT, JOHN, in Kirriemuir, husband of Janet Mackie, parents of John Cuthbert,a sasine, 1639. [NRS.RS35.S2.I.526]

CUTHBERT, JOHN, in Forfar,1691. [NRS.E69.11.1]

CUTHBERT, JOHN, in Tannadice, 1691. [NRS.E69.11.1]

CUTHBERT, WILLIAM, a merchant and bailie of Forfar, deeds, 1707, 1715. [NRS.RD2.93.2; RD2.104.1090]

CUTHBERT, WILLIAM, bailie in Forfar, 1660, 1668; a merchant there 1671; husband of Jean Piggott (born 1638, died 1678), there in 1691; testament, 1695, Comm. St Andrews. [Forfar gravestone] [NRS.E69.11.1; RD4.30.436][AA.F1.1.1/2]

CUTHBERT, WILLIAM, spouse to Elizabeth Craig, was admitted as a burgess and freeman of Forfar, 1688. [AA.F1.1.2]

CUTHBERT, WILLIAM, in Forfar,1691. [NRS.E69.11.1]; a merchant and bailie of Forfar, 1696. [NRS.RD3.86.108; RD4,78.264]

CUTHBERT, WILLIAM, in Forfar, 1759. [NRS.E326.1.169]

CUTHBERT, ..., born 1655, died 1679, husband of Isobel Wood, daughter of bailie George Wood. [Forfar gravestone]

CUTHBERT, ..., a merchant burgess and bailie of Forfar, deceased, husband of Jean Thom, 1721. [NRS.GD47.797]

CUTHILL, DAVID, in Kinnell, 1691. [NRS.E69.11.1]

CUTHILL, JOHN, in Kinnell, 1691. [NRS.E69.11.1]

THE PEOPLE OF STRATHMORE, 1600-1799

CUTTIE, JOHN, in Glamis, 1681. [NRS.E69.11.1]

DA, ALEXANDER, in Kirriemuir, husband of Janet Millar, a sasine,1648. [NRS.RS35.S2.III.47]

DAIKEROIT, JOHN, in Balnabriche, and his wife Janet Windram, testament, 1611, Comm. Brechin. [NRS]

DALGETTY, DAVID, in Easter Ordie, Finavon, testament, 1658, Comm. Brechin. [NRS]

DALGETTY, DAVID, in Rescobie, 1691. [NRS.E69.11.1]

DALGETY, ELSPET, in Orde, Finavon, testament, 1613, Comm. Brechin, [NRS]

DALGETTY, JEAN, 1765. [NRS.CH2.1302.2/17]

DALGETTY, JOHN, in Aberlemno, 1691. [NRS.E69.11.1]

DALL, ALEXANDER, a merchant in Brechin, a deed, 1688. [NRS.RD4.63.205]

DALL, ALEXANDER, in Kirriemuir, husband of Janet Millar, a sasine, 1648. [NRS.RS35.S2.III.47]

DALL, ALEXANDER, in Haugh of Brechin Castle, testament, 1691, Comm. Brechin. [NRS]

DALL, DAVID, in Kirriemuir, a sasine,1698. [NRS.RS35.S3.X.131]

DALL, ISOBEL, sasine, 1658. [AA.F5.85]

DALL, JAMES, the younger, a writer and councillor in Forfar, a sasine, 1669. [NRS.GD1.61.7] [AA.F1.1.2] , in Forfar,1691. [NRS.E69.11.1]

DALL, THOMAS, in Kinnell, 1691. [NRS.E69.11.1]

DALL, WILLIAM, in Kinnell, 1691. [NRS.E69.11.1]

DALL, WILLIAM, from Forfar, was admitted as a member of the Scots Charitable Society of Boston, Massachusetts, in 1760. [NEHGSms]

DALZELL, SIBYLLA, spouse of Hugh Rodger in Kirriemuir,a sasine, 1692. [NRS.RS35.S3.IV.472]

THE PEOPLE OF STRATHMORE, 1600-1799

DALMAHOY, ROBERT, a merchant and saddler in Brechin, testament, 1795, Comm. Brechin. [NRS]

DAND, JOHN, sr., in Craigend of Balnabrich, and his spouse Margaret Syme, testament, 1664, Comm. Brechin. [NRS]

DARGIE, KATHERINE, 1787. [NRS.CH2.1302.2/125]

DARGIE, JOHN, on the Hill of Finavon, testament, 1613, Comm. Brechin. [NRS]

DARGIE, JOHN, in the Mains of Finavon, Oathlaw, and spouse Agnes Peacock, testament, 1662, Comm. Brechin. [NRS]

DAVID, JOHN, in Oathlaw, 1691. [NRS.E69.11.1]

DAVIDSON, EDWARD, in Dunnichen, 1691. [NRS.E69.11.1]

DAVIDSON, ISOBEL, in Haughs of Ballinshore, rebuked, 1716. [NRS.CH2.1302.1.105]

DAVIDSON, JAMES, a wright or brazier in Brechin, spouse Agnes Moffat, a sasine, 1692. [NRS.RS35.S3.IX.185][RP.II.345]

DAVIDSON, JOHN, in Guthrie, 1691. [NRS.E69.11.1]

DAVIDSON, JOHN, in Aberlemno, 1691. [NRS.E69.11.1]

DAVIDSON, THOMAS, in Pitmaddie, Menmuir, testament, 1599, Comm. Brechin. [NRS]

DAVIDSON, WILLIAM, versus John Brown, Forfar Burgh Court, 25/28 August 1784; versus William Mitchell, Forfar Burgh Court, 20 May 1785. [AA.F1.8.1]

DAVIE, ALEXANDER, 1731. [NRS.CH2.1302.185]

DAW, ALEXANDER, in Halton, Kinnell, wife Agnes Paton, testaments, 1605, 1606, Comm. St Andrews. [NRS]

DAW, ANDREW, a smith in the Tenements of Caldham, Brechin, and spouse Katherine Davidson, testament, 1642, Comm. Brechin. [NRS]

DAW, ANDREW, in Oathlaw, 1691. [NRS.E69.11.1]

DAW, JAMES, in Balmadie, in Rescobie, 1691. [NRS.E69.11.1]

DAW, JAMES, a merchant in Brechin, 1691. [RPCS.XVI.605]

DAW, THOMAS, in Carcary, Farnell, testament, 1638, Comm. Brechin. [NRS]

DAW, WILLIAM, in Tenements of Caldham, testament, 1638, Comm. Brechin. [NRS]

DAWSON, JAMES, in Tannadice, 1691. [NRS.E69.11.1]

DAY, THOMAS, in Forfar,1691. [NRS.E69.11.1]

DEAN, ALEXANDER, in Tannadice, 1691. [NRS.E69.11.1]

DEAS, JAMES, a burgess of Brechin, a sasine, 1673. [NRS.RS35.S3.V.128]

DEMPSTER, CHARLES, a burgess of Brechin, a sasine, 1679. [NRS.RS35.S3.VII.107]

DEMPSTER, GEORGE and ISOBELL, in Easter Drums, Brechin, 1610. [RGS.VII.269]

DEMPSTER, GEORGE, a burgess of Brechin, a sasine, 1672, father of George and James. [NRS.RS35.V.93]

DEMPSTER, JAMES, a bailie of Brechin, dead by 1638, spouse of Janet Baillie, parents of Catherine, Janet, and John, a sasine.. [NRS.RS35.S2.I.430]

DEMPSTER, JAMES, burgess of Brechin, spouse Elizabeth Fullarton, sasine, 1637, [NRS.RS35.S2.I.104]; a donor in 1651. [Brechin Cathedral]

DEMPSTER, JAMES, a master of Brechin Grammar School, preceptor of the Maison Dieu in the Cathedral Church in 1684, son of George Dempster, a sasine. [NRS.RS35.S3.VIII.3]

DEMPSTER, JOHN, a burgess of Brechin, testament, 1578, Comm. Edinburgh. [NRS]

DEMPSTER, JOHN, a master of Brechin Grammar School, preceptor of the Maison Dieu in the Cathdral Church a sasine, 1672, son of George Dempster, minister of Brechin fom 1665 to 1676. [NRS.RS35.S3.V.27][F.6.375]

DEMPSTER, JOHN, a skinner in Brechin, a sasine, 1654. [NRS.RS35.S2.IV.428]

THE PEOPLE OF STRATHMORE, 1600-1799

DEMPSTER, JOHN, of Dunnichen, testament, 1760, Comm. Brechin. [NRS]

DEMPSTER, MARION, mother of James Clerk a merchant in Brechin, 1620. [RPCS.XII.216]

DEMPSTER, ROBERT, a saddler burgess of Brechin, 1606. [RPCS.VII.643]

DEMPSTER, ROBERT, a skinner burgess of Brechin, spouse of Lucres Balbirny, testament, 1622, Comm. Brechin. [NRS]

DEMPSTER, ROBERT, bailie of Brechin, relict Nicolas Clark, sasine, 1669. [NRS.RS35.S3.IV.176]

DEUCHAR, ANDREW, in Farnell, 1691. [NRS.E69.11.1]

DEUCHAR, ANDREW, kirk officer of Dunnichen, relict Agnes Dumbreck, testament, 1728, Comm. Brechin. [NRS]

DEUCHARS, DAVID, in Nether Bargillo,Tannadice, 1691. [NRS.E69.11.1]

DEUCHARS, DAVID, in Farnell, 1691. [NRS.E69.11.1]

DEUCHAR, JAMES, in Haugh of Finavon, spouse Christian Lindsay, testament, 1626, Comm. Brechin. [NRS]

DEUCHAR, JAMES, in Lonhead, an elder in Kirriemuir, 1720. [NRS.CH2.1302.1.121]

DEUCHAR, JEAN, in Ground of Logie, 1724. [NRS.CH2.1302.141]

DEUCHAR, ROBERT, in Dunnichen, 1691. [NRS.E69.11.1]

DEUCHAR, ROBERT, servant to David Barron clerk of Kirriemuir, 1745. [NRS.RH11.70.7]

DEUCHARS, ROBERT, in Old Cotton of Gardin, Kirkden, testament, 1747, Comm. St Andrews. [NRS]

DEUCHARS, WILLIAM, in Forfar,1691. [NRS.E69.11.1]

DICK, JOHN, versus Thomas Allerich, Forfar Burgh Court, 16 June 1784, 25 June 1784, 11/18 August 1784. [AA.F1.8.1]

DICKIE, CHARLES, of Newmonthill, provost of Forfar, and his son Charles, deeds, 1707. [NRS.RD3.111.292; RD3.112.8]

THE PEOPLE OF STRATHMORE, 1600-1799

DICKIESON, CHARLES, in Forfar,1691. [NRS.E69.11.1]

DICKIESON, JOHN, a burgess of Forfar, a witness in 1603. [RGS.VI.1404]

DICKESON, RICHARD, a burgess of Forfar, an assizeman in 1600. [RGS.VI.1176]

DICKSON, ALEXANDER, a shoemaker in Forfar, 1681. [AA.F5.125] a cordiner in Forfar,1691. [NRS.E69.11.1]

DICKSON, ALEXANDER, jr, in Forfar, 1691. [NRS.E60.11.1]

DICKSON, ALEXANDER, in Rescobie, 1691. [NRS.E69.11.1]

DICKSON, CHARLES, a maltman in Forfar, spouse Isobel Piggot, sasine, 1646. [NRS.RS35.S2.III.527]

DICKSON, CHARLES, a cordiner and stent master of Forfar, 1689. [AA.F1.1.2]

DICKSON, CHARLES, of Newmonthill, formerly a bailie of Forfar, sasine, 1695. [NRS.RS35.S3.IX.356] [AA.F1.1.2]

DICKSON, CHARLES, a maltman in Forfar,1691. [NRS.E69.11.1]

DICKSON, DAVID, in Forfar, 1614. [RGS.VII.1024]

DICKSON, DAVID, a merchant in Forfar, sasine, 1646. [NRS.RS35.S2.III.523]

DICKSON, DAVID, a bailie of Forfar, 1658, 1661, 1671; burgh commissioner to Parliament, 1660-1661; provost, 1676, 1684. [RPCS.I.122][AA.F1.4.1; F5.111; F1.1.1] [NRS.RD4.38.802; RD4.53.660; RD3.27.132]; a burgess of Forfar, a bond, 1666. [NRS.RD2.17.79] , in Forfar,1691. [NRS.E69.11.1]

DICKSON, DAVID, a vintner in Kirriemuir, deed, 1714. [NRS.RD4.88.940]

DICKSON, DAVID, a hammerman in Forfar, deed, 1715. [NRS.RD4.116.252]

DICKSON, DAVID, versus Hutcheson and Stewart, Forfar Burgh Court, 15 December 1784. [AA.F1.8.1]

DICKSON, HELEN, in Kirriemuir, 1733. [NRS.CH2.1302.199]

THE PEOPLE OF STRATHMORE, 1600-1799

DICKSON, JAMES, a merchant and bailie of Forfar, 1680s [NRS.GD1,61.11] [AA.F1.1.2] in Forfar,1691. [NRS.E69.11.1], deeds, 1702,1714. [NRS.RD3.99.2.127; RD4.88.718]

DICKSON, JAMES, was admitted as a burgess and freeman of Forfar, 1688. [AA.F1.1.2]

DICKSON, JAMES, a cordiner, in Forfar,1691. [NRS.E69.11.1]

DICKSON, JAMES, in Kinnetles, 1691. [NRS.E69.11.1]

DICKSON, JAMES, was served heir to his father William Dickson the town clerk of Forfar, 1744. [AA.F5.145]

DICKSON, JAMES, in Forfar, 1759, 1791. [NRS.E326.1.169]

DICKSON, JOHN, a bailie of Forfar, 1607, 1608. [RPCS.VII.408; VIII.647]

DICKSON, JOHN, a merchant in Forfar, a bond, 1676. [NRS.RD4.38.870]

DICKSON, JOHN, a maltman in Forfar, spouse Elizabeth Strang, sasine, 1676. [NRS.RS35.S3.VI.178]

DICKSON, JOHN, a writer in Forfar, husband of Marjorie Donaldson, deeds, 1683, 1684, 1687. [NRS.RD4.52.145; RD2.64.354; RD4.61.1030] in Forfar,1691. [NRS.E69.11.1]

DICKSON, MARGARET, in Forfar,1691. [NRS.E69.11.1]

DICKSON, PATRICK, of Slatefield, born 1772, died 1801, husband of Isabella Steele, born 1775, died 1838. [Forfar gravestone]

DICKSON, WILLIAM, son of Provost David Dickson of Forfar, deeds, 1676, 1684. [NRS.RD2.42.238; RD4.53.660], clerk in Forfar,1691. [NRS.E69.11.1]

DICKSON, WILLIAM, son of John Dickson, a merchant in Forfar, a deed, 1684. [NRS.RD4.53.660] in Forfar,1691. [NRS.E69.11.1]

DICKSON, WILLIAM, tenant in Lunanhead and Ninewalls, 1686. [AA.F1.1.2]

DICKSON, WILLIAM, a notary public, in Glamis, 1681 [NRS.E69.11.1]

THE PEOPLE OF STRATHMORE, 1600-1799

DICKSON, WILLIAM, a notary public in Tannadice, 1691. [NRS.E69.11.1]

DICKSON, ..., son of the late John Dickson a glover, was admitted as a burgess and freeman of Forfar, 1686. [AA.F1.1.2]

DILLIECLAUS, JOHN, a merchant in Forfar,1691. [NRS.E69.11.1]

DILLIECLOWER, JOHN, in Forfar,1691. [NRS.E69.11.1]

DILLICLOWER, JOHN, in Kinnetles, 1691. [NRS.E69.11.1]

DIN, ANDREW, in Tannadice, 1691. [NRS.E69.11.1]

DIRROW, JAMES, son of James Dirrow, a wright in Brechin, sasine, 1692. [NRS.RS35.S3.IX.118]

DOCTOR, JAMES, a weaver in Herdhill, 1724. [NRS.CH2.1302.143]

DOIG, ALEXANDER, in Glamis, 1681. [NRS.E69.11.1]

DOIG, ANDREW, in Kirriemuir, husband of Mary Guild, a sasine,1637. [NRS.RS35.S2.I.76]

DOIG, ANDREW, a weaver in Kirriemuir, 1786. [NRS.CH2.1302.2/123]

DOIG, DAVID, born 1733, tenant in Drum of Eassie, died 19 September 1783, husband of Hellen Smith, parents of John, Agnes, Andrew, and George Doig. [Nevay gravestone]

DOIG, ELIZABETH, 1787. [NRS.CH2.1302.2/125]

DOIG, FRANCIS, of Reswallie, in Rescobie, 1691. [NRS.E69.11.1]

DOIG, JAMES, in Forfar, 1614. [RGS.VII.1024]

DOIG, JAMES, born 1686, son of Andrew Doig and his wife Jean Wardroper, died 1715. [Nevay gravestone]

DOIG, JAMES, versus Alexander Steele, Forfar Burgh Court, 25 August 1784. [AA.F1.8.1]

DOIG, JAMES, the beadle, 1787. [NRS.CH2.1302.2/125]; kirk-officer in Kirriemuir, testament, 1791, Comm. St Andrews. [NRS] [NRS.CH2.1302.2/117]

THE PEOPLE OF STRATHMORE, 1600-1799

DOIG, JANET, spouse of William Clerk, 1784.
[NRS.CH2.1302.2/103]

DOIG, JOHN, in Myreside, parish of Forfar, testament, 1598, Comm. Edinburgh. [NRS]

DOIG, JOHN, born 1709, in Kirkinch, died 18 September 1780, husband of Agnes Christie. [Nevay gravestone]

DOIG, PETER, born 1780, in Kirkinch, died 28 February 1813, husband of Elizabeth Anderson. [Nevay gravestone]

DOIG, ROBERT, a merchant in Kirriemuir, spouse Anna Stormonth, 1744, 1745. [NRS.RH11.70.7]

DOIG, WILLIAM, born 1640, a maltman, died 1686, wife Helen Adamson died aged 45 years, testament, 1687, Comm. St Andrews, sasines. [Kirriemuir gravestone] [NRS.RS35.S3.VI.93; VII.24; VIII.389]

DOIG, WILLIAM, in Wester Logie, 1742, 1746.
[NRS.RH11.70.7]

DOIG, WILLIAM, in Ground of Langbank, 1745.
[NRS.CH2.1302.247]

DON, ALEXANDER, at the Kirk of Menmuir, testament, 1652, Comm. Brechin. [NRS]

DON, ALEXANDER, a cordiner in Kirriemuir, a sasine, 1693.
[NRS.RS35.S3.IX.404]

DON, GILBERT, in Forfar, 1785. [NRS.E326.3.19]

DON, JOHN, a merchant in Kirriemuir, husband of Eupham Fyfe, a sasine, 1675. [NRS.RS35.S3.VI.64]

DON, JOHN, a merchant in Kirriemuir, son of John Don a merchant there, a sasine, 1692. [NRS.RS35.S3.IX.6]

DON, JOHN, a merchant in Kirriemuir, 1732. [NRS.GD7.2.151]

DON, MARGARET, wife of (1) Thomas Traill, and, by 1727, (2) James Lindsay, dead by 1739, and (3) John Fyfe a merchant in Kirriemuir, died in 1758. [NRS.GD7.2.142/215/236/240]

DONALD, ALEXANDER, in Fotheringham, testament, 1579. Comm. Brechin. [NRS]

THE PEOPLE OF STRATHMORE, 1600-1799

DONALD, DAVID, in Aberlemno, 1691. [NRS.E69.11.1]

DONALD, ALEXANDER, in Luddinch, Kirriemuir, testament,1648, Comm. St Andrews. [NRS]

DONALD, ANDREW, in Cruikitbank, Kirriemuir, husband of Elizabeth Wilson, testament,1637, Comm. St Andrews. [NRS]

DONALD, CATHARINE, spouse of William Milne at the Mill of Kirriemuir, a sasine,1638. [NRS.RS35.S2.I.480]

DONALD, JAMES, a merchant in Kirriemuir, 1742, 1746, [NRS.RH11.70.7]; father of George Donald in Madras, India, sasine, 1777. [NRS.RS35.26.116]

DONALDSON, ANDREW, in Forfar,1691. [NRS.E69.11.1]

DONALDSON, DAVID, a merchant burgess of Brechin, spouse [1] Elizabeth Watt, sasine, 1643, [2] Margaret Gray, 1656]; a bailie of Brechin, was granted the lands of Newton in Forfar by Oliver Cromwell in 1657; father of Elspet and Jean, a sasine. [AA.B1.10.13][RGS.X.586][NRS.RS35.S2.i.101/ v.376] [Brechin Cathedral Monumental Inscription]

DONALDSON, JAMES, in Kirriemuir, 1686. [NRS.RH11.70.1/1, 4]

DONALDSON, JAMES, in Tannadice, 1691. [NRS.E69.11.1]

DONALDSON, JAMES, in Forfar, 1691. [NRS.E60.11.1]

DONALDSON, JAMES, in Glamis, 1691. [NRS.E69.11.1]

DONALDSON, JAMES, a merchant in Kirriemuir, 1741. [NRS.CH2.1302.231]

DONALDSON, JOHN, in Aberlemno, 1691. [NRS.E69.11.1]

DONALDSON, JOHN, sr., merchant in Brechin, 1691. [RPCS.XVI.605]

DONALDSON, JOHN, jr., a merchant in Brechin and chamberlain to the Earl of Panmure, 1691. [RPCS.XVI.605]

DONALDSON, JOHN, in Rescobie, 1691. [NRS.E69.11.1]

DONALDSON, JOHN, in Kirriemuir, testament, 1739, Comm. St Andrews. [NRS]

THE PEOPLE OF STRATHMORE, 1600-1799

DONALDSON, KATHERINE, in High Street, Brechin, 1609.
[RPCS.VIII.335]

DONALDSON, THOMAS, sr. and jr., in Glamis, 1681.
[NRS.E69.11.1]

DONALDSON, WILLIAM, in Tannadice, 1691.
[NRS.E69.11.1]

DONNAT, JAMES, in Montpersie, Kingoldrum, testament, 1679, Comm. Brechin. [NRS]

DORRETT, ALEXANDER, maltman in Brechin, 1691.
[RPCS.XVI.605]

DORWARD, ISOBEL, a witch in Forfar, 1661. [AA.F5.35.3]

DORWARD, JOHN, in Balmadie, Rescobie, 1691.
[NRS.E69.11.1]

DORWARD, JOHN, born 1652, resident of Ground of Balmadies, died 1727. [Guthrie gravestone]

DORWARD, MARGARET, spouse of George Renny in Kirriemuir, a sasine, 1638. [NRS.RS35.S2.I.312]

DOUGALL, ANDREW, in Shedhill, an elder in Kirriemuir, 1720, 1733. [NRS.CH2.1302.1.121/193]

DOUGALL, DAVID, a wright in Kirriemuir, husband of Isobel Hendry or Henderson, a sasine, 1685. [NRS.RS35.S3.VIII.433]

DOUGALL, GEORGE, son of David Dougall, a wright in Kirriemuir, husband of Helen Bruce, a sasine, 1692.
[NRS.RS35.S3.IX.21]

DOUGALL, GEORGE, a feuar in Kirriemuir, 1742, 1745.
[NRS.RH11.70.7]

DOUGALL, GEORGE, a maltster in Kirriemuir, 1716, 1745.
[NRS. CH2.1302.1.105; RH11.70.7]

DOUGALL, JAMES, a merchant in Kirriemuir, husband of Katherine Hendrie, a sasine,1693. [NRS.RS35.S3.IX.505]

DOUGALL, JAMES, son of David Dougall, a wright in Kirriemuir, a sasine, 1692. [NRS.RS35.S3.IX.16]

THE PEOPLE OF STRATHMORE, 1600-1799

DOUGALL, JAMES, a merchant in Kirriemuir, deed, 1714. [NRS.RD4.88.672]

DOUGALL, JAMES, in Meikle Mill, an elder in Kirriemuir, 1720. [NRS.CH2.1302.1.121]

DOUGALL, JAMES, a surgeon apothecary in Kirriemuir, 1741, 1744; a bailie of the Regality, 1744. [NRS.RH11.70.7]

DOUGALL, JOHN, Presbytery bursar, 1718. [NRS.CH2.1302.1.115]

DOUGALL, JOHN, at Meikle Mill, 1719. [NRS.CH2.1302.1.119]

DOUGLAS, DAVID, and his son William, at the Mill of Kirriemuir, a sasine,1638; his spouse Margaret Ogilvie, testament, 1613, Comm. St Andrews. [NRS.RS35.S2.I.517]

DOUGLAS, JANE, 1783, 1786. [NRS.CH2.1302.2/93, 123]

DOUGLAS, JOHN, in Kinnell, 1691. [NRS.E69.11.1]

DOUGLAS, ROBERT, MA, Bishop of Brechin from 1682 to 1684. [F.6.375]

DOUGLAS, ROBERT, of Bridgetoun, sasine, 1744. [AA.F1.4.3]

DOUGLAS, WILLIAM, a surgeon apothecary and provost of Forfar, a deed, 1706, 1718. [NRS.RD4.99.983; GD205.24.164]

DOUNIE, ANDREW, born 1631, a weaver burgess of Brechin, died 6 January 1696. [Brechin Cathedral gravestone]

DOUNIE, DAVID, in Lonhead of Guthrie, spouse Helen Shanks, testament, 1614, Comm. Brechin. [NRS]

DOUNIE, JOHN, in Forfar, 1691. [NRS.E60.11.1]

DOWNIE, JOHN, in Aberlemno, 1691. [NRS.E69.11.1]

DRIMMIE, ALEXANDER, a creelman in Strathcathro, testament, 1628, Comm. Brechin. [NRS]

DROVER, JOHN, in Tannadice, 1691. [NRS.E69.11.1]

DRUMMOND, ANDREW, at the Ford of Fochray, Strathcathro, spouse Isobel Guthrie, testament, 1625, Comm. Brechin. [NRS]

THE PEOPLE OF STRATHMORE, 1600-1799

DRUMMOND, JAMES, Bishop of Brechin from 1684 to 1689. [F.6.376]

DUAR, JAMES, in Glamis, 1681. [NRS.E69.11.1]

DUFFIE, JAMES, in Chapelton, Rescobie, 1691. [NRS.E69.11.1]

DUGALL, WILLIAM, in Oathlaw, 1691. [NRS.E69.11.1]

DUGAT, GILBERT, and Elizabeth Scott, parents of John, James, Mary, and Ann, 1660-1670s. [Nevay gravestone]

DUNCAN, ALEXANDER, and spouse Agnes Bruce in Kingoldrum, testament, 1621, Comm. Brechin. [NRS]

DUNCAN, ALEXANDER, in Methie Inverarity, 1691. [NRS.E69.11.1]

DUNCAN, ALEXANDER, in Tannadice, 1691. [NRS.E69.11.1]

DUNCAN, JAMES, a weaver in Brechin, and his wife Catherine Carr, a sasine, 1664. [NRS.RS35.S3.II.58]

DUNCAN, JAMES, in Glamis, 1681. [NRS.E69.11.1]

DUNCAN, JAMES, in Tannadice, 1691. [NRS.E69.11.1]

DUNCAN, JAMES, tenant in Kindin, 1741. [NRS.RH11.70.7]

DUNCAN, JAMES, a church elder pre-1783. [NRS.CH2.1302.2/97]

DUNCAN, JOHN, Deacon of the Baxter Craft of Brechin, 1609. [RPCS.VIII.690/704]

DUNCAN, JOHN, a brabiner burgess of Brechin, spouse Marion Hall, testament, 1621, Comm. Brechin. [NRS]

DUNCAN, JOHN, of Balfour, Kincoldrum, testament, 1629, Comm. Brechin. [NRS]

DUNCAN, JOHN, a weaver in Brechin, spouse of Janet Stevenson, a sasine, 1637. [NRS.RS35.S2.I.82]

DUNCAN, JOHN, son of John Duncan, a weaver in Brechin, husband of Janet Mathie, a sasine, 1666. [NRS.RS35.S3.III.113]

THE PEOPLE OF STRATHMORE, 1600-1799

DUNCAN, JOHN, jr., versus .... Tindal, Forfar Burgh Court, 18 February 1785. [AA.F1.8.1]

DUNCAN, ROBERT, in Bannaboth, Kirriemuir, testament, 1636, Comm. St Andrews. [NRS]

DUNCAN, ROBERT, a weaver in Brechin, spouse of [1] Isobel, daughter of Robert Bruce at Meikle Cowle, a sasine, 1677, [NRS.RS35.S3.VI.388]; [2] Isobel Williamson, testament, 1685, Comm. Brechin. [NRS]

DUNCAN, THOMAS, a baxter in Brechin, 1609. [RPCS.VIII.704]

DUNCAN, THOMAS, in Ground of Logy, 1745. [NRS.RH11.70.7]

DUNCANSON, DAVID, a baxter burgess of Brechin, 1605. [RPCS.VII.616]

DUNCANSON, JOHN, a baxter in Brechin, a sasine, 1665. [NRS.RS35.S3.II.290]

DUNDAS, JOHN, a merchant in Kirriemuir, testament, 1786, Comm. St Andrews. [NRS]

DUNDAS, Captain LAURENCE, a bailie of Brechin, spouse Helen Ogilvie, a sasine, 1661. [NRS.RS35.S3.I.197]

DURIE, ALEXANDER, in Dunnichen, 1691. [NRS.E69.11.1]

DURIE, JOSHUA, MA, minister of Forfar from 1596 to 1603. [F.5.285]

DRYDEN, JANET, mortcloth and bell, Kirriemuir, 1716. [NRS.CH2.1302.1.103]

DUTHIE, DAVID, in the Steps of Dairsie, formerly in Kirriemuir, a sasine, 1661. [NRS.RS35.S3.I.183]

DUTHIE, ISOBEL, daughter of Thomas Duthie a braboner in Kirriemuir, a sasine, 1642. [NRS.RS35.II.462]

DUTHIE, ISOBEL, spouse of Thomas Hendrie in Kirriemuir, a sasine, 1638. [NRS.RS35.S2.I.229]

DUTHIE, ISOBEL, daughter of John Jack a cordiner in Kirriemuir, a sasine, 1656. [NRS.RS35.S2.V.288]

DUTHIE, JAMES, 1764. [NRS.CH2.1302.215]

DUTHIE, JANET, widow of John Sim,1726.
[NRS.CH2.1302/157]

DUTHIE, JOHN, in Hardhill, 1745. [NRS.RH11.70.7]

DUTHIE, JOHN, at Boat of Whitewell, 1745. [NRS.RH11.70.7]

DUTHIE, JOHN, a wright, and spouse Margaret Strachan, a sasine, 1756. [AA.F5.146]

DUTHIE, JOHN, versus Thomas Allerich, 16 June 1784, 25 June 1784, 18 August 1784, Forfar Burgh Court; versus Robert Masterton, Forfar Burgh Court, 25 August 1784. [AA.F1.8.1]

DUTHIE, MARGARET, daughter of Robert Duthie and spouse of Andrew Ritchie in Kirriemuir, a sasine, 1685. [NRS.RS35.S3.VIII.299]

DUTHIE, PATRICK, a feuar in Kirriemuir,1742, 1745, 1746. [NRS.RH11.70.7]

DUTHIE, ROBERT, born 1620, in Balmadie, died 1667, spouse Euphane Gudlet, died 1668. [Kirkden gravestone]

DUTHIE, ROBERT, in Kirriemuir, husband of Isobel Adamson, a sasine, 1661. [NRS.RS35.S3.I.182]

DUTHIE, THOMAS, a braboner in Kirriemuir, husband of (1) Janet How, (2) Elizabeth Ogilvie, a sasine, 1637; testament,1640, Comm. St Andrews. [NRS] [NRS.RS35.S2.I.174]

DYSART, GEORGE, in Forfar, 1691. [NRS.E69.11.1]

DYSART, or LAIRD, JAMES, a burgess of Forfar, testament, 1593, Comm. Edinburgh. [NRS]

DYSART, THOMAS, a brabiner in Brechin, wife Janet Webster, a sasine, 1684. [NRS.RS35.S3.VIII.45]

EADIE, WILLIAM, born 1740, graduated MA from St Andrews in 1760, minister of Kirriemuir from 1772 until his death on 20 October 1784. Husband of Helen Leslie, parents of Christian, Francis, William Carnegie, and Mary. [F.5.297]

EASSIE, DAVID, in Tannadice, 1691. [NRS.E69.11.1]

EASSIE, WILLIAM, a tailor in Kirriemuir, husband of Lilias Lyn, a sasine,1656. [NRS.RS35.S2.V.73]

EASSON, JOHN, a litster in Kirriemuir, husband of Janet Paterson, a sasine, 1637. [NRS.RS35.S2.I.110]

EASTON, JOHN, a weaver in Forfar, sasine, 1760. [NRS.GD1.369.242]

EASTON, THOMAS, versus James Wood, Forfar Burgh Court, 16/25 June 1784; versus David Allan, Forfar Burgh Court, 4/9 November 1785. [AA.F1.8.1]

EDIE, ALEXANDER, in Aberlemno, 1691. [NRS.E69.11.1]

EDGAR, DAVID, of Keithock, testament,1723, Comm. Brechin. [NRS]

EDMONSTON, DAVID, versus ... Whyte, Forfar Burgh Court, 13 April 1785. [AA.F1.8.1]

EDWARD, AGNES, in Pyper Balgray, Kincaldrum, testament, 1715, Comm. Brechin. [NRS]

EDWARD, ALEXANDER, in Dodova, Kirriemuir, testament, 1614, Comm. St Andrews. [NRS]

EDWARD, ALEXANDER, in Kirriemuir, 1717. [NRS.CH2.1302.1.109]

EDWARD, ANDREW, tenant in Ballochs, 1743, 1745, 1746; testament, 1756, Comm. St Andrews. [NRS.RH11.70.7]

EDWARD, DAVID, 1729. [NRS.CH2.1302.173]

EDWARD, HELEN, in Ednaughtie, 1738. [NRS.CH2.1302.225]

EDWARD, JAMES, in Tannadice, 1691. [NRS.E69.11.1]

EDWARD, JAMES, a man-servant in Kirriemuir, 1783. [NRS.CH2.1302.2/95]

EDWARD, JOHN, in Inchmilne, parish of Kirriemuir, testament, 1614, Comm. St Andrews. [NRS]

EDWARD, JOHN, in Dodowo, parish of Kirriemuir, testament, 1638, Comm. St Andrews. [NRS]

EDWARD, JOHN, in Kirriemuir, 1739, 1742.
[NRS.GD16.42.722; RH11.70.7]

EDWARD, JOHN, sr., in Wester Pearsie, Kingoldrum, testament, 1781, Comm. Brechin. [NRS]

EDWARD, MARGARET, in Kirriemuir, 1724, 1728.
[NRS.CH2.1302.147/165]

EDWARD, ROBERT, in Cruikit-bank, parish of Kirriemuir, testament, 1637, Comm. St Andrews. [NRS]

EDWARD, ROBERT, and his spouse Agnes Findlay, 1718.
[NRS.CH2.1302.1.115]

EDWARD, THOMAS, in Inchmilne, parish of Kirriemuir, testament, 1615, Comm. St Andrews. [NRS]

ELIES, GEORGE, burgh drummer of Forfar, 1660; an alleged witch in Forfar, 1662. [AA.F1.1.1] [RPCS.I.162]

ELIAS, THOMAS, in Tannadice, 1691. [NRS.E69.11.1]

ELIAS, WILLIAM, in Tannadice, 1691. [NRS.E69.11.1]

ELLIOT, JAMES, born about 1572, son of Andrew Elliot of Cuithley, Arbroath, graduated MA from St Andrews in 1592, minister of Forfar from 1618 to his death in 1637. Husband of Eupham Lindsay, parents of Andrew, James, and a daughter, a sasine. [F.5.285][NRS.RS35.S2.I.454, 466]

ELLIS, ALEXANDER, in Rescobie, 1691. [NRS.E69.11.1]

ERSKINE, ALEXANDER, burgess of Brechin, his widow Isabel, daughter of William Ramsay the town clerk there, a sasine, 1643. [NRS.RS35.S2.II.165]

ERSKINE, ALEXANDER, at Brechin Castle, factor to the Earl of Panmure, and Anna Maule, his spouse, testament, 1674, Comm.Brechin. [NRS]

ERSKINE, FRANCIS, in Guthrie, 1691. [NRS.E69.11.1]

ERSKINE, GEORGE, at Brechin Castle, a sasine, 1679.
[NRS.RS35,S3,VII.226]; testament, 1683, Comm.Brechin. [NRS]

ERSKINE, ISOBELL, widow of John Dougall, 1746.
[NRS.RH11.70.7]

ERSKINE, JAMES, Lord Grange, was admitted as a burgess of Forfar, 1709. [NRS.GD124.8.57]

ERSKINE, MARGARET, daughter of Thomas Erskine in Kirriemuir, a sasine, 1643. [NRS.RS35.S2.II.366]

ERSKINE, THOMAS, in Tayock, Brechin, testament, 1592, Comm. Edinburgh. [NRS]

ERSKINE, THOMAS, a tanner in Kirriemuir, husband of Janet Galloway, a sasine, 1639. [NRS.RS35.S2.I.557]

ERSKINE THOMAS, father of Thomas Erskine in Kirriemuir, a sasine, 1642. [NRS.RS35.S2.II.366]

ESPLIN, ALEXANDER, in Forfar,1691. [NRS.E69.11.1]

ESPLIN, ANDREW, in Loanhead of Guthrie, spouse Elspet Buchan, testament, 1637, Comm. Brechin. [NRS]

ESPLIN, ELIZABETH, daughter of the late John Esplin, in Hillhead of Careston, testament, 1718, Comm. Brechin. [NRS]

ESPLIN, FRANCIS, in Guthrie, 1691. [NRS.E69.11.1],

ESPLIN, JAMES, born 1535, kirk officer, died 1630. [Guthrie gravestone]

ESPLIN, JAMES, a cordiner in Forfar, a bond, 1671. [NRS.RD2.31.506]

ESPLIN, JOHN, a tanner burgess of Forfar, 1650. [NRS.GD1.61.4]

ESPLIN, JOHN, was admitted as a burgess of Forfar, 1660. [AA.F1.1.1]

ESPLIN, JOHN, son of Thomas Esplin a cordiner, was admitted as a burgess and freeman of Forfar, 1686. [AA.F1.1.2], in Forfar, 1691. [NRS.E60.11.1]

ESPLIN, JOHN, in Hillhead of Careston, testament, 1710, Comm. Brechin. [NRS]

ESPLIN, MARGARET, in Methie Inverarity, 1691. [NRS.E69.11.1]

ESPLIN, PATRICK, in Heughhead of Guthrie, testament, 1686, Comm. Brechin. [NRS]

THE PEOPLE OF STRATHMORE, 1600-1799

ESPLIN, THOMAS, a councillor of Forfar, 1660. [AA.F1.1.1]

ESPLIN, THOMAS, a cordiner in Forfar, a bond, 1671. [NRS.RD2.31.506]

ESPLIN, WILLIAM, a cordiner burgess of Forfar, son of the deceased John Esplin, a cordiner burgess there, 1687.[NRS.GD1.61.10]

ESSY, JOHN, in Cadham, 1724. [NRS.CH21302/143]

ESSIE, WILLIAM, was imprisoned in Brechin Castle in 1617. [RPCS.XI.57]

FAIR, CHARLES, in Guthrie, 1691. [NRS.E69.11.1]

FAIRLIE, ANDREW, a saddler burgess of Brechin, testament, 1630, Comm. Brechin. [NRS]

FAIRLIE, NORMAND, jr., a donor in 1648. [Brechin Cathedral]

FAIRN, DAVID, in Oathlaw, 1691. [NRS.E69.11.1]

FAIRN, JOHN, in Tannadice, 1691. [NRS.E69.11.1]

FAIRWEATHER, ALEXANDER, in Rescobie, 1691. [NRS.E69.11.1]

FAIRWEATHER, ANDREW, a litster in Brechin, spouse of Isabel Peers, a sasine, 1668. [NRS.RS35.S3.IV.101]

FAIRWEATHER, ANDREW, in the Barns of Glamis, wife Margaret Wilkie, born 1665, died 1688. [Glamis gravestone]

FAIRWEATHER, JAMES, in Rescobie, 1691. [NRS.E69.11.1]

FAIRWEATHER, JAMES, servant to Andrew Taylor in Ballindarge, 1741. [NRS.RH11.70.7]

FAIRWEATHER, JANET, 1731. [NRS.CH2.1302.185]

FAIRWEATHER, JOHN, a flesher burgess of Brechin, spouse Margaret Speid, testament, 1632, Comm. Brechin. [NRS]

FAIRWEATHER, JOHN, a merchant in Brechin, spouse Margaret daughter of James Collace, a sasine, 1652. [NRS.RS35.S2.IV.38]

THE PEOPLE OF STRATHMORE, 1600-1799

FAIRWEATHER, JOHN, in South Muir of Forfar, in Forfar,1691. [NRS.E69.11.1] tacks, 1708. 1718. [AA.F5/23]; a weaver in the Muir of Forfar, husband of ... Anderson, parents of James Fairweather, born 1722, a merchant in Glamis, died 1759. [Forfar MI]

FAIRWEATHER, JOHN, in Tannadice, 1691. [NRS.E69.11.1]

FALCONER, DAVID, of Balmashanner, son of John Falconer thereof, sasine,1735. [NRS.RS35.15.590]; heritor of Balmashanner, 1720. [AA.F5.133]

FALCONER, GEORGE, a cordiner burgess of Brechin, spouse Bessie Skair, testament, 1646, Comm. Brechin. [NRS]

FALCONER, JOHN, in Glamis, 1681. [NRS.E69.11.1]

FALCONER, JOHN, of Balmashanner, parish of Forfar, 1696; testament, 18 August 1703, Comm. St Andrews. [NRS.RD3.85.478]

FALCONER, JOHN, of Balmashanner, a deed, 1706. [NRS.RD4.98.230]

FALL, HARRY, a gypsy in Forfar, 1604. [RPCS.VII.15]

FAME, JAMES, a maltman in Forfar, 1691. [NRS.E60.11.1]

FANUM, DAVID, born 1737, died 1763. [Aberlemno gravestone]

FANUM, JOHN, born 1700, tenant in Nether Melgund, died 1746 sons John and James. [Aberlemno gravestone]

FARQUHARSON, ALEXANDER, a merchant in Kirriemuir, a sasine, 1664. [NRS.RS35.S3.II.134]

FARQUHARSON, ALEXANDER, of Ballo, Kirriemuir, testament, 1683, Comm. St Andrews. [NRS]

FARQUHARSON, ALEXANDER, in Glamis, 1797. [NRS.E326.10.3.24]

FARQUHARSON, ARCHIBALD, and spouse Anna Blair, in Keithock, testament, 1683, Comm. Brechin. [NRS]

FARQUHARSON, CHARLES, 1743. [NRS.RH11.70.7]

THE PEOPLE OF STRATHMORE, 1600-1799

FARQUHARSON, DAVID, in Balkirie, husband of Jean Anderson, born 1732, died 5 March 1776, parents of David, Alexander, Agnes, Isobel, William, Jean, and Margaret Farquharson. [Nevay gravestone]

FARQUHARSON, JAMES, in Alrick, Glen Isla, appointed Charles Farquharson a watchmaker in Dundee, as tutor to his daughter Margaret Farquharson on 11 May 1757. [NRS.C22.71.468]

FARQUHARSON, THOMAS, in Ground of Logie, 1743. [NRS.RH11.70.7]

FAWNES, ALEXANDER, a flesher burgess of Brechin, spouse Margaret Sand, testament, 1610, Comm. Brechin. [NRS]

FAWNES, WILLIAM, a flesher in Brechin, husband of Margaret Mathie, sasine, 1665. [NRS.RS35.S3.II.382]

FEARN, DAVID, sr, burgess of Brechin, spouse Elspet Mylne, testament, 1622, Comm. Brechin. [NRS]

FEARN, DAVID, burgess of Brechin, a sasine, 1661. [NRS.RS35.S3.I.336]

FEARN, DAVID, a cordiner in Brechin, sasine, 1676. [NRS.RS35.S3.VI.110]

FEARN, ELIZABETH, in Rescobie, 1691. [NRS.E69.11.1]

FEARN, JOHN, a bailie of Brechin, a sasine, 1675. [NRS.RS35.S3.VI.18]

FEE, WILLIAM, died 1708, wife Margaret Smith. [Ruthven gravestone]

FENTON, CHRISTINA, spouse of Thomas Brechin a brabiner in Brechin. a sasine, 1637. [NRS.RS35.S2.I.8]

FENTON, GEORGE, in the Meikleton of Guthrie, testament, 1610, Comm. Brechin. [NRS]

FENTON, GILBERT, in Kintyrie, Kirriemuir, testament, 1640, Comm. St Andrews. [NRS]

FENTON, JOHN, in Eastertoun of Guthrie, testament, 1612, Comm. Brechin. [NRS]

THE PEOPLE OF STRATHMORE, 1600-1799

FENTON, JOHN, son of the late George Fenton, in the Meikletoun of Guthries, testament, 1614, Comm. Brechin. [NRS]

FENTON, JOHN, and his spouse Helen Blair, in the Kirkton of Kingoldrum, testament, 1698, Comm. Brechin. [NRS]

FENTON, JOSEPH, in Balgorny, Glamis, 1797. [NRS.E326.10.3.24]

FENTON, KATHERINE, relict of Provost John Skinner, a donor in 1676. [Brechin Cathedral]

FENTON, JOHN, in Balloch, Kirriemuir, testament, 1618, Comm. St Andrews. [NRS]

FENTON, JOHN, a burgess of Brechin, 1628. [RPCS.II.174]

FENTON, JOHN, a merchant in Kirriemuir, husband of Christian Malder, a sasine, 1648. [NRS.RS35.S2.III.96]

FENTON, JOHN, in Tannadice, 1691. [NRS.E69.11.1]

FENTON, JOHN, a merchant in Brechin, a deed, 1697. [NRS.RD4.81.713]

FENTON, JOHN, in Kirriemuir, 1723. [NRS.CH2.1302.139]

FENTON, MARGARET, daughter of John Fenton a merchant in Kirriemuir, and spouse of Alexander Farquharson, son of Robert Farquharson in Braedownie, a sasine, 1648. [NRS.RS35.III.343,]

FENTON, PATRICK, 1773. [NRS.CH2.1302.2/55]

FENTON, ROBERT, burgess of Brechin, spouse Catherine Scott, ssine, 1637, [NRS.RS35.S2.I.103]; father of Agnes, Isobel and Janet, [RGS.VIII.1938]; testament, 1673, Comm. Brechin. [NRS]

FENTON, THOMAS, in Muirton, Kingoldrum, testament, 1629, Comm. Brechin. [NRS]

FENTON, THOMAS, a tanner in Kirriemuir, son of Grisel Galloway, a sasine, 1642. [NRS.RS35.II.315]

FENTON, THOMAS, was admitted as a burgess and freeman of Forfar, 1686; a litster and councillor of Forfar, 1688. [AA.F1.1.2], a dyer in Forfar, 1691. [NRS.E60.11.1]

FENTON, THOMAS, in Tannadice, 1691. [NRS.E69.11.1]

THE PEOPLE OF STRATHMORE, 1600-1799

FENTON, WILLIAM, a church elder before 1783. [NRS.CH2.1302.2/97]

FERGUSON, ALEXANDER, in Kinnell, 1691. [NRS.E69.11.1]

FERGUSON, ANDREW, a merchant, 1746. [NRS.RH11.70.7]

FERGUSON, DAVID, minister at Farnell, papers, 1720, [NRS.CS271.72097]; testament, 1753, Comm. Brechin. [NRS]

FERGUSON, JOHN, in Tannadice, 1691. [NRS.E69.11.1]

FERGUSON, WILLIAM, servant to James Bursh of Cadham, was admitted as a burgess of Forfar, 1661. [AA.F1.1.1]

FERRIER, ALEXANDER, in Farnell, 1691. [NRS.E69.11.1]

FERRIER, ANDREW, in Kinnell, 1691. [NRS.E69.11.1]

FERRIER, DAVID, in Kinnell, 1691. [NRS.E69.11.1]

FERRIER, HENRY, in Farnell, 1691. [NRS.E69.11.1]

FERRIER, JOHN, in Kinnell, 1691. [NRS.E69.11.1]

FERRIER, JOHN, in Farnell, 1691. [NRS.E69.11.1]

FERRIER, THOMAS, in Farnell, spouse Isobel Erskine, testaments, 1658, Comm. Brechin. [NRS]

FERRIER, THOMAS, in Oathlaw, 1691. [NRS.E69.11.1]

FERRIER, WILLIAM, in Farnell, 1691. [NRS.E69.11.1]

FYFFE, ALEXANDER, a merchant in Brechin, 1620, [RPCS.XII,215]; spouse Margaret Langlands, a sasine, 1637. [NRS.RS35.S2.I.101]

FIFE, ANDREW, in Forfar, 1753. [NRS.E326.1.169]

FYFE, CHRISTIAN, spouse of John Fullarton a tailor in Kirriemuir, a sasine,1692. [NRS.RS35.S3.IX.66]

FYFE, EUPHAME, spouse of John Don a merchant in Kirriemuir, a sasine, 1675. [NRS.RS35.S3.VI.64, etc]

FIFE, EUPHEMIA, in Kirriemuir, 1732. [NRS.GD7.2.151]; spouse of Andrew Steill a merchant in Kirriemuir, testament, 1737, Comm. St Andrews. [NRS]

THE PEOPLE OF STRATHMORE, 1600-1799

FYFE, GEORGE, a mealmaker in Kirriemuir, husband of Bessie Gourlay, a sasine, 1661. [NRS.RS35.S3.I.201, etc]

FYFE, GEORGE, a shoemaker in Kirriemuir, 1722, testament, 1742, Comm. St Andrews. [NRS.CH2.1302.133]

FIFE, GEORGE, a weaver in Kirriemuir, 1745. [NRS.RH11.70.7]

FYFE, GEORGE, born 1753, died 1836. [Forfar gravestone]; versus William Nicoll, Forfar Burgh Court, 5 October 1784. [AA.F1.8.1]

FYFFE, JAMES, in Sandyford, Kirriemuir, husband of Helen Adam, testament, 1602, Comm. Edinburgh. [NRS]

FYFFE, JAMES, a cordiner in Brechin, a sasine, 1666. [NRS.RS35.S3.II.380]

FYFFE, JAMES, in Kirriemuir, May 1686. [NRS.RH11.70.1/2]

FIFE, JAMES, in Rescobie, 1691. [NRS.E69.11.1]

FIFE, JAMES, in Kirriemuir, 1721. [NRS.CH2.1302.127]

FIFE, JAMES, son and heir of the late James Fife a flesher in Kirriemuir, 1742. [NRS.RH11.70.7]

FIFE, JAMES, a feuar in Kirriemuir, 1744. [NRS.RH11.70.7]

FYFE, JANET, spouse of Patrick Gairdner in Kirriemuir, sasine, 1676. [NRS.RS35.S3.VI.330]

FYFE, JANET, spouse of James Henderson a merchant in Kirriemuir, sasine, 1692. [NRS.RS35.S3.IX.144]

FYFFE, JOHN, a glover in Brechin, husband of Margaret Wallace, a sasine, 1665. [NRS.RS35.S3.II.265]

FYFE, JOHN, the elder, in Kentyrie, parish of Kirriemuir, testament, 1687, Comm. of St Andrews. [NRS]

FIFE, JOHN, in Rescobie, 1691. [NRS.E69.11.1]

FYFE, JOHN, a merchant in Kirriemuir, husband of Catharine Kerr, 1692. [NRS.RS35.S3.IX.526]

FYFE, JOHN, a tailor in Kirriemuir, husband of Christian Fife, a sasine, 1692. [NRS.RS35.S3.IX.66]

THE PEOPLE OF STRATHMORE, 1600-1799

FYFE, JOHN, son of John Fyfe, a tailor in Kirriemuir, a sasine, 1698. [NRS.RS35.S3.X.97]

FIFE, JOHN, a merchant in Kirriemuir, and son David, 1733, 1744, 1745. [NRS.CH2.1302.193; RH11.70.7]

FIFE, JOHN, a shoemaker in Kirriemuir, 1745. [NRS.RH11.70.7]

FIFE, JOHN, a merchant in Kirriemuir, husband of the late Margaret Don, 1758. [NRS.GD7.2.241]

FIFE, JOHN, versus the heir of Thomas Fife, Canongate, Edinburgh, 20 April 1785. [AA.F1.8.1]

FYFFE, ROBERT, father of James Fyffe, a cordiner in Brechin, a sasine, 1666. [NRS.RS35.S3.II.380]

FIFE, ROBERT, a witness in Forfar, 1777, a petition, Forfar Burgh Court, 16 June 1784. [NRS.NRAS#124/4/1/78][AA.F1.8.1]

FIFE, WILLIAM, born 1739 in Kirriemuir, a weaver who enlisted in Major James Clephane's Company of the 78th [Fraser's Highlanders] Regiment in Dundee on 21 February 1757, probably fought in the French and Indian Wars in North America. [NRS.GD125.22.16/17]

FILLAN, JOHN, a baxter at the Meikle Mylne of Brechin, 1609. [RPCS.VIII.699]

FINDALE, JAMES, a shoemaker in Forfar, testament, 29 September 1796, Comm. St Andrews. [NRS]

FINDLASON, DAVID, a smith in Brechin, spouse Janet Dakers, a sasine, 1620. [NRS.RS35S1.I.160]

FINLASON, HENRY, brother of Thomas Findlason, skinner in Brechin, a sasine, 1631. [NRS.RS35.S1.VIII.239]

FINDLASON, JOHN, brother of Thomas Findlason, skinner in Brechin, a sasine, 1631. [NRS.RS35.S1.VIII.239]

FINLASON, THOMAS, a skinner in Brechin, a sasine, 1631. [NRS.RS35.S1.VIII.239]

FINDLAY, DAVID, in Tannadice, 1691. [NRS.E69.11.1]

FINDLAY, EUPHAN, in Lednathie, 1726. [NRS.CH2.1302/155]

FINDLAY, JOHN, versus ...... Ross, Forfar Burgh Court, 28 November 1785. [AA.F1.8.1]

FINDLAY, MARGARET, in Rescobie, 1691. [NRS.E69.11.1]

FINDLAY, ROBERT, in Tannadice, 1691. [NRS.E69.11.1]

FINDLAYSON, DAVID, a merchant burgess of Brechin, spouse Violet Ritchie, testament, 1613, Comm. Brechin. [NRS]

FINDLAYSON, DAVID, and spouse Christian Fraser, in the Tenements of Careston, testament, 1632, Comm. Brechin. [NRS]

FISHER, ALEXANDER, in Fanno, in Rescobie, 1691. [NRS.E69.11.1]

FISHER, MICHAEL, provost of Forfar, and his daughter Margaret, sasine, 1699. [NRS.RS35.S3.X.217] [AA.F1.1.2], in Forfar, 1691. [NRS.E60.11.1]

FITCHET, DAVID, in Windedge, Oathlaw, testament, 1669, Comm. Brechin. [NRS]

FITCHET, DAVID, in Farnell, 1691. [NRS.E69.11.1]

FITCHET, WILLIAM, and his wife Catharine Cable in Kirriemuir, a sasine,1661. [NRS.S3.I.282]

FITCHET, WILLIAM, son of William Fitchet, a maltman in Kirriemuir, a sasine,1693. [NRS.RS35.S3.III.413]

FITCHETT, WILLIAM, a maltman in Kirriemuir, spouse Katherine Cable, 1703. [NRS.RS35.10.570]

FITHIE, THOMAS, a merchant in Kirriemuir, a sasine, 1638. [NRS.RS35.S2.I.346]

FLEMING, ALEXANDER, in Woodhead, Kirriemuir, husband of Christian Peter, testament, 1621, Comm. St Andrews. [NRS]

FLEMING, ALEXANDER, in Glamis, 1681. [NRS.E69.11.1]

FLEMING, ALEXANDER, versus ... Mitchell, Forfar Burgh Court, 1/3 September 1784; versus Burnet and Webster, Forfar Burgh Court, 4 November 1785. [AA.F1.8.1]

FLEMING, DAVID, in Denhead in Methie Inverarity, 1691. [NRS.E69.11.1]

THE PEOPLE OF STRATHMORE, 1600-1799

FLEMING, ISOBEL, a servant in Kirriemuir, 1718. [NRS.CH2.1302.1.115]

FLEMING, JANET, in Kirriemuir, 1722. [NRS.CH2.1302.133]

FLEMING, JOHN, versus Andrew Binny, Forfar Burgh Court, 1/13 April 1785. [AA.F1.8.1]

FLEMING, WILLIAM, in Methie Inverarity, 1691. [NRS.E69.11.1]

FLETCHER, JAMES, in Farnell, 1691. [NRS.E69.11.1]

FLETCHER, ROBERT, jr., of Ballinshoe, Kirriemuir, 1745, 1747. [NRS.RH11.70.7]

FOD, ALEXANDER, in Ordy, Finavon, testament, 1628, Comm. Brechin. [NRS]

FOD, JOHN, a burgess of Forfar, testament, 6 May 1641, Comm. St Andrews. [NRS]

FOD, PATRICK, of the Weavers Incorporation of Forfar, 1791. [NRS.CS311.1669]

FOD, THOMAS, in Forfar, 1759. [NRS.E326.1.169]

FORBES, ANDREW, in Farnell, 1691. [NRS.E69.11.1]

FORBES, DANIEL, a merchant in Brechin, relict Isobel Langsandie, sasine, 1687. [NRS.RS35.S3.VIII,497]

FORD, ALEXANDER, treasurer of Forfar, 1688. [AA.F1.1.2]

FORD, DAVID, born 1712, tenant in Dunnichen, died 1784, spouse Isobel Fauld, born 1714, died 1783, children Nicol, Ann, Isobel, and David. [Dunnichen gravestone]

FORD, JOHN, was admitted as a burgess of Forfar 11 June 1660; schoolmaster of Forfar, 1660-1663. [AA.F1.1.1]

FORD, DAVID, versus Alexander Robertson, Forfar Burgh Court, 5 October 1784. [AA.F1.8.1]

FORD, JEAN, 1787. [NRS.CH2.1302.2/125]

FORD, JOHN, versus his debtors, Forfar Burgh Court, 29/30 October 1784. [AA.F1.8.1]

FORD, WILLIAM, in Tannadice, 1691. [NRS.E69.11.1]

FORDELL, JAMES, in Millden, Kirriemuir, 1686. [NRS.RH11.70.1/2]

FORDELL, JOHN, in Millden, Kirriemuir, a deed, 1686. [NRS.RD11.70.1/2]

FORDELL, JOHN, in Kinwhirrie, Kirriemuir, 1686; testament, 1685, Comm. St Andrews. [NRS.RH11.70.1/2]

FORDELL, JOHN, son of the late Alexander Fordell of Buckhood, 1745. [NRS.RH11.70.7]

FORREST, HENRY, treasurer of Forfar, 1706-1707. [AA.F5.4]

FORREST, JAMES, deacon of the Tailors Incorporation of Forfar, 1684; councillor there, 1688. [RBF#217] [AA.F1.1.2]

FORREST, JOHN, a burgess of Forfar, sasine, 1660. [NRS.RS35.S3.I.7, 23] [AA.F1.1.1]

FORREST, THOMAS, a wright and councillor of Forfar, 1680s. [AA.F1.1.2][NRS.RD2.68.34] in Forfar, 1691. [NRS.E60.11.1]

FORREST, WILLIAM, born 1748, a clothier in Kirriemuir, died 1819, spouse Margaret Hood, born 1761, died 1809. [Kirriemuir gravestone]

FORRESTER, Mr GEORGE, in Muirside of Lour, parish of Forfar, testaments,3/8 April 1629, Comm. St Andrews. [NRS]

FORRESTER, ISABEL, in Forfar, 1691. [NRS.E60.11.1]

FORRESTER, MARGARET, or CLARK, born 1768, died 1824. [Kirriemuir gravestone]

FORSYTH, JAMES, in Kirriemuir, 1721. [NRS.CH2.1302.127]

FORSYTH, JAMES, a maltman in Kirriemuir, with a brewery at Kirkton of Airlie, 1774. [NRS.GD16.28.374]

FOSTER, ALEXANDER, in Tannadice, 1691. [NRS.E69.11.1]

FOWLAR, BEATRIX, spouse of James Fraser a merchant in Kirriemuir, a sasine, 1692. [NRS.RS35.S3.IX.148]

FOULAR, DAVID, in Forfar, 1691. [NRS.E60.11.1]

FOWLER, HELEN, in Kirriemuir, 1721. [NRS.CH2.1302.127]

THE PEOPLE OF STRATHMORE, 1600-1799

FOULAR, JOHN, in Forfar, 1691. [NRS.E60.11.1]

FOWLER, MARGARET, spouse to David Robertson in Forfar, testament, 1684, Comm. St Andrews. [NRS]

FOULLAR, THOMAS, in Forfar, 1759. [NRS.E326.1.169]

FOULLO, ELSPET, in Guthrie, 1691. [NRS.E69.11.1]

FRASER, DAVID, a merchant in Kirriemuir, 1741, 1744. [NRS.RH11.70.7]

FRASER, EUPHAM, spouse of James Wood of Kintyre, a merchant in Kirriemuir, a sasine, 1685. [NRS.RS35.S3.VIII.445]

FRASER, HELEN, daughter of the late James Fraser in Kintyrie, 1746. [NRS.RH11.70.7]

FRASER, ISOBEL, daughter of James Fraser a merchant in Kirriemuir, and spouse of John Proctor at New Mill of Menis, sasine,1692. [NRS.RS35.S3.IX.253]

FRASER, JAMES, in Kirriemuir, a sasine, 1656. [NRS.RS35.V.332]

FRASER, JAMES, a maltman in Kirriemuir, son of James Fraser a merchant there, a sasine,1692. [NRS.RS35.S3.IX.518]

FRASER, JAMES, a merchant in Kirriemuir, husband of Beatrix Fowlar, a sasine,1668. [NRS.RS35.S3.IV.39]

FRASER, JAMES, father of James Fraser, a merchant in Kirriemuir, a sasine,1693. [NRS.RS35.S3.IX.255]

FRASER, JAMES, son of James Fraser in Kirriemuir, a sasine, 1656. [NRS.RS35.S2.V.332]

FRASER, JAMES, in Kirriemuir, 1733. [NRS.GD205.25.184]

FRASER, JAMES, in Kyntyrie, parish of Kirriemuir, testament, 1738, Comm. St Andrews. [NRS]

FRASER, JAMES, eldest son of the late James Fraser of Kintyrie and his spouse Mary Craig, 1742. [NRS.RH11.70.7]

FRASER, JOHN, a merchant in Kirriemuir, a sasine, 1692. [NRS.RS35.S3.IX.228]

FRASER, JOHN, collector and boxmaster of the Cordiner Trade of Forfar, 1692. [NRS.GD1.61.12] [AA.F1.1.2], a shoemaker in Forfar, 1691. [NRS.E60.11.1]

FRASER, JOHN, son of James Fraser a merchant in Kirriemuir, and spouse of Margaret Crichton, a sasine,1692. [NRS.RS35.S3.IX.255, etc]

FRASER, JOHN, a poor man in Kirriemuir, 1716. [NRS.CH2.1302.1.105]

FRASER, PAUL, minister at Strathcathro and Chantour of Brechin, testament, 1609, Comm. Brechin. [NRS]

FRASER, ROBERT, and spouse Katherine Buchan, at Cant's Mill, Kincoldrum, testament, 1628, Comm. Brechin. [NRS]

FRASER, ROBERT, son of James Fraser a merchant in Kirriemuir, a sasine, 1692. [NRS.RS35.S3.IX.148]

FRENDERETH, CATHARINE, daughter of John Frendereth in Kirriemuir, and spouse of James Mader a merchant there, sasines, 1643. [NRS.RS35.S2.II.307, etc]

FRENDERETH, JOHN, in Kirriemuir, a sasine,1621. [NRS.RS35.S1.I.135, etc]

FRENDERETH, MARGARET, spouse of John Tyrie in Kirriemuir, a deed,1648. [NRS.RD35.S2.III.190]

FULLARTON, HENRY, born around 1566 son of David Fullarton a skipper burgess of Dundee, graduated MA from St Andrews in 1586, minister of Forfar from 1607 to his death in 1618. Father of William. [F.5.285][RPCS.VIII.99/647]

FUTY, JAMES, in Forfar, 1614. [RGS.VII.1024]

GAIR, JAMES, in Tannadice, 1691. [NRS.E69.11.1]

GAIRDNER, JAMES, a maltman burgess of Brechin, spouse Agnes Austin, testament, 1621, Comm. Brechin. [NRS]

GAIRDNER, JAMES, a flesher in Brechin, a sasine, 1681. [NRS.RS35.S3.VII.460]

GAIRDNER, JOHN, father of John Gairdner, a wright in Brechin, spouse Agnes Lyon, a sasine, 1637. [NRS.RS35.SI.VIII.231]

THE PEOPLE OF STRATHMORE, 1600-1799

GAIRDNER, JOHN, sr., burgess of Brechin, testament, 1649, Comm. Brechin. [NRS]

GAIRDNER, JOHN, a wheelwright in Brechin, husband of [1] Isobel Baillie, testament, 1668, Comm. Brechin, [2] Catharine Mather, a sasine, 1631, [NRS.RS35.S1.VIII.231], a donor in 1682. [Brechin Cathedral]

GAIRDNER, JOHN, a maltman burgess of Brechin, spouse Agnes, sasine 1673. [NRS.RS35.S3.V.230]

GAIRDNER, JOHN, a merchant burgess of Brechin, spouse Margaret Watson, testament, 1674, Comm.Brechin. [NRS]

GAIRDNER, WILLIAM, a flesher in Brechin, 1656, sasine, 1666. [RGS.X.550][NRS.RS35.S3/I.368]

GALL, ALEXANDER, in Tannadice, 1691. [NRS.E69.11.1]

GALL, JAMES, born 1740, a shoemaker in Forfar, died 1781, wife Ann Cuthbert, born 1742, died 1826. [Forfar gravestone]

GALL, JOHN, in Methie Inverarity, 1691. [NRS.E69.11.1]

GALL, JOHN, in Tannadice, 1691. [NRS.E69.11.1]

GALLOWAY, GRISEL, mother of Thomas Fenton a tanner in Kirriemuir, sasine, 1643. [NRS.RS35.S2.II.315]

GALLOWAY, WILLIAM, in Craigend of Balnabreich, Brechin, testament, 1594, Comm. Edinburgh. [NRS]

GARDEN, DAVID, in Tannadice, 1691. [NRS.E69.11.1]

GARDINE, JOHN, a collector in Forfar, 1687. [AA.F1.1.2]

GARDYNE, JOHN, of Lawton, married Elizabeth, daughter of Sir John Arbuthnott of that Ilk, in 1643. [Kirkden inscription]

GARDINER, JOHN, a wright in Brechin, spouse Isobel Baillie, sasine, 1631. [NRS.RS35.S1.VIII.231]

GARDNER, EUPHAN, daughter of Patrick Gardner a maltman in Kirriemuir, 1699. [NRS.RS35.S3.X.227]

GARDNER, JOHN, jr., son and heir of John Gardner sr. in St Michael's Hill, Brechin, 1691.[RP.II.345]

THE PEOPLE OF STRATHMORE, 1600-1799

GARDNER, JOHN, in Kirriemuir, husband of Jean Lyall, 1693. [NRS.RS35.S3.IX.405]

GARDNER, JOHN, a maltman in Kirriemuir, 1699. [NRS.RS35.S3.X.174]

GARDNER, PATRICK, in Kirriemuir, husband of Janet Fife, 1676. [NRS.RS35.S3.VI.330]

GARDNER, PATRICK, 1743. [NRS.RH11.70.7]

GARDNER, THOMAS, in Kirriemuir, 1732. [NRS.GD7.2.151]

GARDNER, VIOLET, spouse David Windram sr., in Hall Carcary, Farnell, testament, 1621, Comm. Brechin. [NRS]

GARLAND, ALEXANDER, in Windyedge, Dunnichen, testament, 1598, Comm. Brechin. [NRS]

GARLAND, JOHN, in Windyedge, Dunnichen, testament, 1647, Comm. Brechin. [NRS]

GARVIE, JANET, relict of Alexander Cuthbert, in Heuchhead of Guthrie, testament, 1613, Comm. Brechin. [NRS]

GEDDES, ANDREW, minister at Farnell, testament, 1719, Comm. Brechin. [NRS]

GELLATLY, CHRISTIAN, relict of David Ogilvy of Templehall, parish of Forfar, testament, 1595, Comm. St Andrews. [NRS]

GELLATLY, JOHN, versus his debtors, Forfar Burgh Court, 23 February 1785. [AA.F1.8.1]

GELLIE, ALEXANDER, a cordiner burgess of Brechin, 1620. [RPCS.XII.215]; spouse Christian Strachan, testament, 1601, Comm.Brechin. [NRS]

GELLIE, JAMES. a cordiner in Brechin, spouse Janet Black, testament, 1613, Comm. Brechin. [NRS]

GENTLEMAN, JAMES, burgess of Brechin, relict Margaret Clark, sasine, 1673. [NRS.RS35.S3.V.327]

GENTLEMAN, JAMES, a messenger in Brechin, sasine, 1667. [NRS.RS35.S3.III.394]

GENTLEMAN, JAMES, son of James Gentleman, a burgess of Brechin, a sasine, 1673. [NRS.RS35.S3.V.327]

THE PEOPLE OF STRATHMORE, 1600-1799

GIB, ALEXANDER, in Kirriemuir, 1741. [NRS.RH11.70.7]

GIBSON, AGNES, spouse Roger Sturrock in Auchterlony, Dunnichen, testament, 1626, Comm. Brechin. [NRS]

GIBSON, ALEXANDER, in Drumgley, Glamis, 1797. [NRS.E326.10.3.24]

GIBSON, ALEXANDER, born 1762, died 1838, spouse Margaret Wyllie, born 1762, died 1805. [Kirriemuir gravestone]

GIBSON, ANDREW, and his wife Isobel Dickson, in Kirriemuir, 1686. [NRS.RH11.70.1/2]

GIBSON, CHRISTIAN, spouse to Walter Mearns in Farnell, testament, 1621, Comm. Brechin. [NRS]

GIBSON, DAVID, a merchant burgess of Forfar, spouse Janet Hoy, testament, 13 June 1628, Comm. St Andrews. [NRS]

GIBSON, DAVID, of Wester Lownie, born 1577, died 1657. [Dunnichen gravestone]

GIBSON, DAVID, a weaver in Brechin, a sasine, 1685. [NRS.RS35.S3.VIII.256]

GIBSON, DAVID, in Dunnichen, 1691. [NRS.E69.11.1]

GIBSON, DAVID, a merchant in Kirriemuir, 1742, 1744, 1745. [NRS.RH11.70.7]

GIBSON, JAMES, a weaver in Brechin, a sasine, 1685. [NRS.RS35.S3.VIII.256]

GIBSON, JAMES, in Oathlaw, 1691. [NRS.E69.11.1]

GIBSON, JOHN, a brabiner at the Meikle Mill of Brechin, father of David and James, a sasine, 1661. [NRS.RS35.S3.I.221]

GIBSON, WILLIAM, in Forfar, 1691. [NRS.E60.11.1]

GIBSON, WILLIAM, in Glamis, 1691. [NRS.E69.11.1]

GIBSON, WILLIAM, in Farnell, 1691. [NRS.E69.11.1]

GILBERT, JOHN, in Carmuir, Kirriemuir, testament, 1673, Comm. St Andrews. [NRS]

GILL, GEORGE, a soldier, 1718. [NRS.CH2.1302.1.115]

THE PEOPLE OF STRATHMORE, 1600-1799

GLASFORD, JOHN, minister at Strathcathro, testament, 1746, Comm. Brechin. [NRS]

GLASFORD, MARJORY, relict of Andrew Knox minister at Kinnaird, testament, 1762, Comm. Brechin. [NRS]

GLASS, JOHN, a tailor in Forfar, husband of Betty Larons, born 1761, died 1798. [Forfar gravestone]

GLENDAY, GEORGE, a wright in Kirriemuir, 1742. [NRS.RH11.70.7]

GLENDAY, GEORGE, a cooper in Kirriemuir, 1745. [NRS.RH11.70.7]

GLENDAY, GEORGE, born 1704, farmer, died 1763, wife Janet Nichol. [Glamis gravestone]

GLENDAY, Mr JOHN, Dean of Cashel and Prebend of St Michael's, Dublin, a donor in 1690. [Brechin Cathedral]

GLENDAY, JOHN, a weaver in Denhead of Logie, Kirriemuir, 1746. [NRS.RH11.70.7]

GLENDAY, PATRICK, in Langbank, Kirriemuir, husband of Margaret Ogilvie, testament, 1617, Comm. St Andrews. [NRS]

GLOVER, THOMAS, minister at Guthrie, testament, 1625, Comm. Brechin. [NRS]

GOODFELLOW, DAVID, born 1613, died 1683, servant to the Earl of Southesk, his spouse Janet Gellatlie, died 1683, testament, 1683, Comm. Brechin. [NRS][Kinnaird gravestone]

GOODLET, ALEXANDER, in Tirbinnes, 1733, 1742, 1746. [NRS.CH2.1302.193; RH11.70.7]

GOODLET, THOMAS, born 1770, died 1837, spouse Ann Black, born 1778, died 1810. [Kirriemuir gravestone]

GORDON, ANN, a servant in Kirriemuir, 1720. [NRS.CH2.1302.1.123]

GORDON, DAVID, a shoemaker in Kirriemuir, husband of Catharine Watson, sasine, 1677. [NRS.RS35.S3.VI.459]

GORDON, DAVID, a shoemaker in Kirriemuir, 1741. [NRS.RH11.70.7]

THE PEOPLE OF STRATHMORE, 1600-1799

GORDON, ELIZABETH, in Kirriemuir, 1747. [NRS.RH11.70.7]

GORDON, JAMES, in Kirriemuir,sasine, 1637. [NRS.RS35.S2.I.37]

GORDON, JAMES, son of Adam Gordon, brother of James Gordon in Kirriemuir, sasine, 1637. [NRS.RS35.S2.I.37]

GORDON, JAMES, in Farnell, 1691. [NRS.E69.11.1]

GORDON, JAMES, a merchant in Kirriemuir, 1742, 1747. [NRS.RH11.70.7]

GORDON, JANET, in Kirriemuir, 1786. [NRS.CH2.1302.2/123]

GORDON, JOHN, in Forfar, 1691. [NRS.E60.11.1]

GORDON, MARGARET, a young woman at Meikle Miln, Kirriemuir, 1728. [NRS.CH2.1302.167]

GORDON, PETER, in Crathienaird, 1745. [NRS.RH11.70.7]

GORDON, ROBERT, in Tannadice, 1691. [NRS.E69.11.1]

GORDON, THOMAS, son of George Gordon of Auchmuthie, was admitted as a burgess of Forfar, 1661. [AA.F1.1.1]

GORDON, THOMAS, a tanner in Kirriemuir, a sasine, 1676. [NRS.RS35.S3.VI.83]

GORDON, WILLIAM, in Forfar,1691. [NRS.E69.11.1]

GOUCK, ALEXANDER, in Kinnetles, 1691. [NRS.E69.11.1]

GOUK, ALEXANDER, late tenant in Greenlaw, Farnell, schoolmaster at Kinnaird, testament, 1760, Comm. Brechin. [NRS]

GOULD, HELENA, in Forfar, 1691. [NRS.E69.11.1]

GOURLAY, DAVID, in Forfar, 1691. [NRS.E60.11.1]

GOURLAY, ELIZABETH, spouse of George Fyfe in Kirriemuir, sasine, 1661. [NRS.RS35.S3.I.201]

GOWAN, AGNES, in Glamis, 1681. [NRS.E69.11.1]

GRAHAM, Mr GEORGE, in Methie Inverarity, 1691. [NRS.E69.11.1]

GRAHAM, GEORGE, in Kirriemuir, 1740. [NRS.GD7.2.178]

GRAHAM, JEAN, spouse of Thomas Bursie in Kirriemuir, sasine,1637. [NRS.RS35.S2.I.160]

GRAHAM, MARGARET, in Methie Inverarity, 1691. [NRS.E69.11.1]

GRANT, ALEXANDER, born 1760, farmer in Kintyrie, died 1834. [Kirriemuir gravestone]

GRANT, HENRY, in Tannadice, 1691. [NRS.E69.11.1]

GRANT, MARY, a servant in Turfbeg, Forfar, 1765. [NRS.CH2.1302.245]

GRANT, WILLIAM, in Moss-side of Ballinshoe, 1783. [NRS.CH2.1302.2/107]

GRAY, AGNES, in Tannadice, 1691. [NRS.E69.11.1]

GRAY, ALEXANDER, in Kinnetles, 1691. [NRS.E69.11.1]

GRAY, ALEXANDER, in Tannadice, 1691. [NRS.E69.11.1]

GRAY, ALEXANDER, in Cotterton of Middleton, wife Giles Brown, born 1706, died 1764. [Kirkden gravestone]

GRAY, ANDREW, of Lour, Constable of Forfar, 1611. [RPCS,VIII.308]

GRAY, ANNA, wife of William Luke a notary in Forfar, heir to her father William Gray a writer in Forfar, 9 June 1643. [NRS.Retours.Forfar]

GRAY, CHARLES, in Forfar, 1785, 1791; versus Alexander Robertson, Forfar Burgh Court, 11 May 1785. [AA.F1.8.1][NRS.E326.3.19]

GRAY, CHARLES, a brew-house owner in Kingston, Forfar, 1793-1808. [NRS. NA7604]

GRAY, DAVID, merchant in Brechin, spouse Margaret Allan, a sasine, 1686. [NRS.RS35.VIII.495]

GRAY, DAVID, versus .... Winter, Forfar Burgh Court, 22 September 1784; versus John Hunter, Forfar Burgh Court, 22/29/31 December 1784, 14 January 1785; in Forfar, 1785, 1791. [NRS.E326.3.19][AA.F1.8.1]

THE PEOPLE OF STRATHMORE, 1600-1799

GRAY, ELSPET, spouse John Smart in Balgray, Kincaldrum, testament, 1614, Comm. Brechin. [NRS]

GRAY, ELSPET, spouse to David Watt a maltman, a donor in 1649. [Brechin Cathedral]

GRAY, EUPHEMIA, heir portioner to her father William Gray a writer in Forfar, 9 June 1643. [NRS.Retours.Forfar]

GRAY, GEORGE, sheriff clerk of Forfar, a bond, 1671. [NRS.RD3.27.349]

GRAY, GEORGE, versus Charles Findlay, Forfar Burgh Court, 22 September 1784. [AA.F1.8.1]

GRAY, HENRY, a saddler in Brechin, husband of Barbara Livingstone, sasine, 1692. [NRS.RS35.S3.IX.118]

GRAY, ISOBEL, heir portioner to her father William Gray a writer in Forfar, 9 June 1643. [NRS.Retours.Forfar]

GRAY, JAMES, in Forfar, 1691. [NRS.E60.11.1]

GRAY, JOHN, a writer and notary in Forfar, husband of (1) Isobel Cramond, (2) Anna Gray, sasine, 1654; bailie, 1660. [NRS.RS35.S2.IV.484, etc][AA.F1.1.1]

GRAY, JOHN, son of John Gray, a writer in Forfar, sasine, 1670. [NRS.RS35.S3.IV.386]

GRAY, JOHN, versus Andrew Binny, Forfar Burgh Court, 30 November 1785. [AA.F1.8.1]

GRAY, MICHAEL, of Turfbef, parish of Forfar, testament, 1684, Comm. St Andrews. [NRS]

GRAY, PATRICK, a surgeon in Forfar, son of the late William Gray of Inverighly, advocate, sasine, 1741. [AA.F1.4.3]

GRAY, ROBERT, was admitted as a burgess of Forfar, 1688. [AA.F1.1.2], sheriff major in Forfar, 1691. [NRS.E60.11.1]

GRAY, ROBERT, versus Robert Fife, Forfar Burgh Court, 1/13 April 1785, 23 February 1785, 27 May 1785. [AA.F1.8.1]

GRAY, WILLIAM, sheriff clerk of Forfar, sasine, 1637. [NRS.RS35.S2.I.48, etc][AA.f1.4.1]

GRAY, WILLIAM, clerk of Forfar, 1648. [NRS.GD1.64.2]

THE PEOPLE OF STRATHMORE, 1600-1799

GRAY, WILLIAM, of Invereightie, 1672. [AA.F5.117]

GRAY, WILLIAM, sheriff clerk of Forfar, deeds, 1671, 1688. [NRS.RD3.28.99; RD4.63.424]

GRAY, WILLIAM, a meal-dealer in Brechin, husband of Agnes Skinner, sasine, 1686. [NRS.RS35.S3.VIII.442]

GRAY, WILLIAM, son of John Gray, a writer in Forfar, a deed of factory, 1676. [NRS.RD3.40.282]

GRAY, WILLIAM, the younger, of Invereightie, contract, 1695. [AA.F5.119]

GRAY, WILLIAM, in Forfar, 1753, 1759. [NRS.E326.1.169]

GRAY, bailie, versus James Milne, Forfar Burgh Court, 11 November 1785. [AA.F1.8.1]

GREEN, ROBERT, in Muirhouse, Kirriemuir, husband of Christian Wallace, testament, 1615, Comm. St Andrews. [NRS]

GREEN, WALTER, a smith in Drumclum, Kirriemuir, spouse Margaret Smyth, testament, 1613, Comm. St Andrews. [NRS]

GREENHILL, ALEXANDER, in Mains of Bridgetoun, sasine witness, 1744. [AA,F1.4.3]

GREENHILL, JOHN, in Glamis, a servant of the Earl of Strathmore, a sasine witness, 1698. [NRS.GD68.1.370]

GREIG, ANDREW, versus ... Archer, Forfar Burgh Court, 20 May 1785. [AA.F1.8.1]

GREIG, JOHN, a maltman in Brechin, a donor in 1644., 1656. [Brechin Cathedral][RGS.X.550]

GREIG, JOHN, burgess of Brechin, reict Janet Petrie, 16..., [NRS.RS35.S2.IV.336]

GREIG, JOHN, in Forfar, a deed, 1705. [NRS.RD2.90/2.46]

GRIEVE, ALEXANDER, tacksman at the Meikle Mill of Kirriemuir, 1742, 1745, 1746. [NRS.RH11.70.7]

GRIEVE, JAMES, schoolmaster in Kinnell, Angus, 1690, [SHS.4.2]; there in 1691. [NRS.E69.11.1]

GREWAR, ELIZABETH, in Kingoldrum, relict of David Wilkie in Ballow, testament, 1707, Comm. Brechin. [NRS]

THE PEOPLE OF STRATHMORE, 1600-1799

GRUAR, ISABEL, in Tannadice, 1691. [NRS.E69.11.1]

GRUAR, WILLIAM, in Tannadice, 1691. [NRS.E69.11.1]

GRUB, AGNES, spouse of William Brodie in Kirriemuir, sasine, 1665. [NRS.RS35.S3.II.348]

GRUBB, Mr JAMES, a schoolmaster in Kirriemuir, 1691. [NRS.E69.11.1]

GUILD, ALEXANDER, in the parish of Kirriemuir, testament, 1620, Comm. St Andrews. [NRS]

GUILD, ISABEL, in Kirriemuir, 1728. [NRS.CH2.1302.167]

GUILD, JAMES, a pundler, 1661. [AA.F1.1.1]

GUILD, JAMES, minister at Strathcathro, testaments, 1678, 1694, Comm. Brechin. [NRS]

GUILD, JANET, a poor blind woman in Kirriemuir, 1762. [NRS.CH2.1302.2/7]

GUILD, JOHN, versus David Adamson, Forfar Burgh Court, 16 November 1785. [AA.F1.8.1]

GUILD, MARY, spouse of Andrew Doig in Kirriemuir, sasine, 1637. [NRS.RS35.S2.I.76]

GUILD, WILLIAM, in Forfar,1691. [NRS.E69.11.1]

GUTHRIE, ALEXANDER, minister at Strathcathro, and wife Magdalen Carnegy, testament, 1663, Comm. Brechin. [NRS]

GUTHRIE, DAVID, in Glamis, 1691. [NRS.E69.11.1]

GUTHRIE, DAVID, late of Carsebank, parish of Forfar, testament, 1716, Comm. St Andrews. [NRS]

GUTHRIE, DAVID, versus ... Bowen, Forfar Burgh Court, 31 December 1784, 2 February 1785. [AA.F1.8.1]

GUTHRIE, ELSPETH, an alleged witch in Forfar, 1661. [RPCS.I.122]

GUTHRIE, DAVID, of Carsebank, in Rescobie, 1691. [NRS.E69.11.1]

GUTHRIE, FRANCIS, Keeper of the Sasines in Forfar, relict Margaret Jarden, sasine, 1685. [NRS.RS35.S3.VIII.262, etc]

GUTHRIE, FRANCIS, of Guthrie, spouse Bethie Guthrie testament, 1666, Comm. Brechin. [NRS]

GUTHRIE, GIDEON, of Halkerton, was admitted a burgess of Forfar on 26 June 1660. [AA.F1.1.1]

GUTHRIE, HARRY, schoolmaster in Forfar, sasine, 1643. [NRS.RS35.S2.II.220]

GUTHRIE, HARRY, only son of Gideon Guthrie, was admitted as a burgess of Forfar, 26 June 1660. [AA.F1.1.1]

GUTHRIE, HELEN, an alleged witch in Forfar, 1661; found guilty and sentenced to death at Forfar on 13 November 1662. [RPCS.I.122][AA.F5.35]

GUTHRIE, HELEN, in Tannadice, 1691. [NRS.E69.11.1]

GUTHRIE, ISABEL, in Glamis, 1691. [NRS.E69.11.1]

GUTHRIE, ISABEL, daughter of David Guthrie of Carsebank, testament, 1754, Comm. St Andrews. [NRS]

GUTHRIE, JAMES, in Tannadice, 1691. [NRS.E69.11.1]

GUTHRIE, JANET, spouse of David Rodger a merchant in Kirriemuir, sasine, 1679. [NRS.RS35.S3.VII.24]

GUTHRIE, JEDSON, of Blaberhill, parish of Forfar, testament, 14 October 1614, Comm. St Andrews. [NRS]

GUTHRIE, JOHN, cordiner in Brechin, 1608. [RPCS.VIII.664]

GUTHRIE, JOHN, heir to his father Francis Guthrie of Guthrie, 1665. [NRS.Retours,Forfar,412]

GUTHRIE, Captain JOHN, burgess of Brechin, spouse Christian Wilson, sasine, 1681. [NRS.RS35.VII.313]

GUTHRIE, PATRICK, in Cotton Dod, Rescobie, 1691. [NRS.E69.11.1]

GUTHRIE, THOMAS, bailie of Forfar, 1661, 1664, deeds, 1666, 1671; provost of Forfar, father of Elizabeth Guthrie, spouse of Henry Lindsay, sasine, 1672. [RPCS.I.122][AA.F1.1.1] [RGS.XI.566][NRS.RS35.S3.V.47, 50, etc; RD4.16.710, RD4.30.436]

THE PEOPLE OF STRATHMORE, 1600-1799

GUTHRIE, THOMAS, a maltman in Forfar, a bond, 1666.
[NRS.RD2.17.79]

GUTHRIE, WILLIAM, a maltman burgess of Forfar, died on 13 July 1648, husband of Catherine Dickson, testament,18 August 1649, Comm. St Andrews. [Forfar gravestone] [NRS]

GUTHRIE, WILLIAM, a burgess of Forfar, 1691.
[NRAS#124/4/1/66]

GUTHRIE, ………,of Guthrie, in Guthrie, 1691. [NRS.E69.11.1]

HACKNEY, ANDREW, in Cotton of Lour, parish of Forfar, husband of Elspeth Balfour, testament, 4 August 1692, Comm. St Andrews. [NRS] , in Rescobie, 1691. [NRS.E69.11.1]

HACKNEY, ANDREW, in Kinnetles, 1691. [NRS.E69.11.1]

HABRON, JOHN, in Kinnell, 1691. [NRS.E69.11.1]

HALBETT, ALEXANDER, in Kinnetles, 1691. [NRS.E69.11.1]

HALIBURTON, GEORGE, DD, Bishop of Brechin from 1678 to 1682. [F.6.375]

HALKETT, THOMAS, in Pluckerston, 1741, 1745.
[NRS.RH11.70.7]

HALKETT, THOMAS, a weaver in Kirriemuir, testament, 1790, Comm. St Andrews. [NRS] [NRS.CH2.1302.2/113, 123]

HALL, JOHN, a burgess of Brechin, relict Christian Wilson, parents of William, a sasine, 1679. [NRS.RS35.S3.VII.42]

HAMILTON, ALEXANDER, Writer to the Signet, was admitted as a burgess of Forfar on 18 May 1714.
[NRS.GD1.79.11]

HAMPTON, JOHN, a cordiner in Brechin, 1691.
[RPCS.XVI.605]

HANSON, ROBERT, in Kirriemuir,1774.
[NRS.CH2.1302.2/111]

HANTON, DAVID, in Kirriemuir, June 1686.
[NRS.RH11.70.1/3]

HANTON, DAVID, in Tannadice, 1691. [NRS.E69.11.1]

HANTON, JAMES, in Balloch, Kirriemuir, testament, 1656, Comm. St Andrews. [NRS]

HANTON, JAMES, in Knows of Glen Prosen, parish of Forfar, testament, 1720, Comm. St Andrews. [NRS]

HANTON, JANET, in Kirriemuir, 1716. [NRS.CH2.1302.1.105]

HANTON, ROBERT, in Kirriemuir, 1786. [NRS.CH2.1302.2/123]

HANTON, THOMAS, in Tannadice, 1691. [NRS.E69.11.1]

HARDY, WILLIAM, a notary in Brechin, 1606. [RPCS.VII.643]

HARIEL, DAVID, born 1638, died on 15 June 1680, father of Agnes. [Forfar gravestone]

HASWELL, CATHARINE, spouse of James Rodger in Kirriemuir, sasine, 1643. [NRS.RS35.S2.II.438]

HASWELL, HELEN, spouse of David Cromb in Kirriemuir, sasine, 1643. [NRS.RS35.S2.II.544]

HASWELL, JOHN, in Kirriemuir, husband of (1) Margaret Schewan, (2) Janet Smart, father of Thomas, sasine, 1620. [NRS.RS35.S1.I.130]

HASWELL, JOHN, a flesher, son of John Haswell in Kirriemuir, husband of Elizabeth Croll, sasine, 1620. [NRS.RS35.S1.I.130]

HASWELL, JOHN, uncle of John Haswell in Kirriemuir, sasine, 1631. [NRS.RS35.S1.VIII.155]

HASWELL, JOHN, in Kirriemuir, son of Thomas Haswell there, husband of Katherine Ogilvie, sasine, 1686. [NRS.RS35.S3.VIII.448, etc]

HASWELL, MARGARET, in Kirriemuir, 1745. [NRS.RH11.70.7]

HASWELL, THOMAS, in Kirriemuir, portioner of Tarbirne, son of John Haswell in Kirriemuir, husband of Elizabeth Morgan, sasine, 1637. [NRS.RS35.S2.I.15, etc]

HASWELL, THOMAS, grandfather of Thomas Haswell in Kirriemuir, sasine, 1639. [NRS.RS35.S2.I.452]

THE PEOPLE OF STRATHMORE, 1600-1799

HAWTOUN, ARTHUR, a burgess of Brechin, relict Margaret Dickson, sasine, 1674. [NRS.RS35.S3.V.304]

HAY, ALEXANDER, versus James Welsh, Forfar Burgh Court, 29 December 1784,14/26 January 1785; 2/18/23 February 1785. [AA.F1.8.1]

HAY, ANDREW, born 1680, in Pickerton of Guthrie, died 1724, wife Janet Adam. [Guthrie gravestone]

HAY, DAVID, in Ballindarg, Kirriemuir, testament, 1686, Comm. St Andrews. [NRS]

HAY, GEORGE, at the Burnside of Kirriemuir and the Mill thereof, husband of Agnes Proctor, sasine, 1685. [NRS.RS35.S3.VIII.448]

HAY, GEORGE, in Glamis, 1681. [NRS.E69.11.1]

HAY, GEORGE, at Burnside of Kirriemuir, relict Agnes Proctor, a sasine, 1704. [NRS.RS35.X.496]

HAY, JAMES, at the Mill of Kirriemuir, May 1686. [NRS.RH11.70.1/2]

HAY, JAMES, at Meikle Mill, Kirriemuir, a deed, 1701. [NRS.RD3.96.127]

HAY, JOHN, in Glamis, 1681. [NRS.E69.11.1]

HAY, JOHN, versus Baxter and Smith, Forfar Burgh Court, 5 November 1784; versus .... Yeaman, Forfar Burgh Court, 24 December 1784; versus ... Nicoll, Forfar Burgh Court, 19 January 1785; 30 November 1785. [AA.F1.8.1]

HEATTON, ALEXANDER, in New Muir, Forfar, testament, 4 April 1683, Comm. St Andrews. [NRS]

HEGGIE, JOHN, schoolmaster in Forfar, spouse Margaret Lindsay, a bond, 1666, sasine, 1668. [NRS.RD4.17.632; RS35.S3.IV.121]

HEIGH, ALEXANDER, a glover in Forfar, 1661, a skinner, a bond, 1666; spouse Margaret Lindsay, sasine, 1676; was admitted as a burgess of Forfar, 1661. [AA.F1.1.1][NRS.RD2.16.402; RS35.S3.VI.383]

THE PEOPLE OF STRATHMORE, 1600-1799

HENDERSON, ALEXANDER, in Forfar, 1691.
[NRS.E60.11.1]

HENDERSON, ANDREW, town herd of Forfar, 1680s.
[AA.F1.1.2]

HENDERSON, DAVID, a merchant in Brechin, husband of Grisel Milne, sasine,1699. [NRS.RS35.S3.X.249]

HENDERSON, FRANCIS, in Forfar, 1726.
[NRS.GD45.16.1460]

HENDERSON, HELEN, spouse of Thomas Piggot a merchant in Kirriemuir, sasine, 1661. [NRS.RS35.S3.I.303]

HENDERSON, ISABEL, spouse of David Dougall a wright in Kirriemuir, sasine, 1692. [NRS.RS35.S3.IX.218]

HENDERSON, JAMES, a merchant in Brechin, husband of Margaret Strachan, sasine, 1670. [NRS.RS35.S3.IV.319]

HENDERSON, JAMES, in Forfar,1691. [NRS.E69.11.1]

HENDERSON, JAMES, a merchant in Kirriemuir, husband of Janet Fife,sasine, 1692. [NRS.RS35.S3.IX.144]

HENDERSON, JAMES, an Excise officer in Kirriemuir, 1728.
[NRS.CH2.1302.169]

HENDERSON, JOHN, was admitted as a master and freeman of the Incorporation of Tailors of Forfar on 4 December 1656.
[RBF#215], a tailor in Forfar, 1691. [NRS.E60.11.1]

HENDERSON, JOHN, son of John Henderson a tailor, was admitted as a burgess and freeman of Forfar, 1688. [AA.F1.1.2]

HENDERSON, JOHN, a merchant in Forfar, 1680s. [AA.F1.1.2]

HENDERSON, JOHN, in Rescobie, 1691. [NRS.E69.11.1]

HENDERSON, MARGARET, spouse of Henry Straitton in Kirriemuir, sasine, 1649. [NRS.RS35.S2.III.249]

HENDERSON, THOMAS, and spouse Janet Duncan, in Finavon Wood, Oathlaw, testament, 1663, Comm. Brechin.
[NRS]

HENDERSON, WILLIAM, in Forfar, 1691. [NRS.E60.11.1]

HENDERSON, WILLIAM, in Methie Inverarity, 1691.
[NRS.E69.11.1]

HENDERSON, WILLIAM, surgeon in Kirriemuir, 1731.
[NRS.CH2.1302.185]

HENDRY, ALEXANDER, a maltman in Brechin, husband of Bessie Donaldson, sasine, 1639. [NRS.RS35.S2.I.366]

HENRIE, ALEXANDER, a merchant in Brechin, 1691.
[RPCS.XVI.605]

HENDRY, CATHARINE, spouse of John Milne a hammerman in Kirriemuir, a sasine, 1653. [NRS.RS35.S2.IV.29]

HENDRY, CHARLES, in Kirriemuir, 1721.
[NRS.CH2.1302.127]

HENDRY, DAVID, a maltman in Brechin, sasine, 1666.
[NRS.RS35.S3.III.54]

HENDRY, DAVID, a merchant in Forfar, deeds, 1683, 1687, 1688, 1690. [NRS.RD4.52.822; RD2.68.721/973; RD3.67.429; RD2.71.479]; in Forfar,1691. [NRS.E69.11.1]

HENRY, DAVID, in Tannadice, 1691. [NRS.E69.11.1]

HENDRY, ELIZABETH, in Kirriemuir, 1732.
[NRS.CH2.1302.189]

HENDRY, GEORGE, a tanner and cordiner in Kirriemuir, husband of Janet Paull, a sasine, 1637. [NRS.RS35.S2.I.51, etc]

HENDRY, GEORGE, in Kirriemuir, April 1686.
[NRS.RH11.70.1/2]

HENDRY, ISABEL, spouse of James Straiton a weaver in Kirriemuir, a sasine,1637. [NRS.RS35.S2.I.121]

HENDRY, ISOBEL, spouse of David Dougall a wright in Kirriemuir, a sasine, 1686. [NRS.RS35.S3.VIII.433]

HENRY, JOHN, spouse Bessie Robert, in Over Balgay, Kincaldrum, testament, 1612, Comm. Brechin. [NRS]

HENDRY, JOHN, in Kirriemuir, a sasine, 1632.
[NRS.RS35.S1.VIII.150]

THE PEOPLE OF STRATHMORE, 1600-1799

HENDRY, JOHN, son of the late John Hendry, in Hayston, Kirriemuir, testament, 1649, Comm. St Andrews. [NRS]

HENDRY, JOHN, in Kirriemuir, son of William Hendry there, husband of Isobel Ogilvie, a sasine, 1664. [NRS.RS35.S3.II.61]

HENDRY, JOHN, a merchant in Brechin, husband of Lilias Clark, sasine, 1672. [NRS.RS35.S3.V.280, etc]

HENDRY, JOHN, in the Roods of Kirriemuir, a sasine, 1673. [NRS.RS35.S3.V.138]

HENDRY, JOHN, a cordiner in Kirriemuir, son of George Hendry a cordiner there, spouse of Margaret MacPherson, a sasine, 1666. [NRS.RS35.S3.III.166, etc]

HENDRY, JOHN, son of John Hendry in Kirriemuir, a sasine, 1631. [NRS.RS35.S1.VIII.172]

HENDRY, JOHN, son of John Hendry, a cordiner in Kirriemuir, sasine, 1680, 1686. [NRS.RS35.S3.VII.429; RH11.70.1/2]

HENDRY, JOHN, mort-cloth, Kirriemuir, 1716. [NRS.CH2.1302.1.105]

HENDRY, KATHERINE, spouse of James Dougall a merchant in Kirriemuir, a sasine, 1694. [NRS.RS35.S3.IX.506]

HENDRY, KATHRYN, in Kirriemuir, 1741. [NRS.RH11.70.7]

HENDRIE, THOMAS, spouse Grizel Thomson born 1578, died 1636. [Eassie gravestone]

HENDRY, THOMAS, in Kirriemuir, husband of Isobel Duthie, a sasine, 1638. [NRS.RS35.S2.I.229, etc]

HENDRY, THOMAS, a merchant in Kirriemuir, husband of Magdalene Ogilvy, a sasine, 1672. [NRS.RS35.S3.V.100]

HENDRY, THOMAS, brother of John Hendry in Roods of Kirriemuir, a sasine, 1672. [NRS.RS35.S3.V.138]

HENDRY, THOMAS, in Kirriemuir, 1732. [NRS.GD7.2.151]

HENDRY, WILLIAM, in Kirriemuir, a sasine, 1664. [NRS.RS35.S3.II.61]

HEPBURN, JAMES, in Cotton Dod, in Rescobie, 1691. [NRS.E69.11.1]

THE PEOPLE OF STRATHMORE, 1600-1799

HEPBURN, JAMES, a smith in Forfar, 1708. [NRS.AC8/102]

HEPBURN, JOHN, a smith in Forfar, 1691. [NRS.E60.11.1]

HEPBURN, JOHN, in Balmadie, in Rescobie, 1691. [NRS.E69.11.1]

HEPBURN, JOHN, versus Henry, Forfar Burgh Court, 17 November 1784. [AA.F1.8.1]

HEPBURN, THOMAS, a shoemaker in Kirriemuir, a sasine, 1693. [NRS.RS35.S3.IX.548]

HEPBURN, THOMAS, a smith in Forfar, 1687. [AA.F1.1.2], a hammerman in Forfar, 1691. [NRS.E60.11.1]

HERALD, DAVID, a weaver in Clackmilne, 1745. [NRS.RH11.70.7]

HERD, MATILDA, spouse of Thomas Mitchell jr. in Potterhill, Kinnaird, testament, 1621, Comm. Brechin. [NRS]

HERRIS, GILBERT, spouse Catherine Soutar, in Kinnell, testament, 1659, Comm. Brechin. [NRS]

HERRES, JAMES, in Kinnell, 1691. [NRS.E69.11.1]

HERRES, THOMAS, in Kinnell, 1691. [NRS.E69.11.1]

HESWALL, ISOBEL, spouse of James Hill in Kirriemuir, was served heir to her grandfather John Heswall, 1741. [NRS.RH11.70.7]

HESWELL, JOHN, in Kirriemuir, husband of Margaret Schewan, a sasine,1637. [NRS.RS35.S2.I.15]

HEW, JOHN, in Rescobie, 1691. [NRS.E69.11.1]

HILL, ANDREW, in Denmylne, Forfar, husband of Margaret Fyfe, testament, 18 October 1687, Comm. St Andrews. [NRS]

HILL, DAVID, in Memus, Kirriemuir, testament,1613, Comm. St Andrews. [NRS]

HILL, JAMES, in Kirriemuir, dead by 1740. [NRS.GD7.2.178]

HILL, JAMES, in Kirriemuir, 1744. [NRS.RH11.70.7]

HILL, JOHN, at the Clockmill, 1746. [NRS.RH11.70.7]

HILL, JOHN, a wright in Kirriemuir, husband of Katherine Barron, a sasine, 1757. [NRS.RS35.18/469, etc]

HILLOCKS, DAVID, a weaver in Sparrowcroft, Forfar, 1798. [NRS.NA7340]

HOBART, JOHN, a cordiner in Kirriemuir, husband of Margaret Cadger, a sasine, 1750. [NRS.RS35.17/105]

HOBB, WILLIAM, born 1744, died 1815, wife Margaret Winter, born 1754, died 1816. [Forfar gravestone]

HODGE, ISABEL, in Forfar, 1691. [NRS.E69.11.1]

HODGE, JAMES, in Farnell, 1691. [NRS.E69.11.1]

HODGE, JOHN, in Kinnell, 1691. [NRS.E69.11.1]

HOG, ALEXANDER, in Locardstoun, Kirriemuir, testament, 1616, Comm. St Andrews. [NRS]

HOGG, ANDREW, a wheelwright in Brechin, husband of Agnes Blackhall,sasine, 1661. [NRS.RS35.S3.1.241]

HOGG, JANET, in Kinnetles, 1691. [NRS.E69.11.1]

HOLP, PATRICK, in Glamis, 1681. [NRS.E69.11.1]

HOME, DAVID, servant to the Earl of Southesk, testament, 1639, Comm. Brechin. [NRS]

HONEY, JOHN, in Kinnell, 1691. [NRS.E69.11.1]

HOOD, ALEXANDER, in Ready, 1741, dead by 1745, relict Isobel Cathro. [NRS.RH11.70.7]

HOOD, ANDREW, in Dunnan, Glamis, 1797. [NRS.E326.10.3.24]

HOOD, JAMES, a fisherman in Forfar, 1777. [NRS.NRAS#124/4/178]

HOOD, DAVID, in the Mains of Glamis, 1797. [NRS.E326.10.3.24]

HOOD, JAMES, in Forfar, 1791. [NRS.E326.1.169]

HOOD, JOHN, in Dyketon, Careston, testament, 1670, Comm. Brechin. [NRS]

THE PEOPLE OF STRATHMORE, 1600-1799

HOOD, ROBERT, spouse Margaret Kinninmonth, in Mains of Finavon, testament, 1679, Comm. Brechin. [NRS]

HOOD, THOMAS, in Finavon, relict Isobel Doig, testament, 1679, Comm. Brechin. [NRS]

HOOD, THOMAS, in Balmadie, Rescobie, 1691. [NRS.E69.11.1]

HORN, JAMES, a hammerman in Glamis, wife Margaret born 1648, died 1676. [Glamis gravestone]

HORN, JAMES, born 1716, at Bridgend of Glamis, died 1773, wife Katherine Shepherd, born 1707, died 1793. [Glamis gravestone]

HORNE, WILLIAM, in Innerighty House, Kinnetles, 1691. [NRS.E69.11.1]

HORNE, WILLIAM, in Kinnetles, 1691. [NRS.E69.11.1]

HORNE, WILLIAM, in Methie Inverarity, 1691. [NRS.E69.11.1]

HORNE, WILLIAM, in Glamis, 1681. [NRS.E69.11.1]

HOWE, ALEXANDER, a tailor in Forfar, 1684. [RBF#218]

HOW, ANDREW, at Hillend of Dod, parish of Forfar, testament, 1712, Comm. St Andrews. [NRS]

HOW, DAVID, born 1707, tenant in Bevellgreen, died 1752, spouse Isobel Jolly. [Aberlemno gravestone]

HOW, ELIZABETH, wife of James Stirling, 1779. [AA.F5.151]

HOWE, WILLIAM, a tailor in Forfar in 1776, husband of Helen Mitchell; versus Anderson and Easton, Forfar Burgh Court, 18, 20 August 1784. [AA.F1.8.1][Forfar gravestone]

HOWAT, JANET, aged 13, daughter of Helen Guthrie, a suspected witch, confession, 1661, imprisoned in Forfar, 1666. [AA.F5.35.3][RPCS.II.129]

HOWIE, JOHN, in Cotton of Glaswell, parish of Kirriemuir, testament, 1725, Comm. St Andrews. [NRS]

HOWIE, WILLIAM, in Strathcathro, 1691. [NRS.E69.11.1]

THE PEOPLE OF STRATHMORE, 1600-1799

HUDSON, THOMAS, in Kirriemuir, 1783.
[NRS.CH2.1302.2/93]

HUME, BEATRIX, deceased, Kirriemuir,1718.
[NRS.CH2.1302.1.113]

HUMMELL, AGNES, spouse of John Benny a shoemaker burgess, 1696. [AA.F5.43]

HUNTER, ALEXANDER, a merchant in Kirriemuir, spouse of Beatrix Anderson, a sasine, 1699. [NRS.RS35.S3.X.206]

HUNTER, ALISON, youngest daughter of the late George Hunter a burgess of Forfar, 1662. [AA.F5.38]

HUNTER, ANDREW, Provost of Forfar, testament, 25 January 1639, Comm. St Andrews. [NRS]

HUNTER, ANDREW, a tanner burgess of Forfar, charter, 1649. [NRS.GD1.61.2]

HUNTER, ANDREW, son of Robert Hunter, was admitted as a burgess of Forfar, 1660. [AA.F1.1.1]

HUNTER, ANDREW, of Dod, in Rescobie, 1691.
[NRS.E69.11.1]

HUNTER, ANDREW, second son of deceased David Hunter of Burnside, testament, 1707, Comm. Brechin. [NRS]

HUNTER, ANDREW, Provost of Forfar, sasine, 1749.
[NRS.RS35.17.23]

HUNTER, ANDREW, son of Andrew Hunter a shoemaker in Forfar, a sasine, 1717. [NRS.RS35.13.130]

HUNTER, ANDREW, son of Thomas Hunter, the elder, a wright in Forfar, a sasine, 1711. [NRS.RS35.12,438]

HUNTER, BESSIE, spouse of Patrick Benny a burgess of Forfar, testament, 29 April 1620, Comm. St Andrews. [NRS]

HUNTER, DAVID, an assizeman in Forfar, 1600; sometime Provost of Forfar, testament, 27 March 1616, Comm. St Andrews; [RGS.VI.1176]

HUNTER, DAVID, provost of Forfar, 1643.[RPCS.VIII.19]

THE PEOPLE OF STRATHMORE, 1600-1799

HUNTER, DAVID, of Burnside, spouse Catharine Campbell, sasine,1631. [NRS.RS35.S1.VIII.42, 224]; testament 1659, Comm. Brechin. [NRS]; 1689. [AA.F5.102], in Forfar, 1691. [NRS.E60.11.1]

HUNTER, GEORGE, a burgess and bailie of Forfar in 1607, 1608, testament, 27 March 1616, Comm. St Andrews. [NRS] [RPCS.VII.408; VIII.647]

HUNTER, GEORGE, son of Andrew Hunter, Provost of Forfar, and his wife Euphame Bennie, testament, 21 January 1629, Comm. St Andrews. [NRS]

HUNTER, GEORGE, a burgess of Forfar, father of Janet and Alison, sasine, 1644. [NRS.RS35.S2.II.534]

HUNTER, JAMES, son of the late William Hunter, burgess of Forfar, testament, 1595, Comm. Edinburgh. [NRS]

HUNTER, JAMES, a burgess of Forfar, testament, 18 February 1598, Comm. St Andrews. [RAS]

HUNTER, JOHN, of Baldovy, Kincaldrum, testament, 1667, Comm. Brechin. [NRS]

HUNTER, JOHN, born 1622, in Castleton, died 1693, wife Elizabeth Jelly, son Andrew. [Eassie gravestone]

HUNTER, JOHN, miller at the Mill of Kinnaird, spouse Elspet Brock, testament, 1700, Comm. Brechin. [NRS]

HUNTER, JOHN, versus Donald and Thornton, Forfar Burgh Court, 2 June 1784, 1791. [AA.F1.8.1][NRS.E326.1.169]

HUNTER, KATHERINE, daughter of the deceased David Hunter of Burnside, testament, 1707, Comm. Brechin. [NRS]

HUNTER, MARGARET, spouse to George Baillie a burgess of Forfar, testament, 1618, Comm. St Andrews. [NRS]

HUNTER, PATRICK, in Kinnell, 1691. [NRS.E69.11.1]

HUNTER, ROBERT, bailie of Forfar, 1660. [AA.F1.1.1]

HUNTER, ROBERT, a wright in Forfar, father of Bessie, sasine, 1698. [NRS.RS35.S3.X.46], in Forfar, 1691. [NRS.E60.11.1]

HUNTER, ROBERT, a day laborer in Forfar, a bond, 1774. [AA.F5.59]

THE PEOPLE OF STRATHMORE, 1600-1799

HUNTER, THOMAS, of Restenneth, 1654. [AA.F5.106]

HUNTER, THOMAS, born about 1643, a councillor and Deacon of the Wrights in Forfar, 1680s. [AA.F1.1.2] in Forfar, 1691. [NRS.E60.11.1]

HUNTER, THOMAS, the elder, a wright in Forfar, a sasine,1717. [NRS.RS35.13.130]

HUNTER, THOMAS, Provost of Forfar, relict Janet Fisher, sasine, 1736. [NRS.RS35.15.555]

HUNTER, THOMAS, a merchant in Kirriemuir, 1745. [NRS.RH11.70.7]

HUNTER, WILLIAM, son of the late William Hunter, a burgess of Forfar, testament, 1595, Comm. Edinburgh. [NRS]

HUNTER, WILLIAM, bailie of Forfar, 1621. [AA.F5.93]

HUNTER, WILLIAM, a skinner in Forfar, son of Andrew Hunter provost of Forfar, spouse Jean Jounken, sasine, 1637. [NRS.RS35.S2.1.83, etc]; relict Jean Junkine, sasine, 1638. [NRS.RS35.S2.I.83]

HUNTER, WILLIAM, provost of Forfar, son of George Hunter, sasine, 1650. [NRS.GD1.61.4][AA.f1.4.5/6]

HUNTER, WILLIAM, son of Andrew Hunter, provost of Forfar, sasine, 1756. [NRS.RS35.18.294]

HUNTER, WILLIAM, in Forfar, 1759, 1785, 1791. [NRS.E326.3.19]

HUTCHEON, ADAM, in Hirdhill, husband of Elizabeth Proctor, a sasine, 1648. [NRS.RS35.S2.III.36, etc]

HUTCHEON, ADAM, in Hirdhill, Kirriemuir, testament, 1673, Comm. St Andrews. [NRS]

HUTCHEON, AGNES, daughter of Alexander Hutcheon in Kirriemuir, spouse of Duncan Laing a merchant there, a sasine,1645. [NRS.RS35.S2.II.452]

HUTCHEON, AGNES, daughter of William Hutcheon a merchant in Kirriemuir, a sasine, 1631. [NRS.RS35.S1.VIII.246]

THE PEOPLE OF STRATHMORE, 1600-1799

HUTCHEON, ALEXANDER, in Forfar, an assizeman in 1600. [RGS.VI.1176]

HUTCHEON, ALEXANDER, maltman in Kirriemuir, spouse Janet Cuthbert, born 1595, died 1655. [Kirriemuir gravestone]

HUTCHEON, ALEXANDER, in Kirriemuir, husband of Janet Findlaw, a sasine, 1637. [NRS.RS35.S2.I.21]

HUTCHEON, ALEXANDER, in the West Roods of Kirriemuir, a sasine, 1692. [NRS.RS35.S3.IX.59]

HUTCHEON, ALEXANDER, a maltman in Kirriemuir, a sasine, 1655. [NRS.RS35.S2.V.10]

HUTCHEON, CHRISTINA, spouse of John Crombe in Kirriemuir, a sasine, 1631. [NRS.RS35.S1.VIII.30]

HUTCHEON, DAVID, the elder, a cordiner in Kirriemuir, sasines, testament, 1635, Comm. St Andrews. [NRS][NRS.RS35.S2.I.456, etc]

HUTCHEON, DAVID, a cordiner in Kirriemuir, son of David Hutcheon, a cordiner there, husband of Isobel Wauch, sasines, 1637. [NRS.RS35.S2.I.16]

HUTCHEON, ISABEL, daughter of William Hutcheon a merchant in Kirriemuir, a sasine,1637. [NRS.RS35.S1.VIII.246]

HUTCHEON, ISOBEL, in Kirriemuir, 1786, 1787. [NRS.CH2.1302.2/123, 125]

HUTCHEON, JAMES, in Kirriemuir, son of David Hutcheon the elder a cordiner there, sasines, 1638. [NRS.RS35.S2.I.139, etc]; testament, 1662, Comm. St Andrews. [NRS]

HUTCHEON, JAMES, son of Walter Hutcheon, brother of Alexander Hutcheon in Kirriemuir, a sasine, 1667. [NRS.RS35.S3.III.174]

HUTCHEON, JANET, daughter of William Hutcheon a merchant in Kirriemuir, and spouse of Thomas Tarbet in Wester Logie a merchant in Kirriemuir, sasines,1631. [NRS.RS35.VIII.245, etc]

HUTCHEON, JANET, spouse of John Adam a tanner in Kirriemuir, a sasine, 1637. [NRS.RS35.S2.I.136]

THE PEOPLE OF STRATHMORE, 1600-1799

HUTCHEN, JOHN, and wife, died 1668. [Brechin Cathedral gravestone]

HUTCHEON, MARGARET, daughter of Alexander Hutcheon in Kirriemuir, a sasine, 1667. [NRS.RS35.S3.III.264]

HUTCHEON, MARGARET, daughter of Thomas Hutcheon in Wester Tarbirne, spouse of Archibald Cuthbert in Kirriemuir, sasines, 1643. [NRS.RS35.S2.II.412, etc]

HUTCHEON, MARGARET, relict of Robert Volum in Kirriemuir, sasines, 1698. [NRS.RS35.X.60]

HUTCHEON, MARJORIE, spouse of Gilbert Smythe a merchant in Kirriemuir, a sasine, 1654. [NRS.RS35.S2.IV.401]

HUTCHEON, PATRICK, a brabonar in Cotton of Lour, parish of Forfar, testament, 9 March 1607, Comm. St Andrews. [NRS]

HUTCHEON, ROBERT, son of Alexander Hutcheon in the West Roods of Kirriemuir, a sasine, 1692. [NRS.RS35.S3.IX.59]

HUTCHEON, ROBERT, tenant in Kinquherrie, 1743, 1745. [NRS.RH11.70.7]

HUTCHEON, WILLIAM, in Kirriemuir, testament, 1620; husband of Isobel Alexander, testament, 1620, Comm. St Andrews. [NRS]

HUTCHEON, WILLIAM, sr and jr, in Forfar, 1691. [NRS.E60.11.1]

HUTCHESON, ELIZABETH, in Guthrie, 1691. [NRS.E69.11.1]

HUTCHESON, HELEN, spouse John Dorward, in Blairs of Drumbarrow, Dunnichen, testament, 1632, Comm. Brechin. [NRS]

HUTCHESON, JOHN, in Forfar, 1691. [NRS.E60.11.1]

HUTCHESON, MARGARET, in Peggerton of Guthrie, testament, 1698, Comm. Brechin. [NRS]

HUTCHISON, PETER, born 1747, tenant in Mireside of Nevay, died 14 February 1816, husband of Jean Gray, parents of Janet, Jean, Catharine, Alexander, Elizabeth, and Peter Hutchison. [Nevay gravestone]

THE PEOPLE OF STRATHMORE, 1600-1799

HUTTON, DAVID, in Oathlaw, 1691. [NRS.E69.11.1]

HUTTON, JOHN, in Forfar, 1691. [NRS.E60.11.1]

INCHEAK, JANET, spouse William Shepherd, died 1652. [Eassie gravestone]

INGLIS, ANDREW, in Potterhill, Kinnaird, testament, 1728, Comm. Brechin. [NRS]

INNERARITY, JAMES, a merchant burgess of Brechin, and spouse Elspet Syme, testament, 1647, Comm. Brechin. [NRS]

INNERMITTIE, DAVID, in Kinnell, 1691. [NRS.E69.11.1]

INNERMITTIE, JOHN, in Kinnell, 1691. [NRS.E69.11.1]

INVERARITY, HENRY, born 1678, tenant in Framedrum, died 1766, wife [1] Agnes Wood, 1688-1723, [2] Margaret Black, 1695-1767, children John, Agnes, and Elizabeth. [Aberlemo gravestone]

INNES, Dr JOHN, a physician in Brechin, husband of Barbara Ramsay, parents of Margaret, sasine, 1684; a donor in 1678; testament, 1677, Comm. Brechin. [Brechin Cathedral] [NRS.RS35.S3.VIII.5]

IRELAND, CATHERINE, daughter of Thomas Ireland schoolmaster in Alyth, spouse of James Rattray a glover in Kirriemuir, sasine, 1676. [NRS.RS35.S3.VI.212]

IRELAND, JOHN, in Burnside, Forfar, 1691. [NRS.E60.11.1]

IRELAND, JOHN, in Guthrie, 1691. [NRS.E69.11.1]

IRELAND, WILLIAM, born 1747, a land surveyor, died Fofar 1808. [Guthrie gravestone]

IRONS, CATHERINE, spouse of Abraham Piggott notary and clerk of the regality of Kirriemuir, a sasine, 1637. [NRS.RS35.S2.I.25]

IRVINE, ROBERT, born 1710, died 1775, wife Ann Watson, children John, Robert, John, Katherine, Margaret, Isobel, Thomas, Jean, Agnes, James, and Ann. [Guthrie gravestone]

IRVINE, PATRICK, in Kirriemuir, 1783. [NRS.CH2.1302.2/93]

JACK, ALEXANDER, in Guthrie, 1691. [NRS.E69.11.1]

THE PEOPLE OF STRATHMORE, 1600-1799

JACK, DAVID, in Glamis, 1681. [NRS.E69.11.1]

JACK, JOHN, in Aberlemno, 1691. [NRS.E69.11.1]

JACK, ELSPETH, spouse of John Mitchell a brabiner in Kirriemuir, a sasine, 1649. [NRS.RS35.S2.III.504]

JACK, ELSPETH, daughter of John Jack a cordiner in Kirriemuir, sasine, 1692. [NRS.RS35.S3.IX.390]

JACK, JAMES, in Kincaldrum, testament, 1705, Comm. Brechin. [NRS]

JACK, JOHN, a cordiner in Kirriemuir, husband of Isobel Duthie, a sasine, 1656. [NRS.RS35.S2.V.288]

JACK, JOHN, schoolmaster in Aberlemno, Angus, 1690. [SHS.4.2]

JACK, PETER, versus Robert Masterton, Forfar Burgh Court, 30 November 1785. [AA.F1.8.1]

JAKE, JOHN, born 1537, in Balkeru, died on 30 August 1597. [Nevay gravestone]

JAFFREY, ALEXANDER, a writer in Forfar, a sasine, 1752. [NRS.RS35.17.443]

JAFFREY, JOHN, a writer in Forfar, formerly a bailie thereof, spouse of Elizabeth Hunter, son of Alexander Jaffrey, a writer there, 1744, 1745. [NRS.RH11.70.7; RS35.16.551, etc; NRAS#124/4/1/75]

JAFFREY, MAGDALENE, daughter of the late Alexander Jaffrey provost of Forfar, testaments, 1775, 1776, Comm. St Andrews. [NRS]

JAMES, GEORGE, in Farnell, 1691. [NRS.E69.11.1]

JAMES, JOHN in Strathcathro, 1691. [NRS.E69.11.1]

JAMIE, ALEXANDER, the elder, treasurer of Brechin, 1691. [RPCS.XVI.605]

JAMIESON, ALEXANDER, a maltman in Brechin, husband of Margaret Langsandie, sasine, 1686. [NRS.RS35.S3.VIII.498]

JAMIESON, ALEXANDER, in Kinnell, 1691. [NRS.E69.11.1]

THE PEOPLE OF STRATHMORE, 1600-1799

JAMIESON, ANDREW, a messenger in Redford, parish of Forfar, deed, 1714. [NRS.RD4.89.65]

JAMIESON, DOUGAL, a maltman and bailie of Brechin, husband of Isobel Skinner, parents of Walter, John, Barbara, and Isobel, sasine,1642; in Brechin, 1656. [NRS.RS35.S2.II.22, etc] [RGS.X.550]

JAMIESON, ELSPETH, in Kirriemuir, 1746. [NRS.RH11.70.7]

JAMIESON, JAMES, in Guthrie, 1691. [NRS.E69.11.1]

JAMIESON, JAMES, bailie to Archibald, Duke of Douglas, of the Regality of Kirriemuir, 1745. [NRS.RH70.11.7]

JAMIESON, JOHN, in Carcary, Farnell, spouse Elspet Bunyon, testament, 1637, Comm. Brechin. [NRS]

JAMIESON, JOHN, bailie of Brechin, son of Dougal Jamieson, father of John, Dougal, Isobel, and Walter, sasine, 1656, [NRS.RS35.S2.V.298, etc]

JAMIESON, JOHN, burgh piper of Forfar, 1689. [AA.F1.1.2]

JAMIESON, JOHN, in Rescobie, 1691. [NRS.E69.11.1]

JAMIESON, JOHN, in Forfar, 1785. [NRS.E326.3.19]

JAMIESON, JOHN, minister of the Secession Church in Forfar from 1789 to 1797, later a lexicographer. [NRS.NA22406; E326.1.169]

JAMIESON, MURDOCH, 1742. [NRS.RH11.70.7]

JAMIESON, WALTER, spouse Janet Johnston, in Meikle Carcary, Farnell, testament, 1609, Comm. Brechin. [NRS]

JAMIESON, WALTER, a bailie and kirkmaster, a maltman in Brechin, sasine, 1661; a donor in 1680. [Brechin Cathedral] [NRS.RS35.S3.I.118]

JAPP, ALEXANDER, in Capo, Strathcathro, testament, 1751, Comm. Brechin. [NRS]

JARRON, DAVID, born 1680, tenant farmer, died 1742, wife Magdalene Taws, born 1691, died 1756, daughter Elisabeth, born 1726, died 1761. [Guthrie gravestone]

THE PEOPLE OF STRATHMORE, 1600-1799

JARRON, GEORGE, versus John Tindal, Forfar Burgh Court, 25 June 1784. [AA.F1.8.1]

JEFFREY, ALEXANDER, a bailie of Forfar, deeds, 1706, 1715. [NRS.RD3.109.238; RD2.105.537]

JOHNSON, WILLIAM, versus Thomas Rodger, Forfar Burgh Court, 1 December 1784. [AA.F1.8.1]

JOHNSTON, ALEXANDER, in Wester Brakie, testament, 1617, Comm. St Andrews. [NRS]

JOHNSTON, ANDREW, spouse Christian Kinnear, in Egibert of Farnell, testament, 1631, Comm. Brechin. [NRS]

JOHNSTON, FRANCIS, in Methie Inverarity, 1691. [NRS.E69.11.1]

JOHNSTON, GEORGE, of Herdhill, born 1753, died 1846. [Kirriemuir gravestone]

JOHNSTON, GEORGE, from Kirriemuir, sought in New York during 1782. [NY Gazette, 20.5.1782]

JOHNSTON, HELEN, born 1747, died 1848. [Kirriemuir gravestone]

JOHNSTON, JAMES, in Aberlemno, 1691. [NRS.E69.11.1]

JOHNSTON, JAMES, 1783. [NRS.CH2.1302.2/97]

JOHNSTON, JEAN, in Kinnetles, 1691. [NRS.E69.11.1]

JOHNSTON, JOHN, a webster, spouse Margaret Laing, in Carcary, Farnell, testament, 1613, Comm. Brechin. [NRS]

JOHNSTON, JOHN, in Farnell, 1691. [NRS.E69.11.1]

JOHNSTON, JOHN, in Aberlemno, 1691. [NRS.E69.11.1]

JOHNSTON, MARJORIE, relict of Andrew Da in Nansford, Farnell, testament, 1629, Comm. Brechin. [NRS]

JOHNSTON, THOMAS, a servant, imprisoned in Brechin Tolbooth and banished in 1614. [RPCS.X.233]

JOHNSTON, THOMAS, in Brechin, 1620. [RPCS.XII.215]

JOHNSTON, THOMAS, in Hardhill, 1745. [NRS.RH11.70.7]

THE PEOPLE OF STRATHMORE, 1600-1799

JOLLY, ALEXANDER, a cordiner in Brechin, 1621. [RPCS.XII.427]

JOLLY, JAMES, a cordiner in Brechin, 1621. [RPCS.XII.427]

JOLLY, and STURROCK, versus James Wood, Forfar Burgh Court, 25 June 1784. [AA.F1.8.1]

JORDANE, MARGARET, spouse Patrick Mylne a tailor in Guthrie, testament, 1614, Comm. Brechin. [NRS]

KAY, JANET, spouse John Guthrie in Cotton of Kinnaird, testament, 1625, Comm. Brechin. [NRS]

KEAIR, (?), THOMAS, in South Muir of Forfar, a tack, 1718. [AA.F5/23]

KED, JEAN, in Forfar, 1691. [NRS.E60.11.1]

KEITH, JOHN, born in Kincardineshire, educated at Marischal College, Aberdeen, 1649-1653, minister of Kirriemuir from 1663 to his death in 1668. [F.5.296]

KEITH, WALTER. spouse Agnes Junckin, in Corechie Mill, Dunnichen, testament, 1637, Comm. Brechin. [NRS]

KELLIE, ANDREW, jr. in Langlands of Guthrie, testament, 1642, Comm. Brechin. [NRS]

KELLIE, JAMES, in Guthrie, 1691. [NRS.E69.11.1]

KANDOW, MARGARET, in Kirriemuir, 1744. [NRS.CH2.1302.249]

KENDOW, ROBERT, in Glenorg, parish of Kirriemuir, testament, 1617, Comm. St Andrews. [NRS]

KERMOCK, JOHN, in Kirriemuir, 1741, 1742. [NRS.CH2.1302.231; RH11.70.7]

KERMACK, SYLVESTER, spouse Catherine Dougas, born 1749, died 1796. [Ruthven gravestone]

KERR, ALEXANDER, in Aberlemno, 1691. [NRS.E69.11.1]

KERR, DAVID, in Westfield, Forfar, husband of Isobel Leuchars testament 28 October 1674, Comm. St Andrews. [NRS]

KER, DAVID, in Kirriemuir, 1763. [NRS.CH2.1302.2/11]

KER, ELSPET, in Kirriemuir, 1734. [NRS.CH2.1302.207]

KERR, GEORGE, versus .... Jack, Forfar Burgh Court, 18 August 1784; versus Andrew Millar jr., 25 August 1784, Forfar Burgh Court; versus Masterton and Yeaman, Forfar Burgh Court, 22 September 1784; versus ... Baxter, Forfar Burgh Court, 1 December 1784; versus ... Daldarg, Forfar Burgh Court, 18 February 1785. [AA.F1.8.1]

KERR, HERCULES, a maltman in Brechin, husband of Agnes Skinner, 1676. [NRS.RS35.S3.VI.110]

KERR, JAMES, versus Andrew Dall, Forfar Burgh Court, 11 August1784; Peter Jack, Forfar Burgh Court, 8 September 1784; versus Downie and Mill, Forfar Burgh Court, 15 December 1784; versus Patrick Neish, Forfar Burgh Court, 26 January 1785, 18/23 February1785, 1 April 1785. [AA.F1.8.1]

KER, JOHN, in Methie Inverarity, 1691. [NRS.E69.11.1]

KERR, JOHN, in Farnell, 1691. [NRS.E69.11.1]

KERR, Reverend JOHN, in Forfar, 1753, 1759. [NRS.E326.1.169]

KER, JOHN, a weaver in Ground of Ballinshoe, 1741. [NRS.CH2.1302.235]

KERR, ROBERT, a weaver in Brechin, husband of Katherine Fearn, sasine, 1677. [NRS.RS35.S3.VI.444]

KERR, ROBERT WILLIAM, in Forfar, 1753. [NRS.E326.1.169]

KERR. THOMAS, formerly a carpenter aboard HMS Southampton, then in Forfar, testament, 1794, Comm. St Andrews. [NRS]

KERR, WALTER, a burgess of Forfar, testament, 1577, Comm. Edinburgh. [NRS]

KERR, WILLIAM, a burgess of Brechin, husband of Janet Whyte, sasine, 1661. [NRS.RS35.S3.I.241]

KERR, WILLIAM, in Woodhead of Balmaw, a burgess of Forfar, a tack, 1666. [NRS.RD2.18.437]

THE PEOPLE OF STRATHMORE, 1600-1799

KERR, WILLIAM, son of the late David Kerr in West Fauld of Forfar, was admitted as a burgess and freeman of Forfar, 1685. [AA.F.1.1.2]

KERR, WILLIAM, son of John Kerr the younger in New..., was admitted as a freeman and burgess of Forfar, 1685. [AA.F1.1.2]

KERR, WILLIAM, sr and jr. in Forfar, 1691. [NRS.E60.11.1]

KER, WILLIAM, in Methie Inverarity, 1691. [NRS.E69.11.1]

KERR, WILLIAM, a writer and former Provost of Forfar, husband of Elizabeth Ballingall, sasines, 1736, 1745, 1759. [NRS.RS35.15.505, etc; E326.1.169][AA.F1.4.3/16] [NRAS#124/4/1/75]

KEWNIE, JAMES, a weaver in Ground of Inverquharity, an elder, 1741. [NRS.CH2.1302.235]

KEY, ANDREW, a tanner in Kirriemuir, husband of Agnes Young, a sasine, 1637. [NRS.RS35.S2.I.110]; testament,1648, Comm. St Andrews. [NRS]

KEY, JOHN, a tanner in Kirriemuir, husband of Maidie Piggott, a sasine,1648. [NRS.RS35.S2.III.24]

KEY, JOHN, versus Watt and Findlay, Forfar Burgh Court, 11 August 1784. [AA.F1.8.1]

KEY, Dr PATRICK, born 1752, in Forfar 1785, 1791, died 1806, husband of Anne Binny, born 1757, died 1832. [NRS.E326.3.19][Forfar gravestone]

KID, GEORGE, versus ....Mathers, Forfar Burgh Court, 20 August 1784. [AA.F1.8.1]

KIDD, JAMES, in Glamis, 1681. [NRS.E69.11.1]

KYD, JOHN, in Logie, Kirriemuir, husband of Janet Craik, testament, 1637, Comm. St Andrews. [NRS]

KID, WILLIAM, a burgess of Forfar, testament, 1606, Comm. Edinburgh. [NRS]

KID, WILLIAM, in Oathlaw, 1691. [NRS.E69.11.1]

KEIR, JOHN, in Methie Inverarity, 1691. [NRS.E69.11.1]

THE PEOPLE OF STRATHMORE, 1600-1799

KILGOUR, JAMES, a wright in Brechin, 1691. [RPCS.XVI.605]

KINCAID, JOHN, the witch-pricker of Tranent, was admitted as a freeman of Forfar on 24 September 1661. [AA.F1.1.1]

KINGOW, JAMES, a wheelwright in Brechin, husband of Janet Lindsay, sasine, 1681. [NRS.RS35.S3.VII.299]

KINGOW, WILLIAM, a wheelwright, formerly in Brechin, sasine, 1662. [NRS.RS35.S3.I.309]

KINLOCH, DAVID, of Kilry, 1741, 1745. [NRS.RH11.70.7]

KINLOCH, JOHN, in Logie, Kirriemuir, letters, 1792. [NRS.GD1.931.15]

KINLOCH, THOMAS, of Cairn, was admitted as a burgess of Forfar, 4 June 1789. [NRS.GD1.931.107]

KINLOCH, Major WILLIAM, in Logie, Kirriemuir, letter, 1800. [NRS.GD1.931.73]

KINNEAR, DAVID, in Kinnetles, 1691. [NRS.E69.11.1]

KINNEAR, GEORGE, in Maisondieu, Brechin, 1688, Comm. Brechin. [NRS]

KINNEAR, ROBERT, vicar in Brechin, 1606. [RPCS.VII.643]

KINNEAR, ROBERT, in Brechin, 1620. [RGS.VIII.17]

KINNEAR, ROBERT, vicar of Brechin, sasine, 1666. [NRS.RS35.S3.II.343]

KINNEAR, THOMAS, in Farnell, 1691. [NRS.E69.11.1]

KINNEAR, WILLIAM, a merchant in Brechin, sasine,1684. [NRS.RS35.S3.VIII.18]

KYNNIMONTH, ALEXANDER, of Meathie, minister of Kirriemuir, 1586-1622, died 1630. Husband of Anna, daughter of Sir John Ogilvy of Inverquharity; 1607; husband of Catherine Ogilvie, 1642. [NRS.GD68/1/129; RS35.S2.II.76] [F.5.296][CLC#1686]

KYNNIMONTH, ALEXANDER, the younger, graduated MA from St Andrews in 1619, minister of Kirriemuir 1629 to 1663. Husband of Catherine Ogilvy. [F.5.296]

THE PEOPLE OF STRATHMORE, 1600-1799

KYNNINMONTH, AGNES, spouse to Oliver Fenton in Balloch, Kirriemuir, testament, 1613, Comm. St Andrews. [NRS]

KINNINMONTH, or LOUR, ELIZABETH, daughter and heir of Agnes Cramond in Brechin, 1620. [RGS.VIII.17]

KINNINMONTH, or LOWRIE, ISABEL, in Forfar, testament, 7 August 1662, Comm. St Andrews. [NRS]

KINNINMONTH, JOHN, in Glamis, 1681. [NRS.E69.11.1]

KNIGHT, DAVID, a notary in Brechin, sasine, 1676. [NRS.RS35.S3.VI.339]

KNOX, ALEXANDER, at the Meikle Milne of Brechin, sasine, 1639. [NRS.RS35.S1.I.430]

KNOX, ANDREW, deacon of the glovers of Brechin, husband of Jean Langsandie, sasine, 1686. [NRS.RS35.S3.VIII.497]

KNOX, ANDREW, minister at Kinnaird, testament, 1748, Comm. Brechin. [NRS]

KNOX, JAMES, a skinner in Brechin, sasine, 1654. [NRS.RS35.S2.IV.348]

KNOX, JAMES, a glover in Brechin, husband of Margaret Lowson, sasine, 1666. [NRS.RS35.S3.III.83]

KNOX, JOHN, a burgess of Brechin, sasine, 1661. [NRS.RS35.S3.I.221]

KNOX, JOHN, son of Alexander Knox in Brechin, husband of Catherine Dempster, sasine, 1639. [NRS.RS35.S2.I.430]

KNOX, WALTER, a tailor burgess of Brechin, spouse Elizabeth Watson, testament, 1611, Comm. Brechin. [NRS]

LAING, ALEXANDER, in Shilhill, Kirriemuir, husband of Catharine Wood, testament, 1662, Comm. St Andrews. [NRS]

LAING, CHRISTIAN, a donor in 1641. [Brechin Cathedral]

LAING, CHRISTINE, 1661. [AA.F1.1.1]

LAIRD, ALEXANDER, in Forfar, 1691. [NRS.E69.11.1]

LAIRD, DAVID, in Forfar, 1608. [RPCS.VIII.647]

THE PEOPLE OF STRATHMORE, 1600-1799

LAIRD, JAMES, versus Kebal and Masterton, also William Masterton, sr., Forfar Burgh Court, 18 August 1784. [AA.F1.8.1]

LAIRD, JOHN, in Forfar, 1691. [NRS.E60.11.1]

LAIRD, WILLIAM, in Forfar, 1691. [NRS.E60.11.1], in Ground of Balmashanner, a tack, 1716. [AA.F5/23]

LAIRD, WILLIAM, born 1727, a manufacturer at the West Port of Forfar, died 1823, husband of Helen Lowe, born 1715, died 1790. [Forfar gravestone]

LAIKIE, JOHN, in Muirhead, 1742. [NRS.RH11.70.7]

LAKIE, JOHN, in Kirriemuir, 1783. [NRS.CH2.1302.2/101]

LECKIE, AGNES, spouse to James Robertson in Kirriemuir, 1744. [NRS.RH11.70.7]

LAMB, ANDREW, in Langbank, Forfar, testament, 1619, Comm. St Andrews. [NRS]

LAMB, Mr GEORGE, servant to Andrew, Bishop of Brechin, 1615. [RGS.VIII.17]

LAMB, JAMES, in Kirriemuir, 1785. [NRS.CH2.1302.2/115]

LAMB, JOHN, in Forfar,1691. [NRS.E69.11.1]

LAMB, MARGARET, spouse John Garland in Windyedge if Dunbarrow, Dunnichen, testament, 1632, Comm. Brechin. [NRS]

LAMB, NICOLAS, in Kinnell, 1691. [NRS.E69.11.1]

LAMB, WALTER, burgess of Brechin, spouse Margaret Valentine, testament, 1628, Comm. Brechin. [NRS]

LAMBIE, JOHN, Dean of Brechin, sasine, 1673. [NRS.RS35.S3.V.331]

LAMBIE, PATRICK, in Ballindarg, parish of Kirriemuir, testament, 1621, Comm. St Andrews. [NRS]

LAMMIE, SYLVESTER, minister at Glamis, a sasine, 1663. [NRS.GD68.1.226]

LANGLANDS, ALEXANDER, in Aberlemno, 1691. [NRS.E69.11.1]

THE PEOPLE OF STRATHMORE, 1600-1799

LANGLANDS, ALEXANDER, in Guthrie, 1691.
[NRS.E69.11.1]

LANGLANDS, ISOBEL, in Prentice Wynd, Brechin, 1691.
[RP.II.344]

LANGLANDS, JAMES, in Forfar, 1691. [NRS.E60.11.1]

LANGLANDS, JANET, in Prentice Wynd, Brechin, 1691.
[RP.II.344]

LANGLANDS, JEAN, in Prentice Wynd, Brechin, 1691.
[RP.II.344]

LANGLANDS, JOHN, a litster burgess of Forfar, testament, 26 October 1683, Comm. St Andrews.

LANGLANDS, JOHN, in Aberlemno, 1691. [NRS.E69.11.1]

LANGLANDS, MARGARET, in Prentice Wynd, Brechin, 1691.
[RP.II.344]

LANGSANDIE, JANET, sister of John Langsandie, in Brechin, sasine, 1687. [NRS.RS35.S3.VIII.497]

LANGSANDIE, JOHN, a glover in Brechin, husband of Marjorie Watt, sasine,1664. [NRS.RS35.S3.II.60]

LANGWILL, JOHN, burgess and bailie of Brechin, 1617, husband of Janet Gairdner, sasine,1620. [NRS.RS35.S1.I.176] [RPCS.XI.58]

LANGWILL, KATHERINE, a donor in 1622. [Brechin Cathedral]

LAUDER, JOHN, in Kirriemuir, 1745. [NRS.RH11.70.7]

LAURIE, ROBERT, MA, Bishop of Brechin from 1672 to his death in 1678, sasine. [F.6.375][NRS.RS35.S3.V.145]

LAUSON, JAMES, in Aberlemno, 1691. [NRS.E69.11.1]

LAUSON, JOHN, in Forfar,1691. [NRS.E69.11.1]

LAW, THOMAS, a surgeon apothecary in Forfar, a deed, 1700.
[NRS.RD2.84.842]

LAW, WILLIAM, in Woodend, in Rescobie, 1691.
[NRS.E69.11.1]

LAWSON, ALEXANDER, born 1735, died 1831. [Kirriemuir gravestone]

LAWSON, CATHERINE, relict of Thomas Wilson tenant in Kincaldrum, residing in Cransley, Farnell, testament, 1772, Comm. Brechin. [NRS]

LAWSON, ELSPET, in Kirriemuir, 1786. [NRS.CH2.1302.2/123]

LAWSON, WILLIAM, servant to Walter Jamieson, bailie in Brechin, sasine, 1673. [NRS.RS35.S3.V.255]

LEECH, JOHN, burgess and bailie of Brechin, 1607. [RPCS.VII.448]

LEG, MARGARET, spouse to William Michael in Strathcathro, testament, 1627, Comm. Brechin. [NRS]

LEITCH, JOHN, burgess of Brechin, husband of Grissel Thaine, parents of Andrew, Grizel, Isobel, and Margaret, sasine, 1643. [NRS.RS35.S2.II.230]

LEITH, JOHN, burgess of Brechin, 1608. [RPCS.VIII.31]

LEONARD, DAVID, in Kilhill, Kirriemuir, testament, 1683, Comm. St Andrews. [NRS]

LEONARD, JAMES, a burgess of Brechin, father of James, and John, sasine, 1669. [NRS.RS35.S3.IV.287]

LEONARD, JOHN, in Bow, Kirriemuir, relict Euphan Paul testament, 1674, Comm. St Andrews. [NRS]

LESLIE, ALEXANDER, brother to Sir John Leslie of Newton, was admitted as a burgess of Forfar, 1661. [AA.F1.1.1]

LESLIE, ALEXANDER, of Glasswall, parish of Kirriemuir, testament, 1685, Comm. St Andrews. [NRS]

LESLIE, GRAHAM, in Ballinshoe, 1742. [NRS.RH11.70.7]

LESLIE, PATRICK, burgess of Brechin, testament, 1597, Comm. Edinburgh. [NRS]

LESLIE, PETER, born 1777 in Forfar, son of John Leslie and his wife Agnes Ferrier, settled in Savanna, Georgia, as a shopkeeper, died there on 15 August 1805. [Savanna Death Register]

LESLIE, THOMAS, was admitted as a burgess of Forfar, 1661. [AA.F1.1.1]

LEUCHARS, ANDREW, in Bow, Kirriemuir, wife Helen Rodger, testament, 1685, Comm. St Andrews. [NRS]

LEUCHARS, DAVID, in Farnell, 1691. [NRS.E69.11.1]

LEUCHARS, WILLIAM, a merchant burgess of Brechin, husband of Agnes Adam, testament, 1634, Comm. Brechin. [NRS]

LIDDELL, DAVID, treasurer of Brechin, 1617. [RPCS.XI.58]

LIDDELL, DAVID, a merchant in Brechin, sasine,1648. [NRS.RS35.S2.III.23]

LIDDELL, DAVID, a maltman in Kirriemuir, husband of Helen Arbuthnott, a sasine, 1650. [NRS.RS35.S2.III.395]

LIDDELL, DAVID, son of John Liddell, a merchant in Brechin, husband of Annas Mudie, sasine,1661. [NRS.RS35.S3.I.277]

LIDDELL, DAVID, a bailie of Brechin, sasine,1675. [NRS.RS35.S3.VI.44]

LIDDELL, JOHN, a merchant in Brechin, husband of Margaret Smyth, parents of John, sasine, 1648. [NRS.RS35.S2.III.23, etc]

LIDDELL, THOMAS, in Brechin, 1620; bailie of Brechin, 1621, 1623; a citizen of Brechin, father of Eupham and Margaret, 1631; testament, 1629, Comm. Brechin. [RGS.VIII.17/644] [NRS.RS35.S1.VIII.6][RPCS.XII.450]

LIDDELL, WILLIAM, a hammerman in Kirriemuir, husband of Margaret Peddie, a sasine, 1684. [NRS.RS35.S3.VIII.122]

LIND, ANDREW, in Ballinshoe, 1728. [NRS.CH2.1302.167]

LIND, ISABEL, in Balmakathy, 1736. [NRS.CH2.1302.211]

LINDSAY, AGNES, in Balloch, 1745. [NRS.CH2.1302.245]

LINDSAY, AGNES, versus .... Craik, Forfar Burgh Court, 1 April 1785. [AA.F1.8.1]

LINDSAY, ALEXANDER, from Forfar, settled in Portland, New Hampshire, married Lydia Cross in 1719. [Imm.NE#113]

LINDSAY, ANDREW, a litster in Kirriemuir, testament, 1710, Comm. St Andrews. [NRS]

LINDSAY, ANDREW, a litster in Kirriemuir, testament, 1710, Comm. St Andrews. [NRS]

LINDSAY, ANDREW, in Kirriemuir, testament, 1742. [NRS.RH11.70.7]

LINDSAY, BARBARA, relict of Thomas Futhie son of the late Henry Futhie of Boysack, testament, 1663, Comm. Brechin. [NRS]

LINDSAY, CHRISTIAN, spouse of James Deuchar in Haugh of Finavon, testament, 1626, Comm. Brechin. [NRS]

LINDSAY, DAVID, a wright burgess of Brechin, heir to his father Robert Lindsay a wright burgess of Brechin, 1605; a bailie of Brechin, 1605. [NRS.Retours.Forfar][RPCS.VII.616]

LINDSAY, DAVID, was appointed as Bishop of Brechin in 1620. [RGS.VII.2128]

LINDSAY, DAVID, a bailie of Brechin, 1621, husband of Janet Lyndsay, parents of David, sasine,1639. [NRS.RS35.S2.I.251][RPCS.XII.450]

LINDSAY, DAVID, of Ballinshoe, in Kirriemuir, August 1686. [NRS.RH11.70.1/5]

LINDSAY, DAVID, in Glamis, 1681. [NRS.E69.11.1]

LINDSAY, DAVID, in Tannadice, 1691. [NRS.E69.11.1]

LINDSAY, DAVID, in Rescobie, 1691. [NRS.E69.11.1]

LINDSAY, DAVID, in Essie, 1742. [NRS.RH11.70.7]

LINDSAY, DAVID, a weaver in Kirriemuir, 1786. [NRS.CH2.1302.2]

LINDSAY, ELSPET, a young woman, 1720. [NRS.CH2.1302.1.125]

LINDSAY, ELIZABETH and ALEXANDER, versus Andrew Millar, Forfar Burgh Court, 2 July 1784. [AA.F1.8.1]

LINDSAY, EUPHEMIA, eldest daughter of the deceased James Lindsay a merchant in Kirriemuir, and widow of Thomas Traill a writer in Dundee, ca.1750. [NRS.GD7.2.230]

LINDSAY, HELEN, spouse to David Carnegie minister at Farnell, testament, 1656, Comm. Brechin. [NRS]

LINDSAY, HENDRIE, of Cairns, 1687. [AA.F1.1.2], in Forfar, 1691. [NRS.E60.11.1]

LINDSAY, HENRY, MA, minister in Brechin from 1676 to 1678. [F.6.375]

LINDSAY, Reverend HENRY, in Dunnichen, 1691. [NRS.E69.11.1]

LINDSAY, HENRY, in Aberlemno, 1691. [NRS.E69.11.1]

LINDSAY, ISOBEL, in Kirriemuir, 1744. [NRS.RH11.70.7]

LINDSAY, JAMES, a messenger in Forfar, 1608. [RPCS.VIII.647]

LINDSAY, JAMES, a tailor burgess of Brechin, relict Margaret Skinner, testament, 1649, Comm. Brechin. [NRS]

LINDSAY, JAMES, in Kirriemuir, son of Jean Rodger, 1745. [NRS.RH11.70.7]

LINDSAY, JAMES, sometime at the Meikle Mill of Kirriemuir, and his executor, his grandson, John Lindsay, 1705. [NRS.GD16.4.670]

LINDSAY, JAMES, in Kirriemuir, 1784. [NRS.CH2.1302.2/103]

LINDSAY, JEAN, second daughter of the deceased James Lindsay a merchant in Kirriemuir, 1739; spouse of Thomas Watson a merchant in Kirriemuir, 1756. [NRS.GD7.2.168/238]

LINDSAY, JOHN, at Oathlaw, Finavon, testament, 1613, Comm.Brechin. [NRS]

LINDSAY, JOHN, in Easter Ballinscho, Kirriemuir, testament, 1617, Comm. St Andrews. [NRS]

THE PEOPLE OF STRATHMORE, 1600-1799

LINDSAY, JOHN, in Brechin, 1632. [RGS.VIII.1938]

LINDSAY, JOHN, burgess of Brechin, sasine,1637. [NRS.RS35.S2.I.89, etc]

LINDSAY, JOHN, son of David Lindsay, a bailie of Brechin, husband of Catharine Lindsay, parents of Catharine, and Margaret, sasine, 1648. [NRS.RS35.S2.III.104, etc]

LINDSAY, JOHN, in Lochton, 1663. [AA.F5.39]

LINDSAY, JOHN, was admitted as a burgess of Forfar, 1661. [AA.F1.1.1]; in Forfar,1691. [NRS.E69.11.1]

LINDSAY, JOHN, grandson of John Lindsay, burgess of Brechin, sasine, 1695. [NRS.RS35.S3.IX.485]

LINDSAY, JOHN, versus Alexander Tarbat, 16 June 1784, 6 October 1784; versus ....Adamson, Forfar Burgh Court, 10 November 1784. [AA.F1.8.1]

LINDSAY, JOHN, a flesher in Kirriemuir, 1745, 1746. [NRS.RH11.70.7]

LINDSAY, MARY, a young woman in Kirriemuir, 1722. [NRS.CH2.1302.133]

LINDSAY, PATRICK, Commissary of Brechin, sasine,1631. [NRS.RS35.S1.VIII.24]

LINDSAY, ROBERT, a skinner in Brechin, imprisoned there for rioting in 1617, father of Elizabeth, sasine, 1644. [RPCS.XI.57] [NRS.RS35.S2.II.549]

LINDSAY, ROBERT, in Lochton, 1663. [AA.F5.39]

LINDSAY, ROBERT, formerly a merchant in Dundee, resident of Kirriemuir, testament, 1703, Comm. St Andrews. [NRS]

LINDSAY, THOMAS, in Guthrie, 1691. [NRS.E69.11.1]

LINDSAY, WALTER, a burgess of Forfar, 1603, provost there in 1607. [RGS.VI.1404][RPCS.VII.408]

LINDSAY, WILLIAM, in Muirton muir, parish of Forfar, testament, 18 July 1617, Comm. St Andrews. [NRS]

LINDSAY, WILLIAM, in Brechin, deed, 1688. [NRS.RD4.62.450]

THE PEOPLE OF STRATHMORE, 1600-1799

LINDSAY, WILLIAM, in Dunnichen, 1691. [NRS.E69.11.1]

LINDSAY, WILLIAM, bailie depute of the Regality of Kirriemuir, 1692. [NRS.GD16/13/125]

LINDSAY, WILLIAM, at Logiewishart, parish of Kirriemuir, late Baillie of the Regality of Kirriemuir, testament, 1725, Comm. St Andrews. [NRS.GD16.13.78/125]

LINN, ANDREW, in Ballindarg, 1742. [NRS.RH11.70.7]

LITTLEJOHN, ALEXANDER, in Rescobie, 1691. [NRS.E69.11.1]

LIVINGSTONE, DAVID, heir to his father John Livingstone of Newton, Strathcathro, 1646. [NRS.Retours. Forfar.293]

LOCKIE, WILLIAM, a burgess of Forfar, 1608, [RPCS.VIII.647]; 1625, [UStA. Hay of Leyes MS36]; testament, 18 August 1649, Comm. St Andrews. [NRS]

LOUDOUN, ROBERT, in Glen Prossen, Kirriemuir, testament, 1637, Comm. St Andrews. [NRS]

LOURE, DAVID, in Wodwray, a burgess of Forfar, an assizeman in 1600. [RGS.VI.1176]

LOW, ALEXANDER, versus James Wood, Forfar Burgh Court, 2/ 25 June1784; versus his debtors, Forfar Burgh Court, 27/30 October 1784. [AA.F1.8.1]

LOW, ANDREW, in Forfar, 1691. [NRS.E60.11.1]

LOW, ANDREW, born 1754, tenant in Plivermuir, Ground of Logie, died 1827, spouse Margaret Philp, born 1744, died 1833. [Kirriemuir gravestone]

LOW, or KINNIMOND, ELSPET, a donor in 1620. [Brechin Cathedral]

LOW, GEORGE, in Glamis, 1691. [NRS.E69.11.1]

LOW, JAMES, in Collheugh, 1741. [NRS.RH11.70.7]

LOW, JOHN, born 1725, son of David Low and his wife Jean Doig in Craighead, died 4 December 1728. [Nevay gravestone]

LOW, JOHN, father of John Low, burgess of Brechin, relict Catherine Norrie, sasine, 1639. [NRS.RS35.S2.I.519]

THE PEOPLE OF STRATHMORE, 1600-1799

LOW, JOHN, a smith in Brechin, husband of Margaret Mathew, 1673. [NRS.RS35.S3.V.377]

LOW, JOHN, a smith burgess of Brechin, spouse Magdalene Winzett, testament, 1674, Comm. Brechin. [NRS]

LOW, JOHN, in Kirriemuir, 1686. [AA.F1.1.2]

LOW, MATILDA, spouse James Wylie in Cotton of Futhie, Farnell, testament, 1629, Comm. Brechin. [NRS]

LOW, PATRICK, a plasterer in Kirriemuir, heir to his father William Low a plasterer there, 1769. [NRS.S/H]

LOW, ROBERT, burgess of Brechin, 1605. [RPCS.VII.583/590]

LOW, WILLIAM, a blacksmith in Kirriemuir, 1688. [AA.F1.1.2]

LOW, WILLIAM, a mason in Kirriemuir,1742. [NRS.RH11.70.7]

LOWRIE, or KINNYNMONTH, ISOBEL, in Forfar, testament, 7 August 1662, Comm. St Andrews. [NRS]

LOUSON, JAMES in Strathcathro, 1691. [NRS.E69.11.1]

LOUSON, JOHN, in Methie by Forfar, 1691. [NRS.E60.11.1]

LOWSON, JOHN, born 1680, in Muirnook of Lour, died 1763, wife Catherine Butchart, born 1672, died 1748. [Forfar gravestone], in Forfar,1691. [NRS.E69.11.1]

LUCK, PATRICK, in Glamis, 1681. [NRS.E69.11.1]

LUCKLAW, MARGARET, spouse Colin Alison in Kinnaird, testament, 1739, Comm. Brechin. [NRS]

LUKE, WILLIAM, a notary in Forfar, spouse Anna Gray, sasine, 1643. [NRS.RS35.S2.II.199]

LUKE, WILLIAM, a writer in Forfar, son of William Luke and Anna Gray, sasine, 1654. [NRS.RS35.S3.IV.390]; a writer in Forfar, heir to his mother Anna Gray, 5 January 1671. [NRS.Retours.Forfar]

LUNDIE, ISOBEL, and her three children moved from Kirriemuir to join her husband in Kingsale, Ireland, 1724. [NRS.CH2.1302/143]

THE PEOPLE OF STRATHMORE, 1600-1799

LUNDY, THOMAS, of Glasswell, Baillie of the Regality of Kirriemuir, 1708. [NRS.GD137.3152]

LYALL, ANDREW, in Oathlaw, 1691. [NRS.E69.11.1]

LYALL, ANDREW, in Farnell, 1691. [NRS.E69.11.1]

LYELL, DAVID, in Kinnell, 1691. [NRS.E69.11.1]

LYELL, GIDEON, in West Fanno in Methie Inverarity, 1691. [NRS.E69.11.1]

LYELL, JAMES, in Justinhaugh, parish of Kirriemuir, testaments,1637 and 1651, Comm. St Andrews. [NRS]

LYELL, JAMES, spouse Janet Low, at Careston Mill, testament, 1681, Comm. Brechin. [NRS]

LYELL, JAMES, of Gardyne, testament, 1715, Comm. St Andrews. [NRS]

LYELL, JAMES, in Kirriemuir, April 1686. [NRS.RH11.70.1/1]

LYELL, JAMES, born 1711, an Episcopal clergyman in Kirriemuir, died 1794. [Kirriemuir gravestone]

LYELL, JOHN, bailie depute in Kirriemuir, an elder there, 1717. [NRS.CH2.1302.1.107]

LYELL, JOHN, tenant in Carcary, testament, 1738, Comm. Brechin. [NRS]

LYELL, MARGARET, spouse to Thomas Annand in Kinquhirrie, Kirriemuir, testament, 1616, Comm. St Andrews. [NRS]

LYELL, PATRICK, minister at Guthrie, spouse Barbara Dirow, testament, 1662, Comm. Brechin. [NRS]

LYELL, THOMAS, burgess of Brechin, husband of Catherine Taylor, sasine,1654. [NRS.RS35.S2.IV.338]

LYELL, THOMAS, in Nether Careston, spouse Elspet Deuchar, testament, 1684, Comm. Brechin. [NRS]

LYELL, THOMAS, in Kinnell, 1691. [NRS.E69.11.1]

LYELL, WALTER, spouse Sibella Lambie, in Wester Futhie, Farnell, testament, 1613, Comm. Brechin. [NRS]

THE PEOPLE OF STRATHMORE, 1600-1799

LYELL, ..., of Kinnordie, 1783. [NRS.CH2.1302.2/97]

LYNN, JOHN, in Smyddiehill, Strathcathro, testament, 1682-1683, Comm.Brechin. [NRS]

LYON, ANDREW, burgess of Brechin, relict Isobel Norie, testament, 1657, Comm. Brechin. [NRS]

LYON, Mr DAVID, Commissary of Brechin, 1690. [RPCS.XV.459]

LYON, DAVID, in Aberlemno, 1691. [NRS.E69.11.1]

LYON, DAVID, in Glamis, 1691. [NRS.E69.11.1]

LYON, DAVID, Earl of Airlie, and spouse Lady Grisell Lyon, testament, 1722, Comm. Brechin. [NRS]

LYON, DAVID, a merchant in Kirriemuir, 1706, 1715. [NRS.AC9.216; RD3.145.52]

LYON, FRANCIS, minister of Forfar in 1687. [F.5.285]

LYON, ISABEL, in Kinnetles, 1691. [NRS.E69.11.1]

LYON, JAMES, at Leckoway, attorney for Alexander Erskine a merchant in Montrose, sasine, 1744. [AA.F1.4.3]

LYON, JOHN, in Kilcaldrum in Methie Inverarity, 1691. [NRS.E69.11.1]

LYON, JOHN, in Glamis, 1691. [NRS.E69.11.1]

LYON, JOHN, sheriff clerk of Forfar, in Forfar, 1691. [NRS.E60.11.1] deeds, 1707. [NRS.RD2.93.335/491

LYON, JOHN, a notary in Brechin, 1606, 1620. [RPCS.VII.650] [RGS.VIII.17]

LYON, JOHN, son of John Lyon, a notary public in Brechin, husband of Elizabeth Watt, sasine,1638. [NRS.RS35.S2.I.268]

LYON, JOHN, son of Frederick Lyon of Brigtoun and his wife Dame Jean Stewart, in Kinnettles, Angus, 1652. [RGS.X.28]

LYON, JOHN, a merchant (?), 1660. [AA.F1.1.1]

LYON, JOHN, sheriff clerk of Forfar, sasine, 1686.
[NRS.RS35.S3.VIII.360]

LYON, PATRICK, eldest son of Frederick Lyon of Brigtoun, was granted land in the parish of Kinnettles, Angus, in 1652.
[RGS.X.28]

LYON, Reverend PATRICK, in Rescobie, 1691.
[NRS.E69.11.1]

LYON, PATRICK, the younger, in Kirriemuir, 1717.[NRS.CH2.1302.1.109]

LYON, ROBERT, in Kirriemuir, 1747. [NRS.RH11.70.7]

LYON, SYLVESTER, born in Kirriemuir around 1641, fourth son of John Lyon of Wester Ogil, graduated MA from St Andrews in 1666, minister of Kirriemuir, from 1669 until his death on 1 May 1713. Father of David and a daughter; 1691.
[NRS.E69.11.1]; testaments,1714 and 1719, Comm. St Andrews. [NRS][F.5.296]

LYON, WILLIAM, a bailie of Brechin, 1631. [RGS.VIII.1697]

LYON, WILLIAM, bailie of the Regality of Kirriemuir, 1747.
[NRS.RH11.70.7]

MCADAM, ALEXANDER, a tailor in Kirriemuir, husband of Christian, daughter of James Mather there, a sasine, 1660.
[NRS.RS35.S3.I.51]

MCCOMIE, ANDREW, a messenger in Kirriemuir, testament,1710, Comm. St Andrews. [NRS]

MCCOMIE, ... child of John McComie, mort cloth, 1716.
[NRS.CH2.1302.1.105]

MCCOULL, RACHEL, daughter of John McCoull in Chamberlainhaugh, 1745. [NRS.RH11.70.7; CH2.1302.245]

MCCREICH, JOHN, in Plukerstoun, Kirriemuir, husband of Margaret Bowack, testament, 1614, Comm. St Andrews. [NRS]

MCCULLO, JEAN, in Mid Brae, 1741. [NRS.CH2.1302.231]

MCDONALD, RONALD, in Kirriemuir, 1743.
[NRS.RH11.70.7]

THE PEOPLE OF STRATHMORE, 1600-1799

MACDOUGALL, PATRICK, versus ... Erskine, Forfar Burgh Court, 1 December 1784. [AA.F1.8.1]

MCGRIGOR, JAMES, born 1766, died 1838. [Kirriemuir gravestone]

MACKENZIE, ALEXANDER, in Forfar,1691. [NRS.E69.11.1]

MCKENZIE, ANN, spouse of James Bowman in Kirriemuir, 1733. [NRS.CH2.1302.191]

MACKY, ALEXANDER, in Kirriemuir, 1732. [NRS.GD7.2.151]

MACKIE, JOHN, in Blockerston, Kirriemuir, husband of Janet Palmer, testament, 1617, Comm. St Andrews. [NRS]

MACKIE, ALEXANDER, in Kirriemuir, formerly servant to William Rait minister at Kingoldrum, husband of Christina Smyth, parents of Jean, and Margaret, sasines,1631. [NRS.RS35.S1.VIII.161, etc]

MACKIE, THOMAS, in Oathlaw, 1691. [NRS.E69.11.1]

MCKINGO, ALEXANDER, a mason in Forfar, was admitted as a burgess and freeman of Forfar, 1690. [AA.F1.1.2]

MCLEAN, JOHN in Farnell, 1691. [NRS.E69.11.1]

MCLEAN, JOHN, in Glamis Castle, 1797. [NRS.E326.10.3.24]

MACNAB, JAMES, in Rescobie, 1691. [NRS.E69.11.1]

MCNICOLL, THOMAS, in Burlyleave, 1719. [NRS.CH2.1302.1.119]

MCPHERSON, JOHN, in Glamis, 1691. [NRS.E69.11.1]

MCPHERSON, MARGARET, in Kirriemuir, 1729. [NRS.CH2.1302.171]

MADER, ARTHUR, the younger, in Bothers, parish of Brechin, spouse Sara Peddie, testament, 1609, Comm. Brechin. [NRS]

MADER, CATHERINE, spouse to James Allan a bailie, a donor in 1688. [Brechin Cathedral]

MAIR, DAVID, in Kirriemuir, 1747. [NRS.RH11.70.7]

THE PEOPLE OF STRATHMORE, 1600-1799

MAITLAND, JOHN, a merchant in Brechin, husband of Agnes Hendry, sasine, 1680. [NRS.RS35.S3.VII.313]

MALCOLM, ANDREW, in Bagray, Kincaldrum, testament,1624, Comm.Brechin. [NRS]

MALCOLM, DAVID, in Forfar, 1691. [NRS.E60.11.1]

MALCOLM, JAMES, born 1679, weaver on Ground of Turin, died 1764, wife Agnes Smart, born 1689, died 1762. [Rescobie gravestone]

MALCOLM, JAMES, born 1765, died 1827, husband of Elisabeth Mitchell. [Forfar gravestone]

MALCOLM, JOHN, a tailor in Forfar, a deed, 1687. [NRS.RD4.61.1030] , in Forfar,1691. [NRS.E69.11.1]

MALLOCH, JOHN, versus Baxter and Smith, 17 November 1784; versus .... Tavendale, Forfar Burgh Court, 11 May 1785. [AA.F1.8.1]

MANN, DAVID, a weaver in Forfar, 1753, 1759. [NRS.E326.1.169]

MANN, DAVID, a flax grower in Forfar, 1777. [NRS.NRAS#124/4/1/78]

MANN, DAVID, sr., in Forfar, 1785. [NRS.E326.3.19]

MANN, DAVID, jr., in Forfar, 1785; versus William Davidson, 25 June 1784; versus Andrew Steel, Forfar Burgh Court, 23 February 1785; versus Neave and Webster, Forfar Burgh Court, 26 January 1785; 25 February 1785. [AA.F1.8.1] [NRS.E326.3.19]

MANN, DAVID, a banker and merchant in Forfar, 1792. [AA.ms701/7][NRS.E326.1.169]

MANN, JOHN, in Guthrie, 1691. [NRS.E69.11.1]

MANN, JOHN, a merchant in Forfar, 1781. [NRS.NRAS#124/4/1/2/47]

MANN, JOHN, versus his debtors, Forfar Burgh Court, 11 August 1784. [AA.F1.8.1]

MARNO, JOHN, in Aberlemno, 1691. [NRS.E69.11.1]

MARNOU, ROBERT, in Oathlaw, 1691. [NRS.E69.11.1]

THE PEOPLE OF STRATHMORE, 1600-1799

MARR, ALEXANDER, in Forfar, 1691. [NRS.E69.11.1]

MARTIN, ANDREW, a messenger and burgess of Brechin, 1608. [RPCS.VIII.31]

MARSHALL, ISABEL, spouse David Fyfe in Muirside, 1606, Comm. St Andrews. [NRS]

MERSCHELL, JOHN, graduated MA from Edinburgh University in 1598, minister of Brechin from 1600 to 1607, died before July 1635. Husband of Marjory Smith. [F.5.374][RPCS.VII.616]

MARSHALL, JOHN, a litster in Kirriemuir, a sasine, 1694. [NRS.RS35.S3.IX.433, etc]

MARSHALL, JOHN, a messenger in Kirriemuir, a sasine,1699. [NRS.RS35.S3.X.303]

MARSHALL, JOHN, in Kinnell, 1691. [NRS.E69.11.1]

MARSHALL, MARGARET, in Kirriemuir, 1745, 1746. [NRS.RH11.70.7]

MARSHALL, ROBERT, a maltman in Kirriemuir, a sasine,1694. [NRS.RS35.S3.IX.252]

MARSHALL, THOMAS, a baxter citizen of Brechin, 1605. [RPCS.VII.616]

MARSHALL, THOMAS, a customer in Kirriemuir, husband of Helen Smith, parents of Margaret, a sasine, 1686. [NRS.RS35.S3.VIII.480]

MARSHALL, THOMAS, in Kirriemuir, a deed, 1714. [NRS.RD4.88.940]

MARSHALL, WILLIAM, MA, schoolmaster and minister in Brechin 1633-1639. [F.6.379]

MARSHALL, WILLIAM, a weaver in Brechin, husband of Isobel Walker, sasine, 1680. [NRS.RS35.S3.VII.291]

MARTIN, DAVID, in Kirriemuir, 1784. [NRS.CH2.1302.2/103]

MASSON, JAMES, in Forfar, 1791. [NRS.E326.1.169]

MASON, THOMAS, in Achwiche, Kincaldrum, testament,1623, Comm. Brechin. [NRS]

THE PEOPLE OF STRATHMORE, 1600-1799

MASTERTON, ELIZABETH, versus Robert Milne, Forfar Burgh Court, 17 November 1784. [AA.F1.8.1]

MASTERTON, JAMES, in Forfar, 1691. [NRS.E60.11.1]

MASTERTON, JAMES, born 1773, a butcher in Forfar, died 1802, wife Agnes Miller. [ForfarMI]

MASTERTON, JOHN, in Forfar, 1691. [NRS.E69.11.1]

MASTERTON, JOHN, in Burnside of Turfbeg, sasine, 1735. [NRS.RS35.15.510]

MASTERTON, ROBERT, versus his debtors, Forfar Burgh Court, 16 November 1785. [AA.F1.8.1]

MASTERTON, WILLIAM, jr., versus Thornton and Brown, Forfar Burgh Court, 2 June 1784. [AA.F1.8.1]

MATHER, ALEXANDER, a weaver in Ground of Langbank, Kirriemuir, 1745. [NRS.RH11.70.7; CH2.1302.245]

MATHER, DAVID, a merchant burgess of Forfar, testament, 1658, Comm.Brechin. [NRS]

MATHER, JAMES, a merchant in Kirriemuir, son of ... Mather and Christian Air, parents of Christian and Margaret, a sasine, 1649. [NRS.RS35.S2.III.282]

MATHERS, JOHN, a cordiner in Brechin, husband of Mattie Milne, sasine, 1676. [NRS.RS35.S3.VI.280]

MATHER, THOMAS, brother of James Mather in Kirriemuir, a sasine, 1649. [NRS.RS35.S2.III.282]

MATHERS, JOHN, a cordiner in Forfar, 1655. [NRS.GD1.64.3]

MATTHEW, ANDREW, in Kinnell, 1691. [NRS.E69.11.1]

MATHEW, HELEN, in Kirriemuir, 1783. [NRS.CH2.1302.2/95]

MATHEW, ISOBEL, in Kirriemuir, 1786. [NRS.CH2.1302.2/123]

MATTHEW, JAMES, in Kinnell, 1691. [NRS.E69.11.1]

MATTHEW, JOHN, in Kinnell, 1691. [NRS.E69.11.1]

MATHEW, PATRICK, a bonnetmaker in Brechin, 1606. [RPCS.VII.643]

THE PEOPLE OF STRATHMORE, 1600-1799

MATTHEW, WILLIAM, in Kinnell, 1691. [NRS.E69.11.1]

MATHIE, JOHN, born 1566, died in March 1653. [Brechin Cathedral gravestone]

MATHIE, JOHN, tenant, father of John Mathie, born 1683, died 1699, and Alexander Mathie, born 1690, died 1703. [Kinnaird gravestone]

MATTHIE, WILLIAM, in Caldhame of Bannagarour, Kirriemuir, testament, 1617, Comm. St Andrews. [NRS]

MAULE, ROBERT, a wright in Brechin Castle, testament, 1748, Comm. Brechin. [NRS]

MAXWELL, DAVID, in Methie Inverarity, 1691. [NRS.E69.11.1]

MAXWELL, JAMES, in Dunniken, Glamis, 1797. [NRS.E326.10.3.24]

MAXWELL, JOHN, in Forfar,1691. [NRS.E69.11.1]

MAXWELL, THOMAS, in Methie Inverarity, 1691. [NRS.E69.11.1]

MEARNS, ANDREW, a merchant in Kirriemuir, husband of Catherine Adamson, parents of Jean, a sasine, 1662; testament, 1681, Comm. St Andrews. [NRS.RS35.S3.I.292]

MEARNS, ANDREW, a merchant in Kirriemuir, testament, 1706, Comm. St Andrews. [NRS]

MEARNS, BETTY, in Kirriemuir, 1718. [NRS.CH2.1302.1.115]

MEARNS, JANET, spouse to Andrew Johnston, servant to Walter Mearns in Farnell, testament, 1622, Comm. Brechin. [NRS]

MEARNS, THOMAS, a merchant in Kirriemuir, husband of Beatrix Rodger, a deed, 1697. [NRS.RD4.81.579]

MEARNS, THOMAS, an officer of the Regality of Kirriemuir, 1744. [NRS.RH11.70.7]

MEARNS, WALTER, in Farnell, testament, 1635, Comm. Brechin. [NRS]

THE PEOPLE OF STRATHMORE, 1600-1799

MELDRUM, ANDREW, a tailor in Forfar, 1680. [RBF#216], in Forfar,1691. [NRS.E69.11.1]

MEGIESON, THOMAS, in Kinnordy, Kirriemuir, testament, 1617, Comm. St Andrews. [NRS]

MELVILLE, MARGARET, relict of Sylvester Lamy minister at Easste, testament, 1732, Comm. Edinburgh. [NRS]

MENMURE, JOHN, in Forfar, 1691. [NRS.E60.11.1]

MENZIES, ARCHIBALD, a writer (possibly) in Forfar, 1666. [NRS.GD1.449.110]

MENZIES, ..., in Kirriemuir, 1716. [NRS.CH2.1302.1.105]

MEPTHVEN, ROBERT, in Barbsdale, Glamis, 1797. [NRS.E326.10.3.24]

MICHIE, JAMES, in Kinnetles, 1691. [NRS.E69.11.1]

MIDDLETON, HELEN, in Kirriemuir, 1737. [NRS.CH2.1302.215]

MIDDLETON, PATRICK, a lease, Kirriemuir, 1716. [NRS.CH2.1302.1.103]

MILL, ABRAM, in Kinnetles, 1691. [NRS.E69.11.1]

MILL, ALEXANDER, in Forfar,1691. [NRS.E69.11.1]

MILL, ALEXANDER, in Rescobie, 1691. [NRS.E69.11.1]

MILL, ANDREW, in Pickerton of Balgavies, and spouse Isobel Tulloch, testament, 1667, Comm. Brechin. [NRS]

MILL, JOHN, in Strathcathro, 1691. [NRS.E69.11.1]

MILL, ANDREW, in Fanno, in Rescobie, 1691. [NRS.E69.11.1]

MILL, ARCHIBALD, in Rescobie, 1691. [NRS.E69.11.1]

MILL, DAVID, in Kinnell, 1691. [NRS.E69.11.1]

MILL, DAVID, a maltman in Kirriemuir, 1706. [NRS.AC9.216]

MILL, ELSPET, spouse Thomas Strachan in Easterton of Guthries, testament, 1665, Comm. Brechin. [NRS]

MILL, FRANCIS, in Guthrie, 1691. [NRS.E69.11.1]

THE PEOPLE OF STRATHMORE, 1600-1799

MILL, GEORGE, burgess of Brechin, husband of Agnes Baillie, sasine, 1664. [NRS.RS35.S3.II.57]

MILL, JAMES, in Kirriemuir, June 1686. [NRS.RH11.70.1/4]

MILL, JAMES, in Forfar,1691. [NRS.E69.11.1]

MILL, JAMES, in Kinnetles, 1691. [NRS.E69.11.1]

MILL, JAMES in Strathcathro, 1691. [NRS.E69.11.1]

MILL, JAMES, in Kirriemuir, 1787. [NRS.CH2.1302.2/125]

MILL, JANET, in Forfar, 1691. [NRS.E60.11.1]

MILL, JANET, in Kinnell, 1691. [NRS.E69.11.1]

MILL, JOHN, church officer and donor in 1660. [Brechin Cathedral]

MILL, JOHN, in Kinnell, 1691. [NRS.E69.11.1]

MILL, JOHN, in Strathcathro, 1691. [NRS.E69.11.1]

MILL, JOHN, a tailor in Forfar, 1691. [NRS.E60.11.1]

MILL, JOHN, in Guthrie, 1691. [NRS.E69.11.1]

MILL, JOHN, in Farnell, 1691. [NRS.E69.11.1]

MILL, JOHN, in Oathlaw, 1691. [NRS.E69.11.1]

MILL, JOHN, in Dunnichen, 1691. [NRS.E69.11.1]

MILL, JOHN, a lint wheelwright, hospital master, and a donor in 1692, spouse of Jean Mill; sasine, testaments, 1692 and 1693, Comm. Brechin. [Brechin Cathedral] [NRS.RS35.S3.IX.106]

MILL, PATRICK, in Kinnell, 1691. [NRS.E69.11.1]

MILL, THOMAS, in Woodend, in Rescobie, 1691. [NRS.E69.11.1]

MILL, THOMAS, in Strathcathro, 1691. [NRS.E69.11.1]

MILL, THOMAS, in Forfar, 1791. [NRS.E326.1.169]

MILLER, ALEXANDER, in Kirriemuir, 1717. [NRS.CH2.1302.1.111]

MILLER, ALEXANDER, in Forfar, 1791. [NRS.E326.1.169]

THE PEOPLE OF STRATHMORE, 1600-1799

MILLER, ANDREW, in Glamis, 1691. [NRS.E69.11.1]

MILLER, CHRISTIAN, in Kirriemuir, 1726. [NRS.CH2.1302.159]

MILLER, DAVID, in New Mains of Glamis, 1797. [NRS.E326.10.3.24]

MILLER, GEORGE, a weaver in Kirriemuir, 1745, 1746. [NRS.RH11.70.7]

MILLER, GILBERT, at the Mill of Kirriemuir, husband of Isobel Adamson, parents of Gilbert, a sasine, 1643. [NRS.RS35.S2.II.264]

MILLAR, ISABEL, in Kelhill, 1741. [NRS.CH2.1302.233]

MILLAR, JAMES, in Kirriemuir, 1731. [NRS.CH2.1302.185]

MILLER, JEAN, daughter of the late Robert Miller in Wester Ednaghtie, spouse of George Fife a weaver in Kirriemuir, 1745. [NRS.RH11.70.7]

MILLAR, JOHN, at Halch Milne of Brechin, relict Christian Smith, testament, 1597, Comm. Brechin. [NRS]

MILLER, MARGARET, in Kirriemuir, a sasine,1673. [NRS.RS35.S3.V.375]

MILLAR, NICOLL, a burgess of Brechin, and spouse Agnes Cramond, testament, 1610, Comm. Brechin. [NRS]

MILLAR, THOMAS, born 1688, died 1750, spouse Margaret Blair, born 1688, died 1759, parents of James, Janet, John, Thomas, William, and Alexander. [Farnell gravestone]

MILLESSON, ALEXANDER, a wright in Kirriemuir, husband of Janet Steill, a sasine, 1699. [NRS.RS35.S3.X.181]

MILLISON, JAMES, in Aberlemno, 1691. [NRS.E69.11.1]

MILNE, ABRAHAM, in Chapelton, Kirriemuir, testament, 1640, Comm. St Andrews. [NRS]

MILNE, ABRAHAM, versus ....Oram, Forfar Burgh Court, 30 November 1785. [AA.F1.8.1]

MILNE, ALEXANDER, versus his debtors, Forfar Burgh Court, 16 August 1784. [AA.F1.8.1]

THE PEOPLE OF STRATHMORE, 1600-1799

MILNE, BESSIE, spouse Alexander Shanks in Cotton of Guthrie, testament, 1614, Comm. Brechin. [NRS]

MILNE, CATHERINE, in Kinnordie, 1725. [NRS.CH2.1302/155]

MILNE, DAVID, weaver in Kirriemuir, and husband of Catherine Brandon, a sasine, 1648. [NRS.RS35.S2.III.110]

MILNE, DAVID, son of John Milne, a hammerman in Kirriemuir, a sasine, 1684. [NRS.RS35.VIII.122]

MILNE, DAVID, a maltman in Kirriemuir, husband of Jean Reid, a sasine,1698. [NRS.RS35.S3.X.58]

MILNE, DAVID, in Kirriemuir, 1733. [NRS.CH2.1302.191]

MILNE, DAVID, a hammerman in Kirriemuir, 1745. [NRS.RH11.70.7]

MILNE, GEORGE, a burgess of Forfar, husband of Janet Hunter, sasine, 1644. [NRS.RS35.S2.II.534]

MILNE, GEORGE, a smith in Kirriemuir, husband of Margaret Haberon, sasine, 1653. [NRS.RS35.S2.IV.377]

MILNE, GEORGE, a weaver in Kirriemuir, 1742, 1744. [NRS.RH11.70.7]

MILNE, ISOBEL, in Woodhead, 1717. [NRS.CH2.1302.1.109]

MILNE, Captain JAMES, in Forfar, 1660; spouse Grisel Lindsay, sasine, 1673. [AA.F1.1.1][NRS.RS35.S2.V.311]

MILNE, JAMES, a tailor, was admitted as a burgess and freeman of Forfar, 1690. [AA.F1.1.2]

MILNE, JAMES, husband of Isobel Barnet, and son of Thomas Milne, a cordiner in Kirriemuir, a sasine, 1699. [NRS.RS35.S3.IX.265]; a cordiner in Kirriemuir then in New Miln, husband of Isobel Barnett, 1704. [NRS.RS35.11.96]

MILNE, JAMES, in Pitculler, an elder in Kirriemuir, 1720. [NRS.CH2.1302.1.121]

MILNE, JAMES, a tenant in Kirriemuir, 1741. [NRS.RH11.70.7]

MILNE, JAMES, in Kirriemuir, 1785, 1786. [NRS.CH2.1302.2/117, 123]

THE PEOPLE OF STRATHMORE, 1600-1799

MILNE, JANET, in Kirriemuir,1730. [NRS.CH2.1302.177]

MILNE, JANET, spouse to John Moram, in Kirriemuir, 1734. [NRS.CH2.1302.201]

MILNE, JEAN, daughter of the late Robert Milne sometime in Wester Ednaughtie, 1742. [NRS.RH11.70.7]

MILNE, JOHN, in Forfar, accused of assault, 1611. [RPCS.VIII.308]

MILNE, JOHN, a mealman burgess of Brechin, testament, 1625, Comm. Brechin. [NRS]

MILNE, JOHN, a merchant burgess of Brechin, sasine,1660. [NRS.RS35.S3.I.10, etc]

MILNE, JOHN, and his wife Catherine Hendry, in Kirriemuir, September 1686. [NRS.RH11.70.1/5]

MILNE, JOHN, a tailor in Forfar, 1684; deacon of the tailor trade of Forfar, 1690. [RBF#218][NRS.GD1.61.11] [AA.F1.1.2]

MILNE, JOHN, a tailor in Kirriemuir, husband of Isabel Archieson, a sasine, 1692. [NRS.RS35.S3.IX.158]

MILN, JOHN, born 1688, a farmer, died 1771, wife Elizabeth Suttie, born 1697, died 1773. [Forfar gravestone]

MILNE, JOHN, in Kirriemuir, 1729. [NRS.CH2.1302.171]

MILNE, JOHN, smith in Little Carcary, testament, 1740, Comm. Brechin. [NRS]

MILNE, JOHN, in Kirriemuir, 1744. [NRS.CH2.1302.249]

MILNE, JOHN, deacon of the Tailors of Forfar, son of .... Milne and his spouse Janet Whitelaw, grand-daughter of Alexander Whitelaw a shoemaker in Forfar, sasine, 1735. [NRS.RS35.15.580]

MILNE, KATHARINE, in Lednathie, 1733. [NRS.CH2.1302.191]

MILNE, ROBERT, a weaver in Brechin, husband of Janet Dorrat, parents of Robert, sasine, 1684. [NRS.RS35.S3.VIII.39]

MILNE, THOMAS, burgess of Brechin, testaments, 21 August 1599 and 21 May 1607, Comm. Edinburgh. [NRS]

MILNE, THOMAS, a cordiner in Kirriemuir, a sasine, 1699. [NRS.RS35.53.S3.IX.265]

MILNE, WILLIAM, in Maisondieu, Brechin, testament, 1756, Comm. Brechin. [NRS]

MILNER, THOMAS, son of the late Thomas Milner, tacksman of the water mill and dam, 1661. [AA.F1.1.1]

MITCHELL, ALEXANDER, in Kirriemuir, formerly in Clieff, husband of (1) Catherine Duncan, testament, 1618, Comm. St Andrews. [NRS]; (2) Margaret Crombie, a sasine, 1620, parents of Elizabeth, and Helen. [NRS.RS35.S1.I.161, etc]

MITCHELL, ALEXANDER, in Forfar, 1691. [NRS.E60.11.1]

MITCHELL, ALEXANDER, in Kirriemuir, deed, 1704. [NRS.RD35.11.18]

MITCHELL, ALEXANDER, in Haughs of Ballinshoe, rebuked, 1716. [NRS.CH2.1302.1.105]

MITCHELL, ANDREW, a heritor in Kirriemuir, sasine, 1724. [NRS.RS35.XIII.582]

MITCHELL, ANDREW, in Kirriemuir, husband of Marjorie Norrie, a sasine, 1637. [NRS.RS35.I.90]

MITCHELL, DAVID, a maltman, father of James Mitchell, a maltman in Brechin, sasine, 1637. [NRS.RS35.S2.I.105]

MITCHELL, GEORGE, born 1679, died 1747, a burgess of Brechin, spouse Elizabeth Watt. [Kinnaird gravestone]

MITCHELL, ISABEL and JEAN, were served heir to their brother german John Mitchell a merchant in Kirriemuir, 1743. [NRS.RH11.70.7]

MITCHELL, JAMES, a maltman in Brechin, son of David Mitchell, husband of Marion Hardie, sasine, 1637. [NRS.RS35.S2.I.105]

MITCHELL, JAMES, in Dunnichen, 1691. [NRS.E69.11.1]

MITCHELL, JAMES, in Aberlemno, 1691. [NRS.E69.11.1]

MITCHELL, JAMES, versus Dick and Mathers, Forfar Burgh Court, 20 August 1784. [AA.F1.8.1]

MITCHELL, JOHN, in Kirriemuir, husband of Helen Rodger, sister of David Rodger there, a sasine, 1643. [NRS.RS35.S2.II.417]

MITCHELL, JOHN, in Lednathie, Kirriemuir, testament, 1650, Comm. St Andrews. [NRS]

MITCHELL, JOHN, in Forfar, 1691. [NRS.E60.11.1]

MITCHELL, JOHN, son of John Mitchell, a merchant in Kirriemuir, sasine, 1720. [NRS.RS35.XIII.230]

MITCHELL, JOHN, a baxter in Kirriemuir, 1745. [NRS.RH11.70.7]

MITCHELL, JOHN, a tanner in Kirriemuir, 1786. [NRS.CS96/CS232/misc.20/4-8]

MITCHELL, PATRICK, in Aberlemno, 1691. [NRS.E69.11.1]

MITCHELL, PATRICK, a brewer in Brechin, 1691. [RPCS.XVI.605]

MITCHELL, PATRICK, versus John Smith, Forfar Burgh Court, 9 June 1784. [AA.F1.8.1]

MITCHELL, PETER, and GEORGE, versus John Smith, Forfar Burgh Court, 16 June 1784; versus ..... Sands, 2 February 1785, Forfar Burgh Court; versus David Scott, Forfar Burgh Court, 23 February 1785. [AA.F1.8.1]

MITCHELL, ROBERT, Procurator Fiscal of the Regality of Kirriemuir, 1680s. [NRS.RH11.70.1]

MITCHELL, ROBERT, in Farnell, 1691. [NRS.E69.11.1]

MITCHELL, ROBERT, a merchant in Kirriemuir, 1741, testament, 1744, Comm. St Andrews. [NRS.RH11.70.7; RS35.282]

MITCHELL, THOMAS, in Logie, Kirriemuir, testament, 1620, Comm. St Andrews. [NRS]

THE PEOPLE OF STRATHMORE, 1600-1799

MITCHELL, THOMAS, a merchant in Kirriemuir, son of Agnes Great, and husband of Margaret Adamson, a sasine, 1704. [NRS.RS35.X.385]

MITCHELL, THOMAS, versus .....Masterson and Kebel, Forfar Burgh Court, 18/20 August 1784, 6 October 1784; versus John Neave, 18/25 August 1784, Forfar Burgh Court. [AA.F1.8.1]

MITCHELL, THOMAS, a baker in Kirriemuir, testament, 1792, Comm. Andrews. [NRS]

MITCHELL, WILLIAM, son of William Mitchell a cooper, was admitted as a burgess and freeman of Forfar, 1686. [AA.F1.1.2], in Forfar, 1691. [NRS.E60.11.1]

MITCHELL, WILLIAM, cooper, versus William Nicoll, Forfar Burgh Court, 22 September 1784; versus Neish and Davison, 22 September 1784, Forfar Burgh Court; in Forfar, 1785; versus John Tindal, Forfar Burgh Court, 1 December 1784; versus Adamson and Neish, Forfar Burgh Court, 2 February 1785. [AA.F1.8.1] [NRS.E326.3.19]

MITCHELL, WILLIAM, in Balgorney, Glamis, 1797. [NRS.E326.10.3.24]

MITCHELSON, ALEXANDER, in Methie Inverarity, 1691. [NRS.E69.11.1]

MITCHELSON, DAVID, born in Kirriemuir in 1732, was admitted to the Scots Charitable Society of Boston, Massachusetts, in 1767; "late of New York", died in Edinburgh in 1802. [NEHGSms][Canongate gravestone]

MITCHELSON, JOHN, in East Grange in Methie Inverarity, 1691. [NRS.E69.11.1]

MITCHELSON, JOHN, in Kintyrie, 1725. [NRS,CH2.1302.149]

MOFFAT, THOMAS, the younger, was admitted as a burgess and freeman of Forfar, 1688. [AA.F1.1.2]

MOLISON, ALEXANDER, a wright and elder in Kirriemuir, 1720, 1724. [NRS.CH2.1302.1.121/145]

THE PEOPLE OF STRATHMORE, 1600-1799

MOLISON, ALEXANDER, a merchant in Kirriemuir, substitute bailie of the Regality of Kirriemuir, 1741, 1745.
[NRS.RH11.70.7]

MOLLISON, FRANCIS, a bailie of Brechin, deed,1691; a merchant and bailie in Brechin, sasine,1697; testament, 1722, Comm. Brechin. [RPCS.XVI.604/632] [NRS.RD3.86.302; RS35.S3.IX.289]

MOLISON, JAMES, a merchant in Kirriemuir, testament, 1790, Comm. Edinburgh. [NRS]

MOLISON, JOHN, jr., a dyer in Kirriemuir, 1742.
[NRS.RH11.70.7]

MONCUR, JANET, in Balmakathy, 1738. [NRS.CH2.1302.219]

MONCUR, JOHN, in Balmucketie, Kirriemuir, husband of Isobel Forrest, testament, 1616, Comm. St Andrews. [NRS]

MONRO, FINLAY, a quarrier in Kirriemuir, testament, 1791, Comm. St Andrews. [NRS]

MONRO, WILLIAM, in Forfar, 1785, 1791. [NRS.E326.3.19]

MORES, WILLIAM, in Forfar, 1691. [NRS.E60.11.1]

MORGAN, ALEXANDER, a burgess of Forfar, spouse Marjorie Ogilvie, sasine, 1661; a messenger, a tack, 1666.
[NRS.RS35.S3.I.225; RD2.18.437]

MORGAN, ALEXANDER, sr, and jr in Forfar, 1691.
[NRS.E60.11.1]

MORGAN, ALEXANDER, in Glamis, 1691. [NRS.E69.11.1]

MORGAN, ALEXANDER, son of John Morgan, a bailie of Forfar, spouse Jean Simpson, sasine, 1698. [NRS.RS35.X.82]

MORGAN, JOHN, in Milton of Ascurrie, Kirkden, testament, 1730, Comm. St Andrews. [NRS]

MORGAN, JOHN, born 1755, a blacksmith in Forfar, died 1816. [Forfar gravestone]

MORGAN, PATRICK, in Craichie Mill, testament, 1737, Comm. Brechin. [NRS]

THE PEOPLE OF STRATHMORE, 1600-1799

MORGOUND, JOHN, a bailie of Forfar, 1649. [AA,F1.4.5/6]

MORRIS, THOMAS, born 1767, a brewer in Forfar, died 1830, husband of Anne Dowie, born 1774, died 1814. [Forfar gravestone]

MORRES, WILLIAM, was admitted as a burgess of Forfar, 1660. [AA.F1.1.1]

MORRISON, ALEXANDER, born 1751, a weaver in Kirriemuir, died 1828, spouse Euphemia Fife, born 1761, died 1803. [Kirriemuir gravestone]

MORTIMER, ALEXANDER, spouse Cristian Hutcheon, in Aikenhait, Finavon, testament, 1610, Comm. Brechin. [NRS]

MORTIMER, PATRICK, in Glamis, 1691. [NRS.E69.11.1]

MOUGE, JAMES, a wright in Brechin, testament, 1699, Comm. Brechin. [NRS]

MOWAT, ..., Session clerk, Kirriemuir, 1783. [NRS.CH2.1302.2/97]

MOYELL, HENRY, in Coull, Kirriemuir, testament, 1624, Comm. St Andrews. [NRS]

MUDIE, ANDREW, in Glamis, 1691. [NRS.E69.11.1]

MUDIE, CATHERINE, in Guthrie, 1691. [NRS.E69.11.1]

MUDIE, DAVID, in Forfar, 1691. [NRS.E60.11.1]

MUDIE, DAVID, in Kinnell, 1691. [NRS.E69.11.1]

MUDIE, HENRY, in Careston, parish of Brechin, testament, 1622, Comm. Brechin. [NRS]

MUDIE, JAMES, in Forfar, 1691. [NRS.E60.11.1]

MUDIE, JOHN, in Methie Inverarity, 1691. [NRS.E69.11.1]

MUFFETT, JAMES, in Forfar, 1691. [NRS.E60.11.1]

MUFFETT, JOHN, in Forfar, 1691. [NRS.E60.11.1]

MUFFET, JOHN, in Forfar, 1759. [NRS.E326.1.169]

MOFFETT, THOMAS, in Forfar, 1691. [NRS.E69.11.1]

THE PEOPLE OF STRATHMORE, 1600-1799

MURE, ALEXANDER, in Forfar,1691. [NRS.E69.11.1]

MUIR, DAVID, in Kirriemuir, son of Quentin Muir there, husband of Christina Saunders, a sasine, 1665. [NRS.RS35.S3.II.254]

MUIR, HENRY, a wright in Kirriemuir, 1741; a wright in Kirriemuir, and spouse Mary Crofts, sasine 1760. [NRS.RH11.70.7; RS35.19.170]

MUIR, QUENTIN, in Kirriemuir, husband of (1) Janet Bursie, (2) Margaret Knight, a sasine, 1652. [NRS.RS35.S2.IV.26]

MUIRTON, JOHN, a merchant burgess of Brechin, 1608, a donor 1616. [Brechin Cathedral] [RPCS.VIII.664]

MUIRTON, JOHN, a cordiner, bailie and burgess of Brechin, son of ..... Muirton and Nicolas Carnegie, husband of Euphan Lyon, sasine, 1668. [NRS.RS35.S3.IV.176]

MUIRTON, Major JOHN, son of William Muirton a burgess of Brechin, and nephew of John Muirton a citizen of Brechin, husband of Janet Gordon, sasine, 1648. [NRS.RS35.S2.III.11]

MUIRTON, WILLIAM, burgess of Brechin, 1639.[NRS.RS35.S23.I.268]

MURIESON, JAMES, a cooper, was admitted as a burgess and freeman of Forfar, 1686. [AA.F1.1.2] , in Forfar,1691. [NRS.E69.11.1]

MURESON, PATRICK, in Kirriemuir, testament, 1616, Comm. St Andrews. [NRS]

MURDO, ALEXANDER, in Kirriemuir, testament, 1638, Comm. St Andrews. [NRS]

MURDOCH, ABRAHAM, a weaver in Kirriemuir, brother of George Murdoch a weaver there, husband of Mary Nevay, a sasine,1621. [NRS.RS35.S2.I.431]

MURDOCH, ALEXANDER, a brabiner in Kirriemuir, son of .....Murdoch and his wife Isobel Milne, husband of (1) Isobel Malcolm, (2) Margaret Morphie, a sasine,1631. [NRS.RS35.S1.VIII.150]

MURDOCH, ALEXANDER, a tailor in Kirriemuir, husband of Christian Brechin, a sasine, 1661. [NRS.RS35.S3.I.293]

THE PEOPLE OF STRATHMORE, 1600-1799

MURDOCH, GEORGE, a weaver in Kirriemuir, a sasine,1640. [NRS.RS35.S2.I.431]

MURDOCH, JAMES, a tailor in Kirriemuir, son of Marion Nevay, a sasine, 1686. [NRS.RS35.S3.VIII.319]

MURDO, ALEXANDER, a brewer and elder in Kirriemuir, 1717. [NS.CH2.1302.1.107]

MURDOE, ANDREW, a baxter in Kirriemuir, relict Ann Crichton, sasine, 1765. [NRS.RS35.21/97]

MURRAY, ALEXANDER, heir to his father Sir Robert Murray of Priestfield, in the lands and barony of Melgund, 1672. [NRS.Retours.Forfar.455]

MURRAY, JAMES, in Smyddiehill, Strathcathro, testament, 1611, Comm. Brechin. [NRS]

MURRAY, JAMES, in Guthrie, 1691. [NRS.E69.11.1]

MURRAY, JAMES, tenant in Revelgreen, Oathlaw, testament, 1773, Comm. Brechin. [NRS]

MURRAY, JAMES, versus Hepburn, Low and Baird, Forfar Burgh Court, 11 August1784, 3/13 September 1784; a dyer, 1786. [AA.F1.8.1; F5.152]

MURRAY, JOHN, sr., in Keithock, Brechin, spouse Katherine Dynnes, testament, 1628, Comm. Brechin. [NRS]

MURRAY, JOHN, brother german to the late William Murray, a skinner burgess of Brechin, testament, 1633, Comm. Brechin. [NRS]

MURRAY, JOHN, in Kethik, parish of Brechin, testament, 1636, Comm. Brechin. [NRS]

MURRAY, JOHN, in Methie Inverarity, 1691. [NRS.E69.11.1]

MURRAY, WILLIAM, a skinner in Brechin, imprisoned for rioting there, 1617. [RPCS.XI.57]

MURRAY, WILLIAM, the elder, a burgess of Brechin, husband of Christian Arrot, testament, 1628, Comm. Brechin. [NRS]

MURRAY, WILLIAM, a burgess of Brechin, husband of Agnes Murray, testament, 1629, Comm. Brechin. [NRS]

THE PEOPLE OF STRATHMORE, 1600-1799

MURRAY, WILLIAM, a married man, a smith in Kirriemuir, 1723. [NRS.CH2.1302.139/143]

MUSTARD, DAVID, born 1636, in Balbirnie, died 1694, wife Isobel Smith. [Ruthven gravestone]

MUSTARD, JAMES, with a motherless child, in Kirriemuir, 1716. [NRS.CH2.1302.1.107]

MUSTARD, JOHN, in Ardo, Strathcathro, spouse Isobel Doan, testament, 1687, Comm. Brechin. [NRS]

MUSTARD, JOHN, in Strathcathro, 1691. [NRS.E69.11.1]

MUSTO, WILLIAM, in Rescobie, 1691. [NRS.E69.11.1]

MYLES, JAMES, a tailor in Kirriemuir, spouse Jean ...., 1744. [NRS.RH11.70.7]

MYLES, ROBERT, born 1754, tenant of Hillend and Redhall, died 1826, spouse Catherine Ramsay, born 1766, died 1838. [Kirriemuir gravestone]

NAUCHTIE, ALEXANDER, servant to John Fenton burgess of Brechin, 1628. [RPCS.II.174]

NAUGHTIE, WILLIAM, in Kinnell, 1691. [NRS.E69.11.1]

NAYLOUR, JAMES, son of Thomas Naylour, a burgess of Brechin, sasine, 1676. [NRS.RS35.S3.VI.279]

NAYLOUR, THOMAS, a burgess of Brechin, relict Janet Carnegie, testaments, 1662, 1663, Comm. Brechin. [NRS]

NEAVE, CHARLES, versus David Mands, Forfar Burgh Court, 25 August 1784; versus James Low, Forfar Burgh Court, 9 November 1785. [AA.F1.8.1]

NEAVE, THOMAS, at Inverquharity, parish of Kirriemuir, testament, 1721, Comm. St Andrews. [NRS]

NEAVE, WILLIAM, versus Patrick Neish, Forfar Burgh Court, 2/18/23.2.1785. [AA.F1.8.1]

NEISH, DAVID, spouse Barbara, at Farnell Lw, testament, 1658, Comm. Brechin. [NRS]

NEISH, EUPHAN, a widow in Buttergill, parish of Brechin, testament, 1640, Comm. Brechin. [NRS]

THE PEOPLE OF STRATHMORE, 1600-1799

NEISH, ISABEL, spouse Thomas Grub in Burnside of Auldbar, testament, 1735, Comm. Brechin. [NRS]

NEISH, JAMES, in Csrse Gounie, Aberlemno, 1691. [NRS.E69.11.1]

NEISH, JAMES, in Aberlemno, 1691. [NRS.E69.11.1]

NEISH, JOHN, in Auchterlony, Dunnichen, testament, 1626, Comm.Brechin. [NRS]

NEISH, JOHN, in Middledrums, parish of Brechin, testament, 1663, Comm. Brechin. [NRS]

NEISH, JOHN, in Kirriemuir, 1716. [NRS.CH2.1302.1.103]

NEISH, MARGARET, in Brechin, testament, 1671, Comm. Brechin. [NRS]

NEISH, PATRICK, versus ... Stevens, Forfar Burgh Court, 11 August 1784,1 December 1784. [AA.F1.8.1]

NEVAY, ALEXANDER, burgess of Forfar, testament, 1658, Comm. Brechin. [NRS]

NEVAY, ARCHIBALD, in Drumloy, Glamis, 1691. [NRS.E69.11.1]

NEVAY, DAVID, in Forfar, an assizeman in 1600; a burgess of Forfar, 1608. [RGS.VI.1176][RPCS.VIII.647]

NEVAY, JOHN, born 1792, a weaver and poet .[NRS.NA7414]

NEVAY, MARGARET, only chid of Alexander Nevay, a weaver in Glamis, and his wife Jean Taylor, a bond, 1754. [NRS.GD1.654.27]

NEWTON, ALEXANDER, sometime in Lendich, Kirriemuir, testament, 1650, Comm. St Andrews. [NRS]

NEWTON, ISABEL, daughter of late John Newton in Tulloes, Dunnichen, testament, 1730, Comm. Brechin. [NRS]

NEWTON, JAMES, in Inverquharity, 1728. [NRS.CH2.1302.167]

NEWTON, JOHN, of Kilhill, Kirriemuir, testament, 1635, Comm. St Andrews. [NRS]

NEWTON, THOMAS, in Tannadice, 1691. [NRS.E69.11.1]

THE PEOPLE OF STRATHMORE, 1600-1799

NEWTON, WILLIAM, in Dunnichen, 1691. [NRS.E69.11.1]

NICOLL, ALEXANDER, in Tannadice, 1691. [NRS.E69.11.1]

NICOLL, ALEXANDER, tenant in Milton of Guthrie, spouse Helen Lyall, daughter Agnes Nicoll born 1746, died 1765. [Guthrie gravestone]

NICOLL, ALEXANDER, born 1710, smith in Hatton of Inverarity, died 1787, spouse Margaret Thain, born 1719, died 1786. [Inverarity gravestone]

NICOLL, DAVID, in Granch, in Forfar,1691. [NRS.E69.11.1]

NICOLL, DAVID, in Farnell, 1691. [NRS.E69.11.1]

NICOL, DAVID, a writer in Forfar, 1777. [NRS.NRAS#124/4/1/78]

NICOL, DAVID, versus Adamson and Hastings, Forfar Burgh Court, 20 August 1784. [AA.F1.8.1]

NICHOLL, GEORGE, a litster in Forfar, a deed, 1696. [NRS.RD4.78.59]

NICOLL, GEORGE, a litster in Forfar, father of Elizabeth Nicoll, born 1699, died 1722. [Forfar gravestone]

NICOL, ISABEL, relict of John Mill a tailor, a donor in 1680. [Brechin Cathedral]

NICOLL, ISABELLA, born 1696, daughter of John Nicoll in Burnside Dersie, died in Kirriemuir, 1753. [Kirriemuir gravestone]

NICOLL, JAMES, in Logie Wishart, Kirriemuir, testament, 1617, Comm. St Andrews. [NRS]

NICOLL, JAMES, in Dunnichen, 1691. [NRS.E69.11.1]

NICOLL, JAMES, a writer in Kirriemuir, depute bailie of the Regality of Kirriemuir, 1743, 1746. [NRS.RH11.70.7]

NICOLL, JAMES, in Kirriemuir, 1762. [NRS.CH2.1302.2/9]

NICOLL, JAMES, born 1751, died in Ballindarg, 1826, spouse Margaret Glenday, born 1756, died at Lochside of Balfour, 1815. [Kirriemuir gravestone]

NICOLL, JAMES, versus Charles Neave, Forfar Burgh Court, 7 January 1785. [AA.F1.8.1]

NICHOLL, JOHN, in Balquhally, a burgess of Forfar, an assizeman in 1600. [RGS.VI.1176]

NICOLL, JOHN, in Pitforther, parish of Brechin, and spouse Grissell Mathie, testament, 1673, Comm. Brechin. [NRS]

NICOLL, JOHN, in Dunnichen, 1691. [NRS.E69.11.1]

NICOLL, JOHN, in Methie Inverarity, 1691. [NRS.E69.11.1]

NICOLL, JOHN, in Glamis, 1691. [NRS.E69.11.1]

NICOLL, JOHN, in West Grange in Methie Inverarity, 1691. [NRS.E69.11.1]

NICOLL, JOHN, in Farnell, 1691. [NRS.E69.11.1]

NICOLL, JOHN, Forfar Burgh Court, 24 December 1784. [AA.F1.8.1]

NICOL, JOHN, in Bedfoord,1783. [NRS.CH2.1302.2/97]

NICOLL, PATRICK, in Guthrie, 1691. [NRS.E69.11.1]

NICOLL, PETER, in Kirriemuir, 1742. [NRS.RH11.70.7]

NICOLL, ROBERT, versus William Donald, Forfar Burgh Court, 9 June 1784. [AA.F1.8.1]

NICOL, WILLIAM, trumpeter, was admitted as a burgess of Forfar, 1661. [AA.F1.1.1]

NICOLSON, JAMES, an advocate and Commissary of Brechin, husband of Giles Tullie, sasine, 1642; testament, 1685, Comm. Brechin. [NRS.RS35.S2.II.94, etc]

NICOLSON, JAMES, a writer in Forfar, husband of Christian Kennedy, 1705. [NRS.RS35.11.234]

NICOLSON, WILLIAM, a tacksman in Forfar, 1688. [AA.F1.1.2]; a writer in Forfar, 1696. [NRS.RD3.86.108]; a writer, in Forfar,1691. [NRS.E69.11.1]

NICOLSON, WILLIAM, a writer in Forfar, deed, 1714. [NRS.RD4.89.69]

NISH, JAMES, in Oathlaw, 1691. [NRS.E69.11.1]

THE PEOPLE OF STRATHMORE, 1600-1799

NISH, THOMAS in Careston, 1691. [NRS.E69.11.1]

NISH, WILLIAM, in Forfar,1691. [NRS.E69.11.1]

NISHING, DAVID, in Forfar,1691. [NRS.E69.11.1]

NORRIE, ALEXANDER, burgess of Brechin, sasine,1643. [NRS.RS35.S2.II.259]

NORRIE, DAVID, a bailie of Brechin, husband of Margaret Lindsay, parents of Agnes, sasine, 1613, 1620, 1637. [RGS.VII.890; VIII.17] [NRS.RS35.S2.I.3]

NORRIE, GEORGE, in Brechin, 1608. [RPCS.VIII.664]

NORRIE, JAMES, son and heir of the late Mr Alexander Norrie, Brechin, 1656. [RGS.X.550]

NORRIE, JOHN, treasurer and citizen of Brechin, 1608, a notary public in Brechin, 1613, 1615, 1620.
[RPCS.VIII.664][RGS.VII.890; VIII.17/1260]

NORRIE, JOHN, master of Maison Dieu, a citizen of Brechin, testament, 1627, Comm. Brechin. [NRS]

NORRIE, ROBERT, MA, schoolmaster and minister in Brechin from 1639 to 1642. [F.6.379]

NOUMAN, RICHARD, in Guthrie, 1691. [NRS.E69.11.1]

OAKES, THOMAS, in Forfar, 1778. [NRS.E326.3.19]

OFFICIAR, JAMES, and spouse Janet White, in Cotton of Nether Pitforth, parish of Brechin, testament, 1611, Comm. Brechin. [NRS]

OGILVIE, ALEXANDER, in Langbank, Kirriemuir, husband of Elspet Butchart, testament, 1616, Comm. St Andrews. [NRS]

OGILVIE, ALEXANDER, in Cramond, Kirriemuir, testament,1624, Comm. St Andrews. [NRS]

OGILVIE, ALEXANDER, in Kirriemuir, husband of Bessie, daughter of Alexander Adamson, a sasine, 1637. [NRS.RS35.S2.I.5]

OGILVIE, ALEXANDER, a hammerman in Kirriemuir, husband of Margaret, daughter of Thomas Anderson a merchant there, a sasine, 1665. [NRS.RS35.S3.II.372]

OGILVIE, ALEXANDER, a wright in Kirriemuir, son of Alexander Ogilvie there, husband of Jean Mearns, sasines,1643. [NRS.RS35.S3.II.209, etc]

OGILVIE, ALEXANDER, a merchant and bailie depute of the Regality of Kirriemuir, husband of Beatrix Cabell, sasines, 1642. [NRS.RS35.S3.II.118, etc]

OGILVY, ALEXANDER, at Clock Mill, mort cloth, 1716. [NRS.CH2.1302.1.105]

OGILVIE, ANN, born 1574, daughter of Sir John Ogilvie of Inverquharity and wife of Reverend Alexander Kyninmonth minister of Kirriemuir, died in February 1605. [Kirriemuir gravestone]

OGILVY, ANN, in Kirriemuir, 1728. [NRS.CH2.1302.169]

OGILVIE, ARCHIBALD, in Little Lour in Methie Inverarity, 1691. [NRS.E69.11.1]

OGILVIE, ARCHIBALD, in Methie Inverarity, 1691. [NRS.E69.11.1]

OGILVY, CHARLES, a writer in Forfar, 1750s; 1777. [NRS.GD243.15.15; NRAS#124/4/1/78][AA.F1.4.3/17]

OGILVIE, DAVID, of Glasswall, Kirriemuir, testament, 1613, Comm. St Andrews. [NRS]

OGILVIE, DAVID, of Persie, Kirriemuir, husband of Margaret Arbuthnott, testament, 1614, Comm. St Andrews. [NRS]

OGILVIE, DAVID, bailie-depute of the Regality of Kirriemuir, husband of Margaret Simpson, sasines,1637. [NRS.RS35.S1.VIII.30, etc]

OGILVIE, DAVID, at Miln of Bondarg, Kirriemuir, testament, 1685, Comm. St Andrews. [NRS]

OGILVIE, Sir DAVID, of Clova in Kincaldrum, testament, 1688. Comm. Brechin. [NRS]

OGILVIE, DAVID, in Glamis, 1681. [NRS.E69.11.1]

OGILVY, DAVID, a writer in Kirriemuir, husband of Euphan Nevay, procurator fiscal to the Regality of Kirriemuir, 1716, 1741, 1745. [NRS.CH2.1302.1.105; RH11.70.7]

OGILVY, DAVID, at Coull, brother german to Sir John Ogilvy of Inverarity, bt., 1744. [NRS.RH11.70.7]

OGILVY, ELIZABETH, in Kirriemuir, 1745, 1746. [NRS.RH11.70.7]

OGILVIE, ELSPET, in Forfar,1691. [NRS.E69.11.1]

OGILVIE, GEORGE, bailie of the Regality of Kirriemuir, 1686. [NRS.RH11.70.1]

OGILVY, GEORGE, of Kintyrie, born 1681 probably son of Reverend Thomas Ogilvy in Coupar Angus, graduated MA from St Andrews in 1700, minister of Kirriemuir from 1713 until his death on 3 May 1771. Husband of Janet Trail, parents of Margaret, George, Alexander, John, Thomas, John, Janet, David, James, Susan, Betty, Henry, and William. [F.5.297] [NRS.RH11.70.7; GD7.2.142; GD205.24.161]

OGILVY, ISABEL, in Kirriemuir,1766. [NRS.CH2.1302.2/23]

OGILVIE, JAMES, of Balfour, spouse Helen Clephane, in Kincaldrum, testament, 1613, Comm. Brehcin. [NRS]

OGILVIE, JAMES, of Logie, Kirriemuir, testament, 1685, Comm. St Andrews. [NRS]

OGILVIE, JAMES, a merchant in Kirriemuir, husband of Margaret Peddie, a sasine, 1694. [NRS.RS35.S3.IX.508]

OGILVY, JAMES, a merchant in Kirriemuir,1724. [NRS.CH2.1302/141]

OGILVY, JAMES, in Kirriemuir, 1731. [NRS.CH2.1302.181]

OGILVY, JAMES, in Memus, 1737, [NRS.CH2.1302.215]

OGILVY, JAMES, a laborer in Kirriemuir, 1743. [NRS.RH11.70.7]

OGILVY, JAMES, a merchant in Kirriemuir, 1746. [NRS.RH11.70.7]

THE PEOPLE OF STRATHMORE, 1600-1799

OGILVY, JAMES, of Coull, was admitted as a burgess of Forfar, 1752. [NRS.NRAS.334/8]

OGILVY, JAMES, a wright in Kirrriemuir, 1786. [NRS.CH2.1302.2/123]

OGILVIE, JOHN, in Kirriemuir, 1620. [RGS.VIII.1260]

OGILVIE, Sir JOHN, of Inverquharity, parish of Kirriemuir, testament, 1618; husband of Susanna Haliburton, testament, 1621, Comm. St Andrews. [NRS]

OGILVY, JOHN, MA, minister of Kirriemuir 1623-1629, dead by 1632, father of John. [F.5.296]

OGILVIE, JOHN, son of John Ogilvie, minister in Kirriemuir, a sasine, 1642. [NRS.RS35.S2.II.101]

OGILVIE, JOHN, spouse Janet Seaton, in Meikle Keame, Kincaldrum, testament, 1668. Comm. Brechin. [NRS]

OGILVIE, JOHN, in Kirriemuir, a sasine, 1677. [NRS.RS35.S3.VI.330]

OGILVIE, JOHN, bailie depute of the Regality of Kirriemuir, son of David Ogilvie, bailie depute there, husband of Elspeth Ogilvy, a sasine, 1667; testament,1684, Comm. St Andrews. [NRS.RS35.S3.III.446]

OGILVIE, JOHN, elder son of the late John Ogilvie in Ascurrie, was admitted as a burgess and freeman of Forfar, 1686. [AA.F1.1.2]

OGILVIE, JOHN, in Aberlemno, 1691. [NRS.E69.11.1]

OGILVIE, JOHN, in Farnell, 1691. [NRS.E69.11.1]

OGILVY, JOHN, town clerk of Forfar, a deed, 1702. [NRS.RD3.99.2.246]

OGILVY, JOHN, a messenger in Forfar, a deed, 1705. [NRS.RD2.90/2.644]

OGILVY, JOHN, a surgeon in Forfar, husband of Margaret Ogilvie, sasine, 1756, 1759. [NRS.RS35.18.485; E326.1.169]

OGILVIE, Dr JOHN, in Forfar, 1768, 1771, 1785. [NRS.CS181.7529; GD16.41.962; E326.3.19]

THE PEOPLE OF STRATHMORE, 1600-1799

OGILVY, JOHN, of Inshewan, and spouse Jean Seton, sasine, 1745. [AA.F1.4.3/12]

OGILVY, JOHN, a merchant and weaver in Kirriemuir, a sasine, 1759. [NRS.RS35.19.141, etc]

OGILVIE, MARGARET, eldest daughter of Sir John Ogilvy of Innerquharity, parish of Kirriemuir, testament, 1750, Comm. St Andrews. [NRS]

OGILVIE, PATRICK, schoolmaster in Glamis, 1690, [SHS.4.2]; there in 1691. [NRS.E69.11.1]

OGILVY, PATRICK, tenant in Balkiry, husband of Barbara Storier, born 1719, died 2 October 1752, parents of Jean, James, Margaret, and Elspet Ogilvy. [Nevay gravestone]

OGILVIE, ROBERT, a brewer in Kirriemuir, spouse Margaret Crichton, sasine, 1703; 1722. [NRS.RS35.10/514; CH2.1302.133]

OGILVY, ROBERT, in Forfar, 1759. [NRS.E326.1.169]

OGILVIE, THOMAS, burgess of Brechin, sasine, 1620, spouse Margaret Rollo, testament, 1627, Comm. Brechin. [NRS.RS35.S1.I.165]

OGILVIE, THOMAS, husband of Isobel Rodger, mother of Thomas Bursie, all in Kirriemuir, a sasine, 1637. [NRS.RS35.S2.I.4]

OGILVIE, THOMAS, son of Thomas Ogilvie and his wife Isobel Rodger in Kirriemuir, husband of Isobel Morgone, a sasine, 1637. [NRS.RS35.S2.I.4]

OGILVIE, THOMAS, a writer in Kirriemuir, a deed, 1715. [NRS.RD3.145.315]

OGILVY, THOMAS, in Kirriemuir, 1738. [NRS.CH2.1302.225]

OGILVY, THOMAS, born around 1756, son of William Ogilvy, a wright in Kirriemuir, and his wife Isobel White, graduated MA in 1777, minister of Kirriemuir 1785 until his death on 6 April 1802. Husband of Mary Margaret Robert, parents of Ann, Walter, Mary Lyell, Jean, John, and Jean. [F.5.297][Kirriemuir gravestone]

OGILVY, WALTER, in Kirriemuir, 1786. [NRS.CH2.1302.2/123]

OGILVIE, WILLIAM, a merchant and councillor of Forfar, 1680s. [AA.F1.1.2], in Forfar,1691. [NRS.E69.11.1]

OGILVIE, WILLIAM, son of William Ogilvie a merchant, was admitted as a burgess and freeman of Forfar, 1686. [AA.F1.1.2]

OGILVIE, WILLIAM, in Aberlemno, 1691. [NRS.E69.11.1]

OGILVIE, WILLIAM, in Methie, was admitted as a burgess and freeman of Forfar, 1689. [AA.F1.1.2]; a deed, 1696. [NRS.RD3.86.108]

OGILVY, WILLIAM, a merchant in Forfar, a deed, 1702. [NRS.RD4.91.504]

OGILVY, WILLIAM, a burgess of Forfar, formerly in Methie, a deed, 1705. [NRS.RD4.97.197]

OGILVIE, Dr WILLIAM, in Virginia, was served heir to his mother Janet Webster or Ogilvie, widow of William Ogilvie in Shielhill, 1713. [NRS.S/H]

OGILVY, WILLIAM, a wright in Kirriemuir, 1717. [NRS.CH2.1302.1.107]

OGILVY, WILLIAM, a painter in Forfar, 1745. [NRS.NRAS#124/4/1/75]

OGILVY, WILLIAM, a merchant in Forfar, a sasine,1759. [NRS.RS35.19.14]

OLD, JOHN, in Forfar,1691. [NRS.E69.11.1]

ORCHARD, WALTER, schoolmaster in Glamis, Angus, testament, 1658, Comm. Brechin. [NRS]

ORCHARDSON, ALEXANDER, a saddler in Kirriemuir, 1742, 1745. [NRS.RH11.70.7]

ORCHISON, ALEXANDER, in Kirriemuir, 1718. [NRS.CH2.1302.1.113]

ORCHARDSON, ALEXANDER, spouse Mary, born 1702, died 1752, paents of son Jan died 1748. [Glamis gravestone]

ORKNEY, ALEXANDER, a maltman, in Forfar,1691. [NRS.E69.11.1]

ORKNEY, JAMES, 1660. [AA.F1.1.1]

THE PEOPLE OF STRATHMORE, 1600-1799

ORMOND, THOMAS, in Blairs, Dunnichen, testament, 1743, Comm. Brechin. [NRS]

ORR, PATRICK, a writer in Forfar, 1775. [NRS.GD137.1315]t

OUCHTERLONY, ELSPET, spouse to John Rig minister at Dunnichen, testament, 1629, Comm. Brechin. [NRS]

OCHTERLONIE, GILBERT, a bailie of Brechin, 1605. [RPCS.VII.616]

OCHTERLONIE, JOHN, Provost of Brechin, 1643. [AA.B1.10.13]

OUCHTERLONIE, JOHN, merchant in Brechin, at Brechin Castle, testament, 1747, Comm. Brechin. [NRS]

OCHTERLONIE, PATRICK, son of John Ochterlonie late Provost of Brechin, testament, 1662, Comm. Brechin. [NRS]

OUDNEY, ANDREW, a citizen of Brechin, spouse Maldie Liddell, testament, 1597, Comm. Brechin. [NRS]

OUDNIE, PATRICK, a glover in Brechin, husband of Isabel, daughter of Robert Cowie a citizen of Brechin, sasine, 1675. [NRS.RS35.S3.VI.75]

OWER, MARJORY, in Kirriemuir, 1718. [NRS.CH2.1302.1.115]

PALMER, THOMAS, born 1686, in Gask, died 1734. [Kirkden gravestone]

PARIS, WILLIAM, a citizen of Brechin, an obligation, 1594. [NRS.RD1.46.411]

PAROCH, ANDREW, in Kirriemuir, August 1686. [NRS.RH11.70.1/5]

PATRICK, ALEXANDER, son of Edward Patrick a merchant in Kirriemuir, 1748. [NRS.E778/2]

PATTEN, WILLIAM, versus tradesmen, Forfar Burgh Court, 2 February 1785. [AA.F1.8.1]

PATERSON, AGNES, in Kirriemuir, 1716. [NRS.CH2.1302.1.103]

THE PEOPLE OF STRATHMORE, 1600-1799

PATERSON, GEORGE, in Brechin, spouse Catherine Sievwright, testament, 1647, Comm. Brechin. [NRS]

PATERSON, JAMES, a merchant in Oathlaw, was admitted as a freeman of Forfar 1689. [AA.F1.1.2]; in Oathlaw, 1691. [NRS.E69.11.1]

PATERSON, JOHN, a merchant, relict Margaret Liddell, parents of Thomas, a burgess of Brechin, and David, sasine,1620. [NRS.RS35.S2.I.22]

PATERSON, JOHN, in Kinnell, 1691. [NRS.E69.11.1]

PATTERSON, ROBERT, in Kirriemuir, a deed, 1715. [NRS.RD4.116.478]

PATOUN, ALEXANDER, a burgess, bond, 1621. [AA.F5.93]

PATTON, ALEXANDER, a cordiner in Forfar, a bond, 1669. [NRS.RD3.20.519]

PATTON, ALEXANDER, a brabiner burgess of Forfar, resident in Glasgow, sasine, 1669. [NRS.GD1.61.7]

PATON, JAMES, servant to William Gray in Izakston, parish of Brechin, testament, 1630, Comm. Brechin. [NRS]

PATON, THOMAS, in Dunnichen, 1691. [NRS.E69.11.1]

PEACOCK, GILBERT, in Bog of Finavon, testament, 1606, Comm. Brechin. [NRS]

PEACOCK, JAMES, a wright in Forfar, son of Andrew Peacock in Lecoway, sasine 1760. [NRS.RS35.19.228]

PEARSON, ALEXANDER, of Balmadies, in Rescobie, 1691. [NRS.E69.11.1]; born 1626, died 1701, wife Dame Margaret Murray, born 1625, died 1694. [Balmadies gravestone]

PEARSON, DAVID, burgh clerk of Forfar, 1595. [RGS.VIII.117]

PIERSON, JAMES, of Balmadies, born 1666, died 1745. [Balmadies gravestone]; wife Margaret, daughter of Alexander Lindsay of Evlick, born 1660, died 1714. [Balmadies gravestone]

PEIRSON, JAMES, clerk of Forfar, spouse Margaret Gray, sasine, 1644. [NRS.RS35.S2.II.372; GD1.61.9]

THE PEOPLE OF STRATHMORE, 1600-1799

PIERSON, JAMES, of Balmadies, born 1699, died 1763. [Balmadies gravestone]

PIERSON, JAMES, a merchant in Riga, son of Robert Pierson of Balmadies, a sasine, 1768. [NRS.RS35.22.440]

PEARSON, JOHN, a notary in Forfar, 1621. [RGS.VIII.799]; clerk of Forfar, spouse Margaret Gray, sasine, 1644. [NRS.RS35.S2.II.372]

PIERSON, ROBERT, of Balmadies, born 1700, an advocate, died 1763. [Balmadies gravestone]

PIERSON, THOMAS, born around 1600, second son of Thomas Pierson of Lochlands and his wife Agnes Boswell, graduated MA from St Andrews in 1621, minister of Forfar from 1637 until his death in November 1656. Husband of Elizabeth Maule, parents of David. [F.5.285][NRS.RS35.S2.II.513][AA.F5.105]

PEDDIE, JOHN, portioner of Kinclune, Kingoldrum, relict Margaret Cow, testament, 1621, Comm. Brechin. [NRS]

PEDDIE, MARGARET, relict of James Ogilvie late bailie depute of the Regality of Kirriemuir, testament, 1714, Comm. St Andrews. [NRS]

PEIRRIE, DAVID, a carter in Brechin, 1691. [RPCS.XVI.605]

PEIRRIE, JAMES, in Brechin, dead by 1656. [RGS.X.550]

PEIRRIE, WILLIAM, in Brechin, 1656. [RGS.X.550]

PEERS, WILLIAM, a skinner in Brechin, sasine, 1653. [NRS.RS35.S2.IV.391, etc]

PIERES, JAMES, a merchant and his wife Agnes Cargill, donors in 1630. [Brechin Cathedral]

PERISE, WILLIAM, a citizen of Brechin, testament, 1600, Comm. Edinburgh. [NRS]

PEIRS, JAMES, a merchant citizen of Brechin, and spouse Agnes Cargill, testament, 1629, Comm. Brechin. [NRS]

PERRON, JAMES, a merchant burgess of Brechin, relict Agnes Cargill, testament, 1630, Comm. Brechin. [NRS]

THE PEOPLE OF STRATHMORE, 1600-1799

PERRY, WILLIAM, versus ....Low, Forfar Burgh Court, 15 December 1784. [AA.F1.8.1]

PETER, ALEXANDER, a councillor of Forfar, 1680s. [AA.F1.1.2], in Forfar,1691. [NRS.E69.11.1]

PETER, ALEXANDER, in Guthrie, 1691. [NRS.E69.11.1]

PETER, ALEXANDER, in Woodend, in Rescobie, 1691. [NRS.E69.11.1]

PETER, ANDREW, sr and jr in Dunnichen, 1691. [NRS.E69.11.1]

PETER, BARBARA, in Forfar,1691. [NRS.E69.11.1]

PETER, JAMES, in Dunnichen, 1691. [NRS.E69.11.1]

PETER, JAMES, in Guthrie, 1691. [NRS.E69.11.1]

PETER, JAMES, in Guthrie, 1691. [NRS.E69.11.1]

PETER, JOHN, in Guthrie, 1691. [NRS.E69.11.1]

PETER, JOHN, at the Mill of Inverquharity, 1743. [NRS.RH11.70.7]

PETER, JOHN, pickieman at the Miln of Balmuckity, 1746. [NRS.RH11.70.7]

PETER, ROBERT, an innkeeper in Forfar, 1745. [NRS.NRAS#124/4/1/75]

PETER, WILLIAM, in Kirriemuir, May 1686. [NRS.RH11.70.1/2]

PETER, WILLIAM, in Guthrie, 1691. [NRS.E69.11.1]

PETRIE, ANDREW, in Kinnell, 1691. [NRS.E69.11.1]

PETRIE, DAVID, a cordiner in Forfar, father of Katgerine Petrie wife of Thomas Strachan, a bond, 1669. [NRS.RD3.20.519]

PETRIE, DAVID, in Kinnell, 1691. [NRS.E69.11.1]

PETRIE, JAMES, in Kinnell, 1691. [NRS.E69.11.1]

PETRIE, JAMES, tailor in Moor of Gairn, spouse Helen Duncan, born 1720, died 1782. [Kirkden gravestone]

PETRIE, JOHN, in Kinnell, 1691. [NRS.E69.11.1]

THE PEOPLE OF STRATHMORE, 1600-1799

PETRIE, KATHERINE, 1666. [AA.F5.88/96]

PETRIE, NICOLAS, relict of William Ireland, in Guthrie, 1691. [NRS.E69.11.1]

PETRIE, ROBERT, a schoolmaster in Brechin, father of Janet, sasine, 1661. [NRS.RS35.S3.I.269]

PETRIE, ROBERT, in Farnell, 1691. [NRS.E69.11.1]

PETRIE, WILLIAM, in Kinnell, 1691. [NRS.E69.11.1]

PHILIP, JOHN, in Balgorny, Glamis, 1797. [NRS.E326.10.3.24]

PHILIP, JEAN, wife of John Anderson in Nevay, died 1755. [Nevay gravestone]

PHILP, GEORGE, in Blackbairwall, parish of Kirriemuir, husband of Agnes Guild, testament, 1627, Comm. St Andrews. [NRS]

PHILP, GEORGE, versus Patrick Neish, Forfar Burgh Court, 13 August 1784, 29 December 1784. [AA.F1.8.1]

PIGGOTT, ABRAHAM, a notary public and clerk of the Regality of Kirriemuir, husband of Catherine Irons, parents of Helen, Isobel, John, Margaret, and Maidie, 1601, 1605, 1607, 1620. [RGS.VI.1219; VIII.1260] [CLC#1686] [NRS.GD68/1/126/9; RS35.S1.I.163, etc]

PIGGOTT, ALEXANDER, a merchant in Kirriemuir, husband of Agnes Philp, a sasine,1656. [NRS.RS35.S2.V.207]

PIGOT, ELIZABETH, 1661. [AA.F1.1.1]

PIGGOT, JAMES, a bailie of Forfar, 1649. [AA.F1.4.5/6]

PIGOT, JEAN, born 1638, died 7 May 1678, wife of William Cuthbert. [Forfar gravestone]

PIGOT, MARJORY, born 1766, died 1795. [Forfar Gravestone]

PIGGOTT, THOMAS, a merchant in Kirriemuir, husband of (1) Helen Henderson (2) Margaret Junking, sasines, 1661; 1686. [NRS.RS35.s3.i.303; RH11.70.1/5]

PIGGOT, WILLIAM, farmer at Greystone, 1783. [NRS.CH2.1302.2/103]

PIRIE, BESSIE, in Blechinhill, Kirriemuir, testament, 1616, Comm. St Andrews. [NRS]

PITCAIRN, JOHN, in Farnell, testament, 1656, Comm. Brechin. [NRS]

PITCAIRN, MARGARET, in Forfar,1691. [NRS.E69.11.1]

PITCUTHLIE, ROBERT, a merchant in Kirriemuir, testament, 1686, Comm. St Andrews. [NRS]

PLAYFAIR, JOHN, a litster in Kirriemuir, deed, 1715, testaments, 1717, 1718, Comm. St Andrews. [NRS.RD4.116.313]

POPLIE, JOHN, son of Oliver Poplie of Clett, was admitted as a burgess of Forfar, 1661. [AA.F1.1.1]

PORTER, AGNES, in Kirriemuir, 1716. [NRS.CH2.1302.1.105]

PORTER, GAVIN, a burgess of Forfar, a witness, 1603. [RGS.VI.1404]

PORTER, GEORGE, in Glamis, 1691. [NRS.E69.11.1]

PORTER, GILBERT, a tailor in Forfar, 1658. [RBF#215]

PORTER, LILIAS, in Kirriemuir, 1737. [NRS.CH2.1302.215]

POTTER, JOHN, in Guthrie, 1691. [NRS.E69.11.1]

POTTER, JOHN, born 1702, in Pickerton of Guthrie, died 1760, wife Margaret Duncan, sons Andrew and John. [Guthrie gravestone]

POTTER, PATRICK, in Guthrie, 1691. [NRS.E69.11.1]

POTTER WILLIAM, in Forfar, 1791. [NRS.E326.1.169]

POTTIE, ROBERT, in Farnell, 1691. [NRS.E69.11.1]

PRINGILL, JOHN, a tailor burgess of Brechin, son of William Pringall a burgess there, testament, 1630, Comm. Brechin.

PRINGILL, JOHN, burgess of Brechin, husband of Agnes, daughter of John Bruce, sasine,1664. [NRS.RS35.S3.II.55]

PRINGALL, WILLIAM, burgess of Brechin, and spouse Marjorie Duncan, testament, 1635, Comm. Brechin. [NRS]

THE PEOPLE OF STRATHMORE, 1600-1799

PRIORTE, THOMAS, a burgess of Forfar, an assizeman in 1600. [RGS.VI.1176]

PROCTOR, CHRISTIAN, in Kirriemuir, 1731. [NRS.CH2.1302.181]

PROCTOR, DAVID, in Easter Kinnordie, Kirriemuir, testament, 1683, Comm. St Andrews. [NRS]

PROCTOR, DAVID, in Kirriemuir, 1725. [NRS.CH2.1302.151]

PROCTOR, DAVID, versus ... Reid, Forfar Burgh Court, 11 August 1784. [AA.F1.8.1]

PROCTOR, JAMES, in Glamis, 1691. [NRS.E69.11.1]

PROCTOR, JAMES, burgh officer of Forfar, 1689. [AA.F1.1.2]

PROCTOR, JAMES, in Kinnetles, 1691. [NRS.E69.11.1]

PROCTOR, JAMES, a flesher in Kirriemuir, 1741, 1743. [NRS.RH11.70.7]

PROCTOR, JOHN, in Newmyln, Kirriemuir, testament, 1683, Comm. St Andrews. [NRS]

PROCTOR, JOHN, in Glamis, 1691. [NRS.E69.11.1]

PROCTOR, PATRICK, in Glamis Castle, 1797 [NRS.E326.10.3.24]

PROFFETT, ARCHIBALD, in Methie Inverarity, 1691. [NRS.E69.11.1]

PROFFITT, DAVID, merchant burgess of Brechin, spouse Isabel Fairweather, testament, 1641, Comm. Brechin. [NRS]

PROFFITT, DAVID, a merchant in Brechin, husband of (1) Catherine Lindsay, (2) Margaret Owdny, father of Jean, sasine, 1669. [NRS.RS35.S3.IV.237]

PROFFETT, DAVID, in Methie Inverarity, 1691. [NRS.E69.11.1]

PROFFIT, JAMES, a merchant or cadger in Kirriemuir, an elder there, 1720, 1724, 1741, 1745. [NRS. CH2.1302.1.121/143; RH11.70.7]

PROFFETT, MARGARET in Strathcathro, 1691. [NRS.E69.11.1]

PUNDLER, JOHN, in Aberlemno, 1691. [NRS.E69.11.1]

PYOTT, ALEXANDER, in Guthrie, 1691. [NRS.E69.11.1]

PYOTT, BETHIA, spouse to Alexander Langlands schoolmaster at the Kirk of Guthrie, testament, 1686, Comm.Brechin. [NRS]

PYOTT, CHRISTIAN, spouse to John Croume, in Pickerton of Crosston, Dnnichen, testament, 1610, Comm. Brechin. [NRS]

PYOTT, GEORGE, and spouse Margaret Low, in Syde, Strathcathro, testament, 1642, Comm. Brechin. [NRS]

PYOTT, JOHN, in Methie Inverarity, 1691. [NRS.E69.11.1]

PYOTT, WILLIAM, precentor in Kirriemuir, 1762. [NRS.CH2.1302.2/5]

RAE, JOHN, a maltman burgess of Brechin, father of Margaret, sasine, 1637. [NRS.RS35.S2.I.101]

RAE, ROBERT, in Easter Kinnordie, 1741, 1745. [NRS.RH11.70.7]

RAE, THOMAS, a notary, son of John Rae a maltman burgess of Brechin, testament, 1627, Comm. Brechin. [NRS]

RAE, WILLIAM, in Roods of Kirriemuir, daughter Susanna, 1745. [NRS.RH11.70.7]

RAINNIE, ANDREW, in Kinnell, 1691. [NRS.E69.11.1]

RAINNIE, GEORGE, in Kinnell, 1691. [NRS.E69.11.1]

RAINNIE, JOHN, in Kinnell, 1691. [NRS.E69.11.1]

RAITT, ALEXANDER, in Kinnell, 1691. [NRS.E69.11.1]

RAITT, HENRY, born 1651, son of Reverend David Rait, died 1669. [Kinnaird gravestone]

RAITT, JAMES, in Kinnell, 1691. [NRS.E69.11.1]

RAITT, MARGARET, spouse of Arthur Malder at the Mill of Syde, Strathcathro, testament, 1629, Comm. Brechin. [NRS]

RAIT, WILLIAM, a wright in Brechin, husband of Elizabeth Lindsay, sasine,1644. [NRS.RS35.S2.II.549]

THE PEOPLE OF STRATHMORE, 1600-1799

RAITT, Mr WILLIAM, MA, minister of Brechin from 1644 to 1661, and a donor to the church in 1648. [Brechin Cathedral] [F.6.375] [NRS.RS35.S2.III.132]

RAMSAY, Captain ALEXANDER, a citizen of Brechin, relict Margaret Cramond, 1618, sasine, 1637. [RGS.VII.1914][NRS.RS35.S2.I.17]

RAMSAY, Dr ALEXANDER, the Royal Physician, was granted various lands in Angus including the barony of Gardyne in 1658. [RGS.X.640]

RAMSAY, ALEXANDER, in Forfar,1691. [NRS.E69.11.1]

RAMSAY, ARTHUR, versus Andrew Nicoll, Forfar Burgh Court, 19/26 January1785. [AA.F1.8.1]

RAMSAY, CATHERINE, in Kirriemuir, 1783. [NRS.CH2.1302.2/101]

RAMSAY, DAVID, in Forfar, 1614. [RGS.VII.1024]

RAMSAY, DAVID, a messenger citizen of Brechin, and spouse Margaret Millar, testaments, 1626, 1628, Comm. Brechin. [NRS]

RAMSAY, DAVID, 1661. [AA.F1.1.1]

RAMSAY, DAVID, in Forfar,1691. [NRS.E69.11.1]

RAMSAY, DAVID, in Kirriemuir, 1722. [NRS.CH2.1302.135]

RAMSAY, GEORGE, son of James Ramsay in Muirhead, was admitted as a burgess and freeman of Forfar, 1686. [AA.F1.1.2], in Forfar,1691. [NRS.E69.11.1]

RAMSAY, GEORGE, born 1698, in Castleton, died 1730, spouse Margaret Nicol. [Eassie gravestone]

RAMSAY, GILBERT, treasurer, councillor, and stent master of Forfar, 1680s. [AA.F1.1.2], in Forfar,1691. [NRS.E69.11.1]

RAMSAY, JAMES, in Causewayend of Kirriemuir, testament, 1628, Comm. St Andrews. [NRS]

RAMSAY, JAMES, a citizen of Brechin, husband of Christina Leitch, sasine,1638. [NRS.RS35.S2.I.277]

RAMSAY, JAMES, schoolmaster in Tannadice, 1690. [SHS.4.2]

THE PEOPLE OF STRATHMORE, 1600-1799

RAMSAY, JOHN, a notary in Brechin, 1606; Commissary of Brechin, father of Thomas and Agnes, 1615, sasine,1644. [RPCS.VII.643] [RGS.VII.1167][NRS.RS35.S2.II.358, etc]

RAMSAY, JOHN, of Kettins, spouse Margaret Lauder, testament, 1658, Comm. Brechin. [NRS]

RAMSAY, JOHN, in Forfar, 1745. [NRS.CH12.23.461]

RAMSAY, JOHN, versus Masterton and Webster, Forfar Burgh Court, 9 November 1785. [AA.F1.8.1]

RAMSAY, JOHN, in Forfar, 1791. [NRS.E326.1.169]

RAMSAY, MARGARET, a tacksman of Whitewall, 1688. [AA.F1.1.2] , in Forfar,1691. [NRS.E69.11.1]

RAMSAY, PATRICK, in Cattleburn,1745. [NRS.RH11.70.7]

RAMSAY, THOMAS, a notary public and commissary clerk of Brechin, father of James, sasine,1644. [NRS.RS35.S2.II.358, etc]

RAMSAY, THOMAS, a glover in Brechin, sasine, 1666. [NRS.RS35.S3.III.228, etc]

RAMSAY, THOMAS, in Oathlaw, 1691. [NRS.E69.11.1]

RAMSAY, WALTER, and spouse Jean Collin, in Carcary, Farnell, testament, 1635, Comm. Brechin. [NRS]

RAMSAY, WILLIAM, a notary in Brechin, 1606, 1609. [RPCS.VII.568/643; VIII.704]

RAMSAY, WILLIAM, born 1689, a weaver in Cotton of Kincaldrum, died 1773. [Inverarity gravestone]

RAMSAY, WILLIAM, at the Mill of Noyall (?), 1742. [NRS.RH11.70.7]

RANIE, JAMES, in Kinnell, 1691. [NRS.E69.11.1]

RANIE, WALTER, in Kinnell, 1691. [NRS.E69.11.1]

RANIE, WILLIAM, in Kinnell, 1691. [NRS.E69.11.1]

RANKINE, PETER, in Forfar, 1787, 1791. [NRS.E326.2.19]

RAMSAY, WALTER, relict Jean Collins in Meikle Carcary, Farnell, testament, 1641, Comm. Brechin. [NRS]

RATTRAY, ANN, in Kirriemuir, 1743. [NRS.RH11.70.7]

RATTRAY, JAMES, a glover and bailie-substitute of Kirriemuir, husband of Catherine Ireland, a sasine,1676. [NRS.RS35.S3.VI.212]

RATTRAY, JAMES, in Kirriemuir 1686, husband of Margaret Ogilvie, parents of James there, a sasine, 1693. [NRS.RH11.70.1/1; RS35.S3.IX.227]

RATTRAY, JAMES, bailie substitute of the Regality of Kirriemuir, a sasine,1735. [NRS.RS35.XV.213]

RATTRAY, JAMES, in Forfar, 1785. [NRS.E326.3.19]

REAT, DAVID, in Methie Inverarity, 1691. [NRS.E69.11.1]

REE, JOHN, in Methie Inverarity, 1691. [NRS.E69.11.1]

REID, Captain DAVID, son of Alexander Reid of Turgbeg, sasine, 1775. [NRS.RS35.25.165]

REID, DAVID, in Kirriemuir, 1741. [NRS.RH11.70.7]

REID, GEORGE, in Aberlemno, 1691. [NRS.E69.11.1]

REID, ISOBEL, in Auchterlony, Dunnichen, testament, 1635, Comm. Brechin. [NRS]

REID, JAMES, a brabiner citizen of Brechin, spouse Helen Young, testament, 1610, Comm. Brechin. [NRS]

REID, JAMES, in Ednaughtie, 1738. [NRS.CH2.1302.225]

REID, JANET, heir to her father Alexander Reid a weaver in Forfar, 25 June 1669. [NRS.Retours. Forfar]

REID, JOHN, in Tannadice, 1691. [NRS.E69.11.1]

REID, JOHN, a weaver in Brechin, testament, 1691, Comm. Brechin. [NRS]

REID, JOHN, in Oathlaw, 1691. [NRS.E69.11.1]

REID, JOHN, merchant in Forfar, 1745, husband of Margaret Tindal, 1749. [NRS.NRAS#124/4/1/75; RS35.17.13]

REID, JOHN, a merchant in Forfar, 1777. [NRS.NRAS#124/4/1/78]

THE PEOPLE OF STRATHMORE, 1600-1799

REID, JOHN, a stonecutter in Forfar, 1777. [NRS.NRAS#124/4/1/78]

REID, JOHN, versus .... Peacock, Forfar Burgh Court, 13 April 1785. [AA.F1.8.1]

REID, JOHN, a schoolmaster in Kirriemuir, 1794. [NRS.CS271/66116]

REID, KATHERINE, a limner or portrait painter in London, daughter of Alexander Reid of Turfbeg, sasine, 1775. [NRS.RS35.25.165]

REID, WILLIAM, was admitted as a burgess and freeman of Forfar, 1686. [AA.F1.1.2]

REID, WILLIAM, a weaver in Forfar, sasine, 1750. [NRS.RS35.17.176]

REID, WILLIAM, son of Alexander Reid of Turfbeg, sasine, 1775. [NRS.RS35.25.165]

REID, WILLIAM, versus Soutar and Tindal, Forfar Burgh Court, 9 November 1785. [AA.F1.8.1]

REINALD, CHRISTOPHER, in Forfar,1691. [NRS.E69.11.1]

RENNY, CHRISTOPHER, a cordiner, son of the late Criscall Renny, was admitted as a burgess of Forfar, 1660; treasurer there 1680s; spouse Elizabeth Wood, testament, 1674, Comm. St Andrews. [NRS] [AA.F1.1.1/2]

RENNIE, DAVID, in Forfar,1691. [NRS.E69.11.1]

RENNIE, GEORGE, in Kirriemuir, husband of Margaret Dorward, a sasine, 1638. [NRS.RS35.S2.I.312]

RENNIE, GEORGE, a cordiner in Kirriemuir, husband of Agnes Watson, and son of George Rennie there, a sasine,1667. [NRS.RS35.S3.III.385, etc]

RENNY, JOHN, a tailor in Forfar, 1642. [RBF#217]

RICKARD, DAVID, a weaver in Kirriemuir, husband of Elizabeth Wood, a sasine, 1689. [NRS.RS35.S3.VIII.504]

THE PEOPLE OF STRATHMORE, 1600-1799

RICCARD, GEORGE, spouse Jean Glenday, born 1755, died 1825. [Kirriemuir gravestone];1771. [NRS.CH2.1302.2/47]

RICHARD, JOHN, the younger, and spouse Elspet Peirson, in Keithock, parish of Brechin, testament, 1614, Comm. Brechin. [NRS]

RICKART, ELSPET, in Ballinshoe, 1740. [NRS.CH2.1302.229]

RICKART, WILLIAM, a weaver in the Muirhouse of Balinshoe, 1742, 1745. [NRS.RH11.70.7]

RICHARDSON, WILLIAM, in Nether Chill, parish of Kirriemuir, husband of Katherine Gilbert, testament, 1598, Comm. St Andrews. [NRS]

RIND, ALEXANDER, in Glamis, 1691. [NRS.E69.11.1]

RIND, ALEXANDER, in Kinnell, 1691. [NRS.E69.11.1]

RIND, JAMES, in Caldhame, Kirriemuir, May 1686. [NRS.RH11.70.1/2]

RIND, JAMES, in Glamis, 1691. [NRS.E69.11.1]

RIND, MARGARET, heir to her father Thomas Rind of Clockbridges in the barony of Restenneth, 1697. [NRS.Retours.Forfar.1697]

RYND, MARY, an alleged witch imprisoned in Forfar, 1661, 1663. [AA.F5.35.3][RPCS.I.336]

RIND, WILLIAM, bailie of Forfar, 1608. [RPCS.VIII.647]

RIND, WILLIAM, in Glamis, 1691. [NRS.E69.11.1]

RINCKSON, WILLIAM, and spouse Margaret Tweedale, in Cotton of Dysart, parish of Brechin, testament, 1634, Comm. Brechin. [NRS]

RITCHIE, GEORGE, born 1742, died 1806, wife Catherine Hair, born 1729, died 1803. [Forfar gravestone]

RITCHIE, JAMES, in Kinnell, 1691. [NRS.E69.11.1]

RITCHIE, JAMES, a weaver in Herdhill, 1728, later in Burnside of Kirriemuir, 1743. [NRS.CH2.1.165; RH11.70.7]

RITCHIE, JAMES, in Balmakathy, 1738. [NRS.CH2.1302.219]

THE PEOPLE OF STRATHMORE, 1600-1799

RITCHIE, JEAN, in Kirriemuir, 1722. [NRS.CH2.1302.131]

RITCHIE, JOHN, in Aberlemno, 1691. [NRS.E69.11.1]

RITCHIE, JOHN, in Kinnell, 1691. [NRS.E69.11.1]

RITCHIE, JOHN, in Kinnetles, 1691. [NRS.E69.11.1]

RITCHIE, JOHN, in Forfar, 1785, 1791. [NRS.E326.3.19]

RITCHIE, MARGARET, in Kirriemuir, 1725. [NRS.CH2.1302/151]

RITCHIE, ROBERT, in Kirriemuir, 1716, [NRS.CH2.1302.1.103]

RIVEN, JOHN, died 4 January 1645, husband of [1] Elspet Watt, and [2] Mar. [Nevay gravestone]

ROBB, CHRISTIAN, in Kirriemuir, 1731. [NRS.CH2.1302.185]

ROBB, DAVID, in Glasswell, an elder in Kirriemuir, 1720. [NRS.CH2.1302.1.121]

ROBB, DAVID, in Kirriemuir, 1787. [NRS.CH2.1302.2/125]

ROBB, JAMES, born 1729, died 22 November 1790. [Kirriemuir gravestone]

ROBB, JANET, relict of Alexander Kidd in Langbank, 1741. [NRS.RH11.70.7]

ROBB, JOHN, in Glamis, 1691. [NRS.E69.11.1]

ROB, JOHN, a weaver in Forfar, wife Margaret Mitchell, born 1722, died 1777. [Forfar gravestone]

ROB, JOHN and JAMES, versus James Samson, Forfar Burgh Court, 20/22 April 1785, 25 May 1785. [AA.F1.8.1]

ROBB, WILLIAM, in Aberlemno, 1691. [NRS.E69.11.1]

ROBERT, ANDREW, in Forfar, 1691. [NRS.E69.11.1]

ROBERT, HENRY, town officer of Brechin, spouse Isobell Wyllie, testament, 1665, Comm. Brechin. [NRS]

ROBERT, JAMES, in Forfar, 1785; husband of Katherine Cobb, born 1737, died 1797. [NRS.E326.3.19][FMI]

THE PEOPLE OF STRATHMORE, 1600-1799

ROBERTS, DAVID, versus his debtors, Forfar Burgh Court, 20/27 October 1784; versus Burnet and Sturrock, Forfar Burgh Court, 4 November 1785. [AA.F1.8.1]

ROBERTS, GEORGE and JOHN, versus ...Samson, Forfar Burgh Court, 23 February 1785. [AA.F1.8.1]

ROBERTS, JAMES, versus Alexander Findlay, Forfar Burgh Court, 16 November 1785. [AA.F1.8.1]

ROBERTS, JOHN, in Wester Ednaughtie,1742. [NRS.RH11.70.7]

ROBERT, MARGARET, in Glamis, 1681. [NRS.E69.11.1]

ROBERTSON, ALEXANDER, a burgess of Perth, and a merchant in Kirriemuir, parents of Isobel, a sasine, 1642. [NRS.RS35.S2.II.89]

ROBERTSON, ALEXANDER, graduated MA from King's College, Aberdeen, in 1653, minister of Forfar from 1658 to 1662. [F.5.285]

ROBERTSON, ALEXANDER, in Kirriemuir, 1742. [NRS.RH11.70.7]

ROBERTSON, ANDREW, burgess of Brechin, testament, 1638, Comm. Brechin. [NRS]

ROBERTSON, DAVID, a notary in Forfar, sasine, 1650. [NRS.RS35.S2.III.427]

ROBERTSON, DAVID, in Forfar, spouse Margaret Fowler, testament, 14 November 1684, Comm. St Andrews. [NRS]

ROBERTSON, DAVID, a shoemaker in Brechin, husband of Margaret Glendy, sasine,1693. [NRS.RS35.S3.IX.264]

ROBERTSON, DAVID, versus James Anderson, Forfar Burgh Court, 1 April 1785. [AA.F1.8.1]

ROBERTSON, ISABEL, in Kirriemuir, 1783. [NRS.CH2.1302.2/97]

ROBERTSON, JAMES, in Mountpersie, 1731. [NRS.CH2.1302.183]

ROBERTSON, JAMES, in Kirriemuir, 1744, 1746. [NRS.RH11.70.7]

ROBERTSON, JANET, in Kirriemuir, 1717. [NRS.CH2.1302.1.109]

ROBERTSON, JOHN, son of the late John Robertson, in Auchterlony, Dunnichen, testament, 1626, Comm. Brechin. [NRS]

ROBERTSON, JOHN, a writer in Forfar, sasine, 1680/ 1681. [NRS.RS35.S3.VII.442][AA..F1.1.2; F5.102] , in Forfar,1691. [NRS.E69.11.1]

ROBERTSON, JOHN, of Pitreuchie, 1685. [AA.F1.1.2]

ROBERTSON, JOHN, in Strathcathro, 1691. [NRS.E69.11.1]

ROBERTSON, JOHN, in Kirriemuir parish, 1716. [NRS.CH2.1302.1.103]

ROBERTSON, JOHN, formerly a writer in Forfar, sasine, 1728. [NRS.RS35.14.368]

ROBERTSON, JOHN, in Kirriemuir, 1785. [NRS.CH2.1302.2/117]

ROBERTSON, THOMAS, a notary and writer in Forfar, sasine, 1667. [NRS.RS35.S3.III.255, etc]

ROBERTSON, WILLIAM, a writer in Forfar, 1777, 1791. [NRS.NRAS#124/4/1/78; E326.1.169]

ROBERTSON, WILLIAM, in Forfar, 1785; versus Robert and Hood, Forfar Burgh Court, 18 February 1785. [AA.F1.8.1][NRS.E326.3.19]

ROCH, ANDREW, miller at Caldsyde, 1690. [AA.F1.1.2]

RODGER, BEATRIX, only daughter of David Rodger merchant in Kirriemuir, wife of Thomas Mearns, a sasine,1698. [NRS.GD137/2487]

RODGER, DAVID, sr., a merchant in Kirriemuir, husband of Elizabeth Robertson, a sasine, 1644. [NRS.RS35.S2.II.417, etc]

THE PEOPLE OF STRATHMORE, 1600-1799

RODGER, DAVID, in the Newton of Kirriemuir, husband of Janet Guthrie, a sasine, 1668. [NRS.GD205/22/100; RS35.S3.VI.108]

RODGER, DAVID, versus his debtors, Forfar Burgh Court, 29 December 1784, 2 February 1785; versus John Tindal, Forfar Burgh Court, 18 February 1785; in Forfar, 1791. [AA.F1.8.1][NRS.E326.1.169]

RODGER, HENRY, a merchant in Kirriemuir, husband of Jean Mill, a sasine, 1698. [NRS.RS35.S3.X.107]

RODGER, HENDRY, a merchant and elder in Kirriemuir, 1717; testament, 1728. [NRS.CH2.1302.1.107][NRAS.1750]

RODGER, HUGH, in Kirriemuir, husband of Sybylla Dalzell, a sasine,1653. [NRS.RS35.S2.IV.472]

RODGER, JAMES, in Kirriemuir, husband of Catherine Heswall, sasines, 1644. [NRS.RS35.S2.II.438]

RODGER, JEAN, in Kirriemuir, 1719. [NRS.CH2.1302.1.119]

RODGER, JEAN, in Kirriemuir, 1744, 1745. [NRS.RH11.70.7]

RODGER, JOHN, town officer, drummer and pundler in Forfar, 1680s. [AA.F1.1.2]

RODGER, JOHN, spouse Isobel Guthrie, in Mains of Guthrie, testament, 1671, Comm. Brechin. [NRS]

RODGER, JOHN, in Guthrie, 1691. [NRS.E69.11.1]

RODGER, JOHN, in Kirriemuir,1726. [NRS.CH2.1302.159]

RODGER, JOHN, 'a fugitive from justice', in Kirriemuir, 1728. [NRS.CH2.1302.163]

RODGER, MARGARET, in Kirriemuir, 1724. [NRS.CH2.1302.143]

RODGER, ROBERT, in Kirriemuir, husband of Margaret Piggott, parents of Robert and Margaret, sasines, 1649. [NRS.RS35.S2.III.212, etc]

RODGER, ROBERT, a flesher in Kirriemuir, son of Robert Rodger there, sasines, 1676, 1686. [NRS.RS35.S3.VI.195, etc; RH11.70.1/1]

THE PEOPLE OF STRATHMORE, 1600-1799

RODGER, ROBERT, in Bowhouse, Kirriemuir, testament, 1687, Comm. St Andrews. [NRS]

RODGER, ROBERT, in Glamis, 1681. [NRS.E69.11.1]

RODGER, THOMAS, in Kirriemuir, husband of Agnes Rennie, a sasine, 1661. [NRS.RS35.S3.I.222, etc]

RODGER, THOMAS, in Kirriemuir, 1718. [NRS.CH2.1302.1.113]

RODGER, WILLIAM, at Meikle Milne, Kirriemuir, 1729. [NRS.CH2.1302.173]

RODGER, WILLIAM, versus ... Smith, Forfar Burgh Court, 5 November 1784. [AA.F1.8.1]

ROLLOCK, ROBERT, burgess bailie of Brechin in 1607, and daughter **MARY,** donors in 1623. [Brechin Cathedral]; spouse Margaret Oudney, testament, 1621, Comm. Brechin. [NRS][RPCS.VII.448]

ROSS, AGNES, in Kirriemuir, 1718. [NRS.CH2.1302.1.113]

ROSS, ALEXANDER, in Kirriemuir, 1782. [NRS.CH2.1302.2/91]

ROSS, CHARLES, in Forfar, 1791. [NRS.E326.1.169]

ROSS, DAVID, born 1710, farmer in Engliston of Kinnettles, died 24 December 1757. Erected by his sister Jean Ross in Wester Keillor, wife of Patrick Hill. [Nevay gravestone]

ROSS, GEORGE, a merchant in Brechin, sasine, 1675. [NRS.RS35.S3.VI.11]

ROSS, JAMES, in Kinnell, 1691. [NRS.E69.11.1]

ROSS, JOHN, a merchant burgess of Brechin, father of George, sasine, 1643. [NRS.RS35.S2.II.206]; spouse Katherine Fyfe, testament, 1631, Comm. Brechin. [NRS]

ROSS, JOHN, in Forfar,1691. [NRS.E69.11.1]

ROSS, JOHN, an Excise officer at Kirriemuir, 1731. [NRS.AC9.1160]

ROSS, PATRICK, spouse Janet Donaldson, in Finavon, testament, 1662, Comm. Brechin. [NRS]

THE PEOPLE OF STRATHMORE, 1600-1799

ROSS, PETER, a weaver in Reedford, 1786. [NRS.CH2.1302.2]

ROSSIE, THOMAS, in Kinneris, Idvies, testament, 1652, Comm. Brechin. [NRS]

ROY, JAMES, in Muirhouse of Balmucketie, Kirriemuir, testament, 1617, Comm. St Andrews. [NRS]

RUSSELL, JOHN, in Kinnell, 1691. [NRS.E69.11.1]

RUSSELL, PATRICK and AGNES, in Kirriemuir, 1746. [NRS.RH11.70.7]

RUTHVEN, WILLIAM, in East Dinoon, Glamis, 1691. [NRS.E69.11.1]

SAMPSON, ALEXANDER, in Kirriemuir, 1786. [NRS.CH2.1302.2]

SAMSON, CHRISTOPHER, in Cotterton of Benshie, Kirriemuir, testament, 1614, Comm. St Andrews. [NRS]

SAMSON, DAVID, in Forfar,1691. [NRS.E69.11.1]

SAMSON, DAVID, versus Kabel and Masterton, Forfar Burgh Court, 20 May 1785. [AA.F1.8.1]

SAMSON, JAMES, in Methie Inverarity, 1691. [NRS.E69.11.1]

SAMSON, JOHN, born 1684, late in West Craig, died 1769, wife Jean Boath, born 1686, died 1767. [Forfar gravestone]

SAMSON, JOHN in Forfar,1691. [NRS.E69.11.1]

SAMSON, JOHN, versus ... Roberts, Forfar Burgh Court, 2 March 1785. [AA.F1.8.1]

SAMSON, PETER, born 1698, died 1764, wife Margaret Lundie, born 1697, died 1757. [Forfar gravestone]

SAMSON, WILLIAM, versus .... Roberts, Forfar Burgh Court, 22 October 1784. [AA.F1.8.1]

SAND, DAVID, 1597. [AA.F5.121]

SAND, ELSPET, in Forfar, 1691. [NRS.E60.11.1]

SAND, JAMES, a cordiner in Kirriemuir, husband of Janet Morison, a sasine,1684. [NRS.RS35.S3.VIII.145]

SAND, MARGARET, in Forfar, 1691. [NRS.E69.11.1]

SAND, WILLIAM, a shoemaker in Kirriemuir, 1742. [NRS.RH11.70.7]

SANDEMAN, ALEXANDER, in Braklowburn, parish of Brechin, testament, 1632, Comm. Brechin. [NRS]

SANDERSON, JAMES, born 1663, died 13 May 1731, husband of Barbara Mill, born 1662, died 20 November 1733, parents of Elspeth, Agnes, Ann, Christian, James, and David Sanderson. [Nevay gravestone]

SCATRIE, ALEXANDER, in Dunnichen, 1691. [NRS.E69.11.1]

SCHEILLS, GEORGE, was admitted as a burgess of Forfar, 1661. [AA.F1.1.1]

SCHELLANE, THOMAS, a notary and clerk of Brechin, testament, 1642, Comm. Brechin. [NRS]

SCHEWAN, DAVID, son of Walter Schewan, a notary in Kirriemuir, a sasine, 1642. [NRS.RS35.S2.II.70]

SCHEWAN, DAVID, in Kirriemuir, husband of Janet Adamson, a sasine,1648. [NRS.RS35.S2.III.199]

SCHEWAN, JOHN, servant to the clerk of Brechin in 1604, a notary and clerk of Brechin, spouse Margaret Millar, testament, 1627, Comm. Brechin. [NRS][RPCS.XII.215]

SCHEWAN, THOMAS, a baxter burgess of Brechin, 1605; in Brechin, 1620. [RPCS.VII.601; XII.215]

SCHEWAN, THOMAS, a notary in Kirriemuir, 1620. [RGS.VIII.1260]

SCHEWAN, WALTER, a notary in Kirriemuir, husband of Catherine Balfour, a sasine,1631. [NRS.RS35.S1.VIII.44]

SCOTT, ALEXANDER, a bailie of Forfar, 1658; provost of Forfar, 1661; disposition, 1670. [RPCS.I.74][AA.F1.4.1; F5.122; F1.1.1]

SCOTT, ALEXANDER, tenant in Balmadie, in Rescobie, 1691. [NRS.E69.11.1]

THE PEOPLE OF STRATHMORE, 1600-1799

SCOTT, ALEXANDER in Strathcathro, 1691. [NRS.E69.11.1]

SCOTT, ANDREW, in Easter Muirside of Drums, parish of Brechin, spouse Margaret Speid, testament, 1630, Comm. Brechin. [NRS]

SCOTT, DAVID, a writer in Brechin, husband of Isabel, daughter of Robert Fenton there, sasine, 1673. [NRS.RS35.S3.V.266]

SCOTT, DAVID, a wright in Brechin, 1691. [RPCS.XVI.605]

SCOTT, DAVID, in Kineres, Kirkden, testament, 1728, Comm. St Andrews. [NRS]

SCOTT, GEORGE, in Strathcathro, 1691. [NRS.E69.11.1]

SCOTT, JAMES, in Kinnell, 1691. [NRS.E69.11.1]

SCOTT, JAMES, sr. versus ... Hay, Forfar Burgh Court, 23 March 1785. [AA.F1.8.1]

SCOTT, JEAN, in Kirriemuir, 1777. [NRS.CH2.1302.2/47]

SCOTT, JOHN, son of Thomas Scott, a merchant burgess of Brechin, and his spouse Agnes Mathie, testament, 1627, Comm. Brechin. [NRS]

SCOTT, JOHN, a merchant burgess of Brechin, testament, 1647, Comm. Brechin. [NRS]

SCOTT, JOHN, son of Walter Scott, burgess of Brechin, a sasine, 1652. [NRS.RS35.S2.IV.61]

SCOTT, JOHN, a merchant burgess of Brechin, testament, 1675, Comm. Brechin. [NRS]

SCOTT, JOHN, in Strathcathro, 1691. [NRS.E69.11.1]

SCOTT, JOHN, in Forfar, 1791. [NRS.E326.1.169]

SCOTT, PATRICK, in Glamis, 1691. [NRS.E69.11.1]

SCOTT, WALTER, a burgess of Brechin, father of Catherine, John, and Margaret, sasine,1653. [NRS.RS35.S2.IV.61, etc]

SCOTT, WILLIAM, a burgess of Forfar, 1609. [RPCS.VIII.696]

SCOTT, WILLIAM, a merchant burgess of Brechin, and spouse Margaret Smythe, testament, 1634, Comm. Brechin. [NRS]

SCOTT, WILLIAM, a merchant and skipper in Brechin, sasine, 1653. [NRS.RS35.S2.IV.299]

SCOTT, WILLIAM, a merchant in Forfar, a deed, 1702. [NRS.RD4.90.834]

SCRYMGEOUR, CHRISTIAN, spouse to Oliver Ogilvy in Kirkton of Kincaldrum, testament, 1629, Comm. Brechin.[NRS]

SCRYMGEOUR, GRISSELL, daughter of the late James Scrymgeour of Glaswell, Kirriemuir, testament, 1605, Comm. Edinburgh. [NRS]

SCRYMGEOUR, THOMAS, in Easter Torbyres, 1613. [CLC#1686]

SCRYMGEOUR, THOMAS, a wright in Guthrie, testaments, 1793, 1794, Comm. Brechin. [NRS]

SETON, WILLIAM, in Forfar, 1724, 1743, 1745, 1747. [NRS.CH12.23.342/461/489/541]

SEWELL, THOMAS, a burgess of Brechin, husband of Jean Gordon, sasine, 1661. [NRS.RS35.S3.I.310]

SHANKS, PATRICK, in Rescobie, 1691. [NRS.E69.11.1]

SHEDDEN, PATRICK, born 1755, bailie of Forfar, died 1842, husband of Christian Mands, born 1755, died 1841. [Forfar gravestone]

SHEPHERD, AGNES, in Kirriemuir, 1742. [NRS.RH11.70.7]

SHEPHERD, JAMES, in Kinnell, 1691. [NRS.E69.11.1]

SHEPHERD, JAMES, in Kirriemuir, 1742, 1747. [NRS.RH11.70.7]

SHEPHERD, JAMES, a merchant in Kirriemuir, 1785. [NRS.CS96/CS237/misc.20/3; CS96.1910]

SHEPHERD, JAMES, versus John Malloch, Forfar Burgh Court, 19 January 1785. [AA.F1.8.1]

SHEPHERD, JOHN, in Forfar, 1691. [NRS.E69.11.1]

THE PEOPLE OF STRATHMORE, 1600-1799

SHEPHERD, KATHERINE, in Glamis, relict of James Horn blacksmith, testament, 1794, Comm. St Andrews. [NRS]

SHERIFF, GEORGE, versus Elizabeth Spark, Forfar Burgh Court, 8 September 1784. [AA.F1.8.1]

SHERRALL, JAMES, servant to Robert Cando in Easter Hillend, 1743. [NRS.RH11.70.7]

SHILGREEN, WILLIAM, in Kinnell, 1691. [NRS.E69.11.1]

SHIRES, JOHN, a tiler in Brechin, husband of Elizabeth Bruce, sasine, 1685. [NRS.RS35.S3.VIII.270]

SHORSWOOD, JAMES, in Dunnichen, testament, 1686, Comm. Brechin. [NRS]

SHYRIE, ISOBEL, a witch in Forfar, died 1661. [AA.F5.35.3]

SIBBALD, DAVID, of ...keer, was admitted as a burgess of Forfar, 26 June 1660. [AA.F1.1.1]

SIEVWRIGHT, JOHN, burgess of Brechin, and spouse Catherine Whyte, testament, 1647, Comm. Brechin. [NRS]

SIEVWRIGHT, THOMAS, the elder, burgess of Brechin, testament, 1658, Comm. Brechin. [NRS]

SIM, DAVID, in Strathcathro, 1691. [NRS.E69.11.1]

SIME, DAVID, in Westerton of Strathcathro, testament, 1711, Comm. Brechin. [NRS]

SIME, JAMES, in Aberlemno, 1691. [NRS.E69.11.1]

SIME, JOHN, a tailor burgess of Brechin, and Janet Liche, testament, 1645, Comm. Brechin. [NRS]

SIME, JOHN, schoolmaster at Farnell, testament, 1738, Comm. Brechin. [NRS]

SIMSON, ADAM, a baxter, husband of Margaret Craig, born 1679, died 1715. [Forfar gravestone]

SIMPSON, ALEXANDER, 1666. [AA.F5.40]

SIMSON, ANDREW, sr and jr, in Forfar, 1691. [NRS.E69.11.1]

THE PEOPLE OF STRATHMORE, 1600-1799

SIMPSON, DAVID, in Little Migvie, Kirriemuir, testament, 1621, Comm. St Andrews. [NRS]

SIMSON, DAVID, born 1638, in Milton of Ruthven, died 1673, wife Margaret Whitson. [Ruthven gravestone]

SIMSON, JAMES, in Forfar, 1691. [NRS.E69.11.1]

SIMPSON, JAMES, a writer in Kirriemuir, husband of Beatrix Cabel, parents of Beatrix, a sasine,1699. [NRS.RS35.S3.X.257]

SIMPSON, JOHN, in Migvie, Kirriemuir, husband of Janet Cant, testament,1620, Comm. St Andrews. [NRS]

SIMSON, JOHN, in Forfar,1691. [NRS.E69.11.1]

SIMSON, JOHN, a baker, in Forfar,1691. [NRS.E69.11.1]

SIMSON, JOHN, a weaver, in Forfar,1691. [NRS.E69.11.1]

SIMSON, MARGARET, in Forfar,1691. [NRS.E69.11.1]

SIMSON, PATRICK, in Rescobie, 1691. [NRS.E69.11.1]

SIMPSON, RICHARD, in Migivie, parish of Kirriemuir, husband of Isobel Howie, testament, 1619, Comm. St Andrews. [NRS]

SIMSON, THOMAS, in Aberlemno, 1691. [NRS.E69.11.1]

SIMPSON, WILLIAM, a burgess of Forfar, sasine, 1638. [NRS.RS35.S2.I.322]

SIMSON, WILLIAM, in Forfar,1691. [NRS.E69.11.1]

SIMSON, WILLIAM, in Aberlemno, 1691. [NRS.E69.11.1]

SKAIR, THOMAS, a wright in Kirriemuir, spouse Jean Brand, 1762,1774. [NRS.CH2.1302.2/7; RS35.24/509]

SKENE, GEORGE, in Forfar, 1759, 1762, 1785. [NRS.E326.1.169; E326.3.19; CH12.23.217]

SKENE, Mr JOHN, heir to his father Mr John Skenein Balnabriche, Brechin, in 1602. [NRS.Retours. Forfar.28]

SKEEN, MARGARET, in Forfar, 1691. [NRS.E60.11.1]

SKINNER, AGNES, in Brechin, relict of Oliver Ogilvie in Meikle Kennie, mother of Isobel Ogilvie in Brechin, and spouse

of Hercules Kerr a maltman in Brechin, sasine,1662.
[NRS.RS35.S3.I.336]

SKINNER, ALEXANDER, a burgess of Brechin, husband of Catharine Carnegie, parents of Alexander, Agnes, John, and Laurence, 1639. [NRS.RS35.S2.I.360]

SKINNER, DAVID, a burgess of Brechin, and spouse Barbara Fyfe, testament, 1641, Comm. Brechin. [NRS]

SKINNER, DAVID, a bailie of Brechin, husband of Christian, Gray, parents of Catharine, John, Thomas, and Laurence, sasine, 1649. [NRS.RS35.S2.III.170]

SKINNER, DAVID or JOHN, late Provost of Brechin, testament, 1679, Comm. Brechin. [NRS]

SKINNER, JOHN, a burgess of Brechin, 1620, husband of Catharine, daughter of David Carnegie of Cuikstoun, sasine,1639. [NRS.RS35.S2.I.358][RPCS.XII.215]

SKINNER, JOHN, son of David Skinner a bailie of Brechin, and husband of Elspeth, daughter of David Donaldson a bailie of Brechin, sasine, 1656. [RGS.X.550][NRS.RS35.S2.V.376]

SKINNER, JOHN, Provost of Brechin, husband of Catherine Fenton, sasine, 1668. [NRS.RS35.S3.IV.188]

SKINNER, JOHN, baptised 1662 son of Reverend Laurence Skinner, minister in Brechin from 1687 to 1709. Died in Edinburgh around 1725. Husband of (1) Margaret Little, (2) Jean Guild, parents of Margaret. [F.6.380]

SKINNER, LAURENCE, bailie of Brechin, son of Alexander Skinner, a burgess there, sasine, 1638. [NRS.RS35.S2.I.358]

SKINNER, LAURENCE, born about 1617, eldest son of Laurence Skinner of Navar, graduated MA from St Andrews in 1637, master of the Grammar School of Brechin, preceptor of Maison Dieu in 1643, minister in Brechin from 1650 to his death in August 1691. Husband of Margaret Guthrie, parents of John, Janet, Margaret, Katherine and Anna. Late bailie of Brechin, testament, 1691, Comm. Brechin. [Brechin Cathedral] [F.6.376/380][RP.II.326]

SKINNER, LAURENCE, a glover in Brechin, sasine, 1667. [NRS.RS35.S3.III.365]

THE PEOPLE OF STRATHMORE, 1600-1799

SKINNER, THOMAS, a bailie in 1643. [AA.B1.10.13]

SKINNER, THOMAS, a merchant in Brechin, husband of Elizabeth Erskine, sasine, 1679. [NRS.RS35.S3.VII.51]

SKIRLING, ANDREW, in Kinnetles, 1691. [NRS.E69.11.1]

SKIRLING, EFFIE, in Kinnetles, 1691. [NRS.E69.11.1]

SKIRLING, GEORGE, in Rescobie, 1691. [NRS.E69.11.1]

SKIRLING, JAMES, in Glamis, 1691. [NRS.E69.11.1]

SKIRLING, JAMES, a maltman in Kirriemuir, husband of Isabel Cuthbert, a sasine, 1692. [NRS.RS35.S3.IX.153]

SKIRLING, JAMES, a maltman in Kirriemuir, an elder there in 1720, husband of Elizabeth Cuthbert, sasine, 1726. [NRS.CH2.1302.1.121; RS35.14/141]

SKIRLING, THOMAS, in Methie Inverarity, 1691. [NRS.E69.11.1]

SKIRLING, WILLIAM, a maltman in Kirriemuir, husband of Margaret Marshall, a sasine, 1698. [NRS.GD137/2487; RS35.S3.IX.564]

SKIRLING, WILLIAM, a maltman in Kirriemuir, deed, 1714. [NRS.RD4.88.940]

SMALL, ALEXANDER, in Dameye, 1786. [NRS.CH2.1302.2/123]

SMALL, DAVID, son of Reverend Thomas Small, in Forfar, apprenticeship indentureship, 1676. [NRS.RD3.41.389]

SMALL, JAMES, of Quarrelhill, born 1650, son of Reverend Thomas Small, graduated MA from St Andrews in 1670, minister of Forfar from 1687 to 1716, died after 1729. Husband of (1) Margaret, daughter of Alexander Pierson of Balmadies, parents of Patrick and Katharine, (2) Christian Mitchellhill. 1691. [NRS.E69.11.1][F.5.286]

SMALL, THOMAS, born around 1620, son of George Small of Foveran, graduated MA from St Andrews in 1640, minister of Forfar from 1668 until his death in April 1687, deeds. [F.5.285] [AA.F1.1.2][NRS.RD2.24.119; RD3.41.389]

THE PEOPLE OF STRATHMORE, 1600-1799

SMALL, THOMAS, a cooper in Kirriemuir, 1745, 1746. [NRS.RH11.70.7]

SMART, ALEXANDER, in Drumclune, 1720. [NRS.CH2.1302.1.121]

SMART, CHRISTIAN, spouse to Abraham Mylne in Bagray, Kincaldrum, testament, 1625, Comm. Brechin. [NRS]

SMART, DAVID, in Tannadice, 1691. [NRS.E69.11.1]

SMART, DAVID, in Kirriemuir, 1732. [NRS.GD7.2.151]

SMART, JANET, in Kirriemuir, 1786. [NRS.CH2.1302.2/121]

SMART, JOHN, in Hill of Kirriemuir, husband of Isobel Milne, parents of David Smart there, sasine, 1639; testament, 1640, Comm. St Andrews. [NRS.RS35.S2.I.421]

SMART, THOMAS, in Strathcathro, 1691. [NRS.E69.11.1]

SMYTH, ALEXANDER, a smith and gunmaker in the Tenements of Caldhame, spouse Elspet Carr, tenement, 1642, Comm. Brechin. [NRS]

SMITH, ALEXANDER, in Cotton Dod, in Rescobie, 1691. [NRS.E69.11.1]

SMITH, ALEXANDER, in Kinnell, 1691. [NRS.E69.11.1]

SMITH, ANDREW, in Ladywell, 1742. [NRS.RH11.70.7]

SMITH, DAVID, in Oathlaw, 1691. [NRS.E69.11.1]

SMITH, DONALD, a merchant in Forfar, a bond, 1666. [NRS.RD4.17.630]

SMITH, ELSPET, in Muirhead of Logy, 1745. [NRS.RH11.70.7]

SMITH, GEORGE, treasurer and merchant of Forfar, 1680. [AA.F1.1.2]

SMITH, GEORGE, a merchant, in Forfar,1691. [NRS.E69.11.1], deed, 1714. [NRS.RD4.89.69]

SMITH, GEORGE, versus James Butchart, Forfar Burgh Court, 11 August 1784. [AA.F1.8.1]

THE PEOPLE OF STRATHMORE, 1600-1799

SMYTH, GILBERT, a merchant in Kirriemuir, husband of Marjorie Hutcheon, a sasine, 1654. [NRS.RS35.S2.IV.401]

SMYTH, ISABEL, relict of James Smith a hammerman in Glamis, testament,1659, Comm. Brechin. [NRS]

SMYTH, JAMES, a baxter citizen of Brechin, 1605. [RPCS.VII.616]

SMYTH, JAMES, the younger, a baxter citizen of Brechin, 1605. [RPCS.VII.616]

SMITH, JAMES, tutor to David Smith, 1686. [NRS.RH11.70.1/4]

SMITH, JAMES, a merchant in Forfar, deeds, 1688, 1690. [NRS.RD2.59.432; RD2.71.479] [AA.F1.1.2], in Forfar, 1691. [NRS.E60.11.1]

SMITH, JAMES, in Kinnell, 1691. [NRS.E69.11.1]

SMITH, JAMES, in Oathlaw, 1691. [NRS.E69.11.1]

SMITH, JAMES, in Tannadice, 1691. [NRS.E69.11.1]

SMITH, JAMES, a chapman in Shilhill, 1744. [NRS.CH2.1302.247]

SMITH, JAMES, in Forfar, 1759. [NRS.E326.1.169]

SMITH, JAMES, versus Patrick Jack, Forfar Burgh Court, 3/8 September 1784. [AA.F1.8.1]

SMYTH, JANET, spouse to Patrick Barrie in Wolflaw, Finavon, testament, 1637, Comm. Brechin. [NRS]

SMYTH, JOHN, in Cotton of Glaswell, Kirriemuir, testament, 1621, Comm. St Andrews. [NRS]

SMYTH, JOHN, in Ballindarg, Kirriemuir, testament, 1621, Comm. St Andrews. [NRS]

SMITH, JOHN, a burgess of Brechin, father of Elizabeth, sasine, 1639. [NRS.RS35.S2.I.547]

SMITH, JOHN, son of James Smith at Moss-side of Balinshon, was admitted as a burgess and freeman of Forfar, 1688.[AA.F1.1.2]

SMITH, JOHN, in Glamis, 1691. [NRS.E69.11.1]

THE PEOPLE OF STRATHMORE, 1600-1799

SMITH, JOHN, in Methie Inverarity, 1691. [NRS.E69.11.1]

SMITH, JOHN, a merchant in Forfar, a sasine, 1739. [NRS.GD1.61.15]

SMITH, JOHN, a church elder in Kirriemuir before 1783. [NRS.CH2.1302.2/97]

SMITH, JOHN, versus ... Law, Forfar Burgh Court, 3 September 1784; versus John Tindal, Forfar Burgh Court, 26 January 1785. [AA.F1.8.1]

SMITH, MARGARET, in Ground of Logy, 1745, [NRS.RH11.70.7]

SMITH, ROBERT, in Kinnell, 1691. [NRS.E69.11.1]

SMITH, ROBERT, pickyman at the Mill of Kirriemuir, 1742. [NRS.RH11.70.7]

SMITH, ROBERT, Deacon of the Corporation of Tailors in Forfar, 1788. [NRS.CS271/50949]

SMITH, ROBERT, versus .....Nicoll, Forfar Burgh Court, 14 January 1785, 18 February 1785. [AA.F1.8.1]

SMYTH, THOMAS, in Schilhill, Kirriemuir, testament, 1619, Comm. St Andrews. [NRS]

SMITH, THOMAS, town officer and pundler in Forfar, 1689. [AA.F1.1.2]

SMITH, THOMAS, in Rescobie, 1691. [NRS.E69.11.1]

SMITH, WILLIAM, a town officer of Forfar, 1658. [AA.F1.4.1]

SMITH, WILLIAM, a smith in Kirriemuir, 1741. [NRS.CH2.1302.235]

SMITH, WILLIAM, in Kirriemuir, 1746. [NRS.RH11.70.7]

SOUTAR, JAMES, a merchant in Forfar, 1723. [NRS.CS181/7535]

SUTER, JOHN, in Farnell, 1691. [NRS.E69.11.1]

SOUTAR, ROBERT, versus Alexander Smith, Forfar Burgh Court, 6 November 1784. [AA.F1.8.1]

SPALDEN, SYLVESTER, born 1690, died 9 June 1771, husband of Elspet Morice, born 1690, died 3 April 1762, parents of Henry, John, Jean, Margaret, and Janet Spalden. [Nevay gravestone]

SPALDING, DAVID, a tailor in Kirriemuir, 1745. [NRS.CH2.1302.245/251]

SPALDING, ELSPET, spouse John Peter in Kincaldrum, testament, 1610, Comm. Brechin. [NRS]

SPALDING, JAMES, town officer of Forfar, 1658. [AA.F1.4.1]

SPALDING, JOHN, of the Milne of Kirriemuir, husband of Barbara Blair, a sasine, 1649. [NRS.RS35.S2.III.479]

SPALDING, JOHN, born 1700, a wright at Galafauld, died 1768, spouse Isobel Kenner. [Inverarity gravestone]

SPALDING, THOMAS, in the Ground of Brighton in Kinnetles, 1691. [NRS.E69.11.1]

SPEED, JAMES, in Pitpullokis, parish of Brechin, husband of Margaret Bell, testament, 1612, Comm. Brechin. [NRS]

SPEED, JOHN, versus John Tindal, Forfar Burgh Court, 24 December 1784, 12 January 1785. [AA.F1.8.1]

SPEID, JOHN, of Ardivie, parish of Brechin, testament, 1676, Comm. Brechin. [NRS]

SPEID, RICHARD, the elder, and spouse Elspeth Mather in Pitpullox, testament, 1630, Comm. Brechin. [NRS]

SPEED, RICHARD, a maltman burgess of Brechin, spouse Bessie Watt, testament, 1630, Comm. Brechin. [NRS]

SPEED, ROBERT, in Aberlemno, 1691. [NRS.E69.11.1]

SPEID, ROBERT, in Pitpullox, parish of Brechin, testament, 1610, Comm. Brechin. [NRS]

SPEED, ROBERT, in Brechin, husband of Barbara Rutherford, sasine, 1648. [NRS.RS35.S2.III.171]

SPEID, ROBERT, a maltman in Brechin, husband of Janet Ordie, parents of Robert and Thomas, sasine, 1665. [NRS.RS35.S3.II.266, etc]

THE PEOPLE OF STRATHMORE, 1600-1799

SPEID, THOMAS, in Cotton of Halch, parish of Brechin, testament, 1601, Comm. Brechin. [NRS]

SPEID, THOMAS, a merchant skinner in Brechin, spouse Katherine Gibb, testament, 1621, Comm. Brechin. [NRS]

SPEID, THOMAS, and spouse Helen Arbuthnott, in Muirside, parish of Brechin, testament, 1635, Comm. Brechin. [NRS]

SPENCE, DAVID, in Guthrie, 1691. [NRS.E69.11.1]

SPENS, GEORGE, commissary clerk of Brechin, 1691. [NRS.E69.11.1]

SPENS, JOHN, commissary clerk, procurator fiscal, and town clerk of Brechin, husband of Elspeth Lyon, sasine, 1664; testament, 1691, Comm. Brechin. [NRS.RS35.S3.II.53]

SPENCE, ISOBEL, daughter of the late ... Spence in Gallowhill, 1743. [NRS.RH11.70.7]

SPENCE, ROBERT, in Methie Inverarity, 1691. [NRS.E69.11.1]

SPONNAR, JOHN, in Brechin, spouse Katherine Hall, testament, 1632, Comm. Brechin. [NRS]

SPOTTISWOOD, MARGARET, relict of George Herres of Eassie, testament, 1613, Comm. Edinburgh. [NRS]

STALKER, JOHN, a weaver in Kirriemuir, husband of Margaret Coutie, sasine, 1639; testament,1641, Comm. St Andrews. [NRS.RS35.S2.I.377]

STALKER, JOHN, in Kirriemuir, husband of Elizabeth Shepherd, testament, 1640, Comm. St Andrews. [NRS]

STARBIG, WILLIAM, in Rescobie, 1691. [NRS.E69.11.1]

STARK, ALEXANDER, in Forfar, 1691. [NRS.E69.11.1]

STARK, GEORGE, born 1698, died 1740, wife Jean Rickart, born 1694, died 1754. [Forfar gravestone]

STARK, JOSEPH, versus David Mands, Forfar Burgh Court, 29 December 1784. [AA.F1.8.1]

STEEDMAN, GEORGE, spouse Jean Mitchell, in Pickerton, Dunnichen, testament, 1657, Comm. Brechin. [NRS]

STEILL, ANDREW, a merchant in Kirriemuir, 1717, 1742. [NRS.GD7.2.142; RH11.70.7]

STEILL, DAVID, a shoemaker in Kirriemuir, 1745. [NRS.RH11.70.7]

STEILL, DONALD, a shoemaker in Brechin, son of David Steill in the Mains of Rattray, husband of Marjorie Wood, sasine, 1685. [NRS.RS35.S3.VIII.192]

STEILL, GEORGE, bailie of Brechin, husband of Katherine Baillie, parents of Agnes, and George, sasine, 1654; testament, 1687, Comm. Brechin. [NRS.RS35.S2.IV.428]

STEEL, JAMES, a brewer in Forfar, 1753, 1759. [NRS.E326.1.169]

STEEL, JAMES, jr., in Forfar, 1785; versus Charles Winter, Forfar Burgh Court, 4/9 September 1785, 16/28 November 1785. [AA.F1.8.1] [NRS.E326.3.19]

STEEL, JANET, in Kirriemuir, 1762. [NRS.CH2.1302.2/11]

STEILL, WALTER, a wright in Kirriemuir, husband of Margaret, daughter of James Mather a merchant there, a sasine, 1677. [NRS.RS35.S3.VI.336]

STEENSON, JAMES, a tailor, in Forfar,1691. [NRS.E69.11.1]

STEENSON, JAMES, in Glamis, 1691. [NRS.E69.11.1]

STEPHEN, DAVID, in Methie Inverarity, 1691. [NRS.E69.11.1]

STEPHEN, JAMES, in Forfar,1691. [NRS.E69.11.1]

STEVEN, JAMES, in Bractullo, son of the late David Steven sometime in Carsebank, sasine, 1655. [NRS.GD1.64.3]

STEVEN, JAMES, a weaver, 1666. [AA.F5.40]

STEPHEN, MARGARET, in Herdhill, 1730. [NRS.CH2.1302.179]

STEPHEN, MARGARET, in Kirriemuir, 1738. [NRS.CH2.1302.225]

STEPHEN, WILLIAM, in Herdhill, 1720. [NRS.CH2.1302.1.125]

THE PEOPLE OF STRATHMORE, 1600-1799

STEPHEN, WILLIAM, in Kirriemuir, 1783. [NRS.CH2.1302.2/97]

STEVENSON, ALEXANDER, son of late Alexander Stevenson, a merchant burgess of Brechin, spouse Agnes Findlayson, testament, 1621, Comm. Brechin. [NRS]

STEVENSON, DAVID, weaver in Brechin, spouse Janet Gairdner, son David, sasine, 1638. [NRS.RS35.S2.I.301]

STEVENSON, JAMES, weaver in Brechin, spouse Janet Duncan, sasine, 1686. [NRS.RS35.S3.VIII.405]

STEPHENSON, JAMES, in Farnell, 1691. [NRS.E69.11.1]

STEVENSON, JEAN, daughter of late Alexander Stevenson a merchant burgess of Brechin, testament, 1628, Comm. Brechin. [NRS]

STEVENSON, JOHN, spouse Isobel Clark, in Drumbarrow, Dunnichen, testament, 1610, Comm. Brechin. [NRS]

STEVENSON, JOHN, a brabiner at the Meikle Mill of Brechin, spouse Margaret Walker, testament, 1670, Comm. Brechin.[NRS]

STEVENSON, JOHN, weaver at the Meikle Mill of Brechin, spouse Janet Reid, children Francis, James and John, sasine, 1679. [NRS.RS35.S3.VIII.118]

STEVENSON, ROBERT, weaver in Brechin, spouse Catherine Alexander, children Agnes and Isabel, sasine, 1666. [NRS.RS35.S3.III.85]

STEWART, ALEXANDER, and his wife Agnes McConachie, in Kirriemuir, 1686. [NRS.RH11.70.1/5]

STEWART, DAVID, a mason, in Forfar,1691. [NRS.E69.11.1]

STEWART, DAVID, in Kirriemuir, 1724. [NRS.CH2.1302.141]

STEWART, JAMES, in Kinnell, 1691. [NRS.E69.11.1]

STEWART, JOHN, in Forfar,1691. [NRS.E69.11.1]

STEWART, ROBERT, a wright, son of Peter Stewart in Ground of Lour, a sasine witness, 1744. [AA.F1.4.3]

STEWART, WILLIAM, born 1767, a manufacturer in Kirriemuir, died 1845, spouse Agnes Dalgity, born 1772, died 1827. [Kirriemuir gravestone]

STEWART, WILLIAM, in Cairnleith, Kingoldrum, testament, 1798, Comm. Brechin. [NRS]

STINSON, JOHN, in Balmadie, in Rescobie, 1691. [NRS.E69.11.1]

STIRLING, ANDREW, born 1728, died 1796. [Forfar gravestone]

STIRLING, DAVID, a weaver in Whinniedrum, died 1737. [Aberlemno gravestone]

STIRLING, DAVID, versus William Mann, Forfar Burgh Court, 26 January 1785. [AA.F1.8.1]

STIRLING, JAMES, 1779. [AA.F5.151]

STIRLING, JOHN, in Kirriemuir, 1730. [NRS.CH2.1302.177]

STIVEN, ALEXANDER, a shoemaker in Kirriemuir, 1745. [NRS.RH11.70.7]

STIVEN, GIDEON, in Guthrie, 1691. [NRS.E69.11.1]

STIVEN, JAMES, a tobacconist in Kirriemuir, 1745. [NRS.RH11.70.7]

STIVEN, JOHN, in Guthrie, 1691. [NRS.E69.11.1]

STIVEN, WILLIAM, in Hardhill, 1744. [NRS.RH11.70.7]

STOKE, JOHN, in Glamis, 1691. [NRS.E69.11.1]

STORIER, JOHN, in Kinnell, 1691. [NRS.E69.11.1]

STORMONTH, ANNA, in Kirriemuir, 1745. [NRS.RH70.11.7]

STORMONTH, DAVID, in Lednathy, 1724, 1733. [NRS.CH2.1302/141/191]

STORMONTH, DAVID, a merchant in Kirriemuir, 1742. [NRS.RH11.70.7]

STORMONT, JAMES, in Kirriemuir, 1686. [NRS.RH11.70.1/3]

THE PEOPLE OF STRATHMORE, 1600-1799

STORMONTH, JAMES, in Milldad, Kingoldrum, testament, 1740, Comm. Brechin. [NRS]

STORMONTH, JAMES, of Lednathie, born 1731, died 1817. [Kirriemuir gravestone]

STORMONT, PATRICK, in Wester Kinwherrie, 1745. [NRS.RH11.70.7]

STORMONTH, ROBERT, in Kirriemuir,1745. [NRS.CH2.1302.245]

STORRIOR, DAVID, a petition, Forfar Burgh Court, 16 June 1784. [AA.F1.8.1]

STOT, JEAN, in Kirriemuir, 1726. [NRS.CH2.1302/159]

STOUT, JANET, an alleged witch in Forfar, 1662. [RPCS.I.162]

STRACHAN, CATHERINE, spouse of Walter Barty cotterman in Ascurrie, testament, 1600, Comm. St Andrews. [NRS]

STRACHAN, DAVID, Bishop of Brechin, spouse Anna Barclay, testaments, 1671, 1682, Comm. Brechin. [NRS]

STRACHAN, GEORGE, born 1632, minister, died 1692, wife Janet Thomson, born 1641, died 1691. [Guthrie gravestone]

STRACHAN, GEORGE, in Tannadice, 1691. [NRS.E69.11.1]

STRACHAN, JAMES, in Keithock, testament, 1687, Comm. Brechin. [NRS]

STRACHAN, JAMES, late Commissary of Brechin, testament, 1685, Comm. Brechin. [NRS]

STRACHAN, JOHN, in Criss, Kirriemuir, testament, 1613, Comm. St Andrews. [NRS]

STRACHAN, JOHN, in Cleiff, Kirriemuir, testament, 1619, Comm. St Andrews. [NRS]

STRACHAN, JOHN, in Brechin, testament, 1628, Comm. Brechin. [NRS]

STRACHAN, JOHN, a merchant in Kirriemuir, husband of Margaret, daughter of Robert Rodger there, a sasine, 1676. [NRS.RS35.S3.VI.195]

STRACHAN, JOHN, in Kinnell, 1691. [NRS.E69.11.1]

THE PEOPLE OF STRATHMORE, 1600-1799

STRACHAN, JOHN, in Killhill, 1717. [NRS.CH2.1302.1.107]

STRANG, ALEXANDER, a baxter burgess of Forfar, spouse Elizabeth Williamson, testament, 1577, Comm. Edinburgh. [NRS]

STRANG, ALEXANDER, provost of Forfar, 1647, 1650. [RGS.XI.760][AA.F1.4.1/21]

STRANG, ALEXANDER, a burgess in Forfar, sasine, 1654; provost, 1660. [NRS.RS35.S2.IV.339] [AA.F1.1.1]

STRANG, DAVID, a burgess of Forfar, an assizeman in 1600. [RGS.VI.1176]

STRANG, DAVID, Bishop of Brechin, a donor in 1665. [Brechin Cathedral]

STRANG, ISOBELL, in Forfar,1691. [NRS.E69.11.1]

STRANG, JOHN, in Forfar, 1611, 1614.[RPCS.VIII.308] [RGS.VII.1024]

STRANG, JOHN, schoolmaster in Oathlaw, 1690. [SHS.4.2]

STRANG, JOHN, versus Steel and Kyd, Forfar Burgh Court, 25 August 1784. [AA.F1.8.1]

STRANG, ROBERT, born in Forfar, died in Stockholm, Sweden, on 21 April 1651; letter, 1657. [Forfar parish bell inscription][AA.F5.60]

STRANG, WILLIAM, and Margaret Pattillo,a merchant in Stockholm, Sweden, 1660; letter, 1657. [Forfar parish bell inscription][AA.F5.60]

STRATTON, JAMES, a brabiner in Kirriemuir, husband of Isobel Henry, testament, 1640, Comm. St Andrews. [NRS]

STRATTON, JAMES, in Kirriemuir, husband of Katherine Smyth, testament, 1649, Comm. St Andrews. [NRS]

STROCK, JAMES, in Forfar,1691. [NRS.E69.11.1]

STUART, GEORGE, Forfar wardhouse keyholder, 1661. [AA.F1.1.1]

STUART, MARY, in Kirriemuir, 1786. [NRS.CH2.1302.2/123]

THE PEOPLE OF STRATHMORE, 1600-1799

STUILL, HELEN, spouse John Lawdor in Bractullo, Idvie, testament, 1606, Comm. St Andrews. [NRS]

STURROCK, AGNES, spouse to John Dall in Windiedge, Dunnichen, testament, 1647, Comm. Brechin. [NRS]

STURROCK, ALEXANDER, in Draffin, Dunnichen, testament, 1647, Comm. Brechin. [NRS]

STURROCK, ALEXANDER, councillor of Forfar, 1688. [AA.F1.1.2], in Forfar,1691. [NRS.E69.11.1]

STURROCK, ALEXANDER, in Dunnichen, 1691. [NRS.E69.11.1]

STURROCK, ALEXANDER, versus Millar and Mands, Forfar Burgh Court, 7 January 1785. [AA.F1.8.1]

STURROCK, ANDREW, a cordiner, in Forfar,1691. [NRS.E69.11.1]

STURROCK, DAVID, in Forfar,1691. [NRS.E69.11.1]

STURROCK, DAVID, in Rescobie, 1691. [NRS.E69.11.1]

STURROCK, JAMES, in Dunnichen, 1691. [NRS.E69.11.1]

STURROCK, JOHN, cordiner, 1689. [AA.F1.1.2]

STURROCK, JOHN, an officer of Forfar, 1689. [AA.F1.1.2]

STURROCK, JOHN, tacksman of the Forfar windmill, 1690. [AA.F1.1.2]

STURROCK, JOHN, a brewer, in Forfar,1691. [NRS.E69.11.1]

STURROCK, JOHN, son and heir of William Sturrock and his wife Janet Dysart, and grandson of John Dysart, 1673; charter, 1681. [AA.F5.123/126]

STURROCK, JOHN, 1712. [AA.F5.131]

STURROCK, JOHN, of Pitreuchie, 1776. [AA.F5.150]

STURROCK, MARGARET, in Rescobie, 1691. [NRS.E69.11.1]

STURROCK, PATRICK, a merchant in Forfar, 1745. [NRS.NRAS#124/4/1/75]

THE PEOPLE OF STRATHMORE, 1600-1799

STURROCK, PETER, versus William Burnet, Forfar Burgh Court, 16 November 1785. [AA.F1.8.1]

STURROCK, WILLIAM, treasurer of Forfar, a deed, 1707. [NRS.RD2.93.334]

STURROCK, WILLIAM, a bailie of Forfar, late Deacon of the Shoemakers of Forfar, sasine, 1727. [NRS.GD1.369.237]

STURROCK, WILLIAM, versus James Scott, Forfar Burgh Court, 11 May 1784; versus Scott and Black, Forfar Burgh Court, 20 April 1785, 20 May 1785. [AA.F1.8.1]

STURROCK, Mrs, in Forfar, 1791. [NRS.E326.1.169]

SUTTIE, ANDREW, a burgess of Forfar, 1608. [RPCS.VIII.647]

SUTTIE, CATHERINE,1660. [AA.F1.1.1]

SUTTIE, DAVID, in South Mains of Forfar, a tack, 10 May 1690. [AA.F5/23], in Forfar, 1691. [NRS.E60.11.1]

SUTTIE, DAVID, in Guthrie, 1691. [NRS.E69.11.1]

SUTTIE, GEORGE, charter, 1632. [AA.F5.89]

SUTTIE, GEORGE, in Innerarity in Methie Inverarity, 1691. [NRS.E69.11.1]

SUTTIE, JAMES, sasine of a croft, 1621; sasine of lands on north side of Tolbooth of Forfar, 1637. [AA.F5.27/47]

SUTTIE, JAMES, son of George Suttie, was admitted as a burgess of Forfar, 1660. [AA.F1.1.1]

SUTTIE, JAMES, a cordiner in Forfar, a deed, 1689. [NRS.RS2.70.69]

SUTTIE, JAMES, a brewer, in Forfar,1691. [NRS.E69.11.1]

SUTTIE, PATRICK, born 1578, sometime bailie of Forfar, died on 28 September 1655, his spouse Janet Hunter, born 1604, died on 19 September 1661; charter, 1632. [Forfar gravestone] [NRS.RS35.S2.I.95][AA.F5.89]

SUTTIE, WILLIAM, appointed to carry the (regimental?) colours, 1660; was admitted as a burgess and freeman of Forfar on 2 October 1661. [AA.F1.1.1]

SUTTIE, WILLIAM, in Farnell, 1691. [NRS.E69.11.1]

THE PEOPLE OF STRATHMORE, 1600-1799

SUTTIE, WILLIAM, in Kinnetles, 1691. [NRS.E69.11.1]

SWAN, ELSPETH, a merchant in Forfar, 1688. [AA.F1.1.2], in Forfar,1691. [NRS.E69.11.1]

SYM, ALEXANDER, son of late David Sym in Westerton of Strathcathro, testament, 1722, Comm. Brechin. [NRS]

SYME, JOHN, in Balnabreich, spouse Katherine Speid, testament, 1629, Comm. Brechin. [NRS]

SYMMERS, JAMES, an innkeeper in Forfar, 1745. [NRS.NRAS#124/4/1/75]

SYMPSON, ALEXANDER, in Clocksbriggs, testament, 1607, Comm. Edinburgh. [NRS]

SYMSON, ALEXANDER, son of James Symson a weaver, was admitted as a burgess and freeman of Forfar, 1688. [AA.F1.1.2]

SYMSON, JOHN, in Wester Dod, spouse Eupham Cuthbert, testament, 1683, Comm. St Andrews. [NRS]

SYRIE, ISOBEL, a witch in Forfar, 1661. [RPCS.I.74]

TALBERT, ALEXANDER, in Forfar,1691. [NRS.E69.11.1]

TALBERT, DAVID, a tailor in Forfar, 1684, 1691. [RBF#218][NRS.E69.11.1]

TALBERT, DAVID, in Rescobie, 1691. [NRS.E69.11.1]

TALBERT, JOHN, in Forfar,1691. [NRS.E69.11.1]

TARBAT, ALEXANDER, a weaver in Forfar, 1773; versus his debtors, 6 November 1784, Forfar Burgh Court. [AA.F1.8.1;AA.F5.149]

TARBET, GEORGE, in Forfar, 1691. [NRS.E60.11.1]

TARBET, JOHN, a merchant in Forfar, 1759, 1770. [NRS.E326.1.169; GD253.141.1]

TARBAT, WILLIAM, a merchant in Forfar, 1777. [NRS.NRAS#124/4/1/78]

TAYLOR, ADAM, in Brechin, 1620. [RGS.VIII.17]

TAYLOR, ALEXANDER, in Farnell, 1691. [NRS.E69.11.1]

TAYLOR, ANDREW, an alleged witch in Brechin, 1620. [RPCS.XII.362]

TAYLOR, ANDREW, a wright and a councillor of Forfar, 1680s. [AA.F1.1.2], in Forfar,1691. [NRS.E69.11.1]

TAYLOR, ANDREW, a carrier in Kirriemuir, 1717. [NRS.CH2.1302.1.111]

TAYLOR, GEORGE, a baxter burgess of Brechin, 1605. [RPCS.VII.616]

TAYLOR, ISOBEL, in Woodhead, Kirriemuir, testament, 1616, Comm. St Andrews. [NRS]

TAYLOR, JAMES, a smith burgess of Brechin, relict Katherine Skinner, testament, 1677, Comm. Brechin. [NRS]

TAYLOR, JAMES, a shoemaker in Brechin, and spouse Catherine Mill, testament, 1628, Comm. Brechin. [NRS]

TAYLOR, JAMES, in Farnell, 1691. [NRS.E69.11.1]

TAYLOR, JAMES, in Kinnell, 1691. [NRS.E69.11.1]

TAYLOR, JEAN, in Forfar,1691. [NRS.E69.11.1]

TAYLOR, KATHERINE, in Kirriemuir, 1785, 1786. [NRS.CH2.1302.2/118, 120, 123]

TAYLOR, JOHN, in Drumclune, Kiriemuir, testament, 1617, Comm. St Andrews. [NRS]

TAYLOR, JOHN, in Kinclune, Kingoldrum, testament, 1629, Comm. Brechin. [NRS]

TAYLOR, JOHN, in Forfar,1691. [NRS.E69.11.1]

TAYLOR, PATRICK, in Rescobie, 1691. [NRS.E69.11.1]

TAYLOR, THOMAS, in Farnell, 1691. [NRS.E69.11.1]

TEVENDALE, JOHN, versus ....Adamson, Forfar Burgh Court, 16 June 1784. [AA.F1.8.1]

THOM, ALEXANDER, versus ...Jack, Forfar Burgh Court, 8 September 1784. [AA.F1.8.1]

THOM, DAVID, in Aberlemno, 1691. [NRS.E69.11.1]

THE PEOPLE OF STRATHMORE, 1600-1799

THOM, DAVID, a merchant in Kirriemuir, spouse Katherine Gowan, 1742, 1745. [NRS.RH11.70.7]

THOM, ELSPET, spouse to John Rodger in Muirton of Balfour, Kingoldrum, testament, 1624, Comm. Brechin. [NRS]

THOM, GEORGE, versus his debtors, Forfar Burgh Court, 2 February 1785. [AA.F1.8.1]

THOM, JAMES, a tailor and tacksman in Forfar, 1680s; spouse Margaret Thornton, testament, 1687, Comm. St Andrews. [NRS] [RBF#216] [AA.F1.1.2]

THOM, JAMES, a merchant in Brechin, husband of Katharine Hendry, sasine, 1685. [NRS.RS35.S3.VIII.287]

THOM, JAMES, versus Alexander Millar, Forfar Burgh Court, 18 August 1784; versus Patrick Neish, Forfar Burgh Court, 23 February 1785. [AA.F1.8.1]

THOMS, JOHN, in Rescobie, 1691. [NRS.E69.11.1]

THOM, MARGARET, in Kirriemuir, 1741. [NRS.CH2.1302.231]

THOM, THOMAS, Deacon of the Incorporation of Tailors of Forfar, 1619. [RBF#214]

THOM, WILLIAM, versus ....Law, Forfar Burgh Court, 8 September 1784. [AA.F1.8.1]

THOMSON, AGNES, spouse to Alexander Coull, in Cotton of Melgund, Auldbar, testament, 1600, Comm. Brechin. [NRS]

THOMPSON, ALEXANDER, in Kirriemuir, 1786. [NRS.CH2.1302.2/123]

THOMSON, ANDREW, a maltman burgess of Brechin, spouse Marjorie Hanton, testament, 1613, Comm. Brechin. [NRS]

THOMSON, CATHERINE, relict of John Hood, a smith in Dyketon, Careston, testament, 1671, Comm. Brechin. [NRS]

THOMSON, DAVID, in Methie Inverarity, 1691. [NRS.E69.11.1]

THOMSON, JAMES, and spouse Helen Lawson, in Muirton of Balfour, Kincaldrum, testament, 1612, Comm. Brechin. [NRS]

THOMSON, JAMES, in Kinnell, 1691. [NRS.E69.11.1]

THOMSON, JAMES, born 1673, died 1744 in Cossacks. [Kirriemuir gravestone]

THOMSON, JAMES, minister at Kingoldrum, testament, 1781, Comm. Brechin. [NRS]

THOMSON, JANET, born 1590, died 1652, wife of Thomas Mill in Haltoun of Eassie. [Eassie gravestone]

THOMSON, JEAN, in Kirriemuir, 1729, 1738. [NRS.CH2.1302.173/221]

THOMSON, JOHN, in Rescobie, 1691. [NRS.E69.11.1]

THOMSON, JOHN, was served as heir to his granduncle Thomas Rodger, 1742. [NRS.RH11.70.7]

THOMSON, MARGARET, born 1541, spouse to David Cromb, died on 4 February 1613. [Kirriemuir gravestone]

THORNTON, AGNES, heir portioner to her father Charles Thornton a bailie of Forfar, 1681. [NRS.Retours, Forfar#486]

THORNTON, ALEXANDER, in Methie Inverarity, 1691. [NRS.E69.11.1]

THORNTON, ALEXANDER, versus .... Welsh, Forfar Burgh Court, 1 December 1784. [AA.F1.8.1]

THORNTON, CHARLES, a bailie of Forfar, spouse Elspeth Suitie, sasine, 1653; 1660; a bond, 1666; tiend collector in 1658. [NRS.RS35.S3.IV.191; RD4.17.35] [AA,F1.1.1; F1.4.1]; husband of Elspeth Suttie, sasine, 1701. [NRS.RS35.10.349]

THORNTON, CHARLES, in Kelhill, 1741. [NRS.CH2.1302.233];tenant in Killhill, sasine, 1744. [AA.F1.4.3]

THORNTON, GEORGE, in Kinnetles, 1691. [NRS.E69.11.1]

THORNTON, HENRY, of Tillieqhuam in Aberlemno, 1691. [NRS.E69.11.1]

THORNTON, ISABELLA, heir portioner to her father Charles Thornton a bailie of Forfar, 1681. [NRS.Retours, Forfar#486]

THE PEOPLE OF STRATHMORE, 1600-1799

THORNTON, JAMES, a merchant in Glamis and burgess of Forfar, spouse Isobel Henry, sasine, 1686. [NRS.RS35.S3.VIII.435]

THORNTON, JAMES, weaver in Muirhead of Logy, 1745, 1746. [NRS.RH11.70.7]

THORNTON, JANET, heir portioner to her father Charles Thornton a bailie of Forfar, 1681. [NRS.Retours, Forfar#486]

THORNTON, JOHN, a merchant in Glamis, was admitted as a burgess and freeman of Forfar, 1690. [AA.F1.1.2]; in Glamis, 1691. [NRS.E69.11.1]

THORNTON, JAMES, ground officer of the Lordship of Glamis, testament, 1777, Comm. St Andrews. [NRS]

THORNTON, MARGARET, daughter of Thomas Thornton, son of Thomas Thornton, a wright, mother of James Auld, a burgess of Forfar, and spouse of James Thom, sasine, 1686. [NRS.RS35.S3.VIII.435]

THORNTON, PATRICK, a wright in Forfar, 1689. [AA.F1.1.2] in Forfar, 1691. [NRS.E69.11.1]

THORNTON, PATRICK, a councillor and deacon of the Cordiner Trade of Forfar, 1688, 1692. [NRS.GD1.61.12] [AA.F1.1.2], in Forfar, 1691. [NRS.E69.11.1]

THORNTON, ROBERT, a smith, was admitted as a burgess and freeman of Forfar, 1689. [AA.F1.1.2], in Forfar, 1691. [NRS.E69.11.1]

THORNTON, ROBERT, in Forfar, 1759. [NRS.E326.1.169]

THORNTON, THOMAS, a cordiner burgess of Forfar, 1620. [RPCS.XII.189]

THORNTON, THOMAS, a cordiner and pewterer in Forfar, sasine, 1686. [NRS.RS35.VIII.435]

THOULAS, JAMES, burgess of Brechin, testament, 1631, Comm. Brechin. [NRS]

TINDALL, DAVID, versus his debtors, Forfar Burgh Court, 2 June 1784; a shoemaker in Forfar, 1786.[AA.F1.8.1; F5.152]

THE PEOPLE OF STRATHMORE, 1600-1799

TINDALL, JAMES, versus Patrick Neish, 26 January 1785; versus .... Findlay, Forfar Burgh Court, 2 March 1785. [AA.F1.8.1]

TINDALE, WILLIAM, in Tannadice, 1745. [NRS.RH11.70.7]

TOD, ALEXANDER, in Forfar,1691. [NRS.E69.11.1]

TOD, ISOBEL, in Kirriemuir, 1786. [NRS.CH2.1302.2/123]

TOLMIE, JAMES, an Excise officer in Kirriemuir, 1742. [NRS.RH11.70.7]

TORBET, JAMES, a merchant in Kirriemuir, 1745. [NRS.RH11.70.7]

TORN, WILLIAM, born 1738, a merchant in Forfar, died 1784; versus .... Watt, Forfar Burgh Court, 5 October 1784. [AA.F1.8.1] [Forfar gravestone]

TORRIE, NORMAND, a litster burgess of Brechin, and wife Bessie Malcolm, testament, 1636, Comm. Brechin. [NRS]

TORRIE, ROBERT, son of Norman Torrie, a dyer in Brechin, 1632. [RGS.VIII.1938]

TORRIE, WALTER, servant to Robert Gray in Carcary, Farnell, testament, Comm. Brechin. [NRS]

TOUGH, ROBERT, in Kinnell, 1691. [NRS.E69.11.1]

TRAILL, GEORGE, son of the late Thomas Traill, in Kirriemuir, 1732. [NRS.GD7.21.151]

TRAILL, JAMES, son of John Traill, clerk of Forfar, 1604. [RPCS.VII.564]

TRAILL, JOHN, a notary public in Forfar, 1608, 1609; the common clerk of Forfar, and his sons John and Thomas, sasine, 1631. [RPCS.VIII.647/704][NRS.RS35.S1.VIII.46]

TRAILL, THOMAS, clerk of the Regality of Kirriemuir, and Euphemia Lindsay, daughter of James Lindsay a merchant in Kirriemuir and his wife Margaret Don, marriage contract, 1727. [NRS.GD7.2.142]

TRAYL, WILLIAM, , in Kinnell, 1691. [NRS.E69.11.1]

TRUMBLE, JAMES, in Strathcathro, 1691. [NRS.E69.11.1]

THE PEOPLE OF STRATHMORE, 1600-1799

TRUMBELL, JOHN, the younger of Ardrum in Aberlemno, 1691. [NRS.E69.11.1]

TRUMBLE, JOHN, in Strathcathro, 1691. [NRS.E69.11.1]

TULLOCH, JANET, spouse to John Adam in Pickerton of Guthrie, testament, 1686, Comm. Brechin. [NRS]

TULLOCH, JOHN, a merchant in Brechin, a donor in 1643. [Brechin Cathedral]

TULLOW, JOHN, in Tenements of Caldham, parish of Brechin, and spouse Elizabeth Tanndale, testament, 1633, Comm. Brechin. [NRS]

TURNBULL, JOHN, sr, of Strathcathro, testament, 1720, 1718, Comm. Brechin. [NRS]

TURNBULL, JOHN, jr, of Strathcathro, testaments, 1716, 1718, Comm. Brechin. [NRS]

TURNBULL, PETER, of Strathcathro, spouse Margaret Jonkine, testament, 1669, Comm. Brechin. [NRS]

TYRIE, JAMES, portioner of Hillhead of Kirriemuir, husband of Isobel Edward, sasine, 1709. [NRS.RS35.12.147]

TYRIE, JANE, in Kirriemuir, 1783. [NRS.CH2.1302.2/93]

TYRIE, JOHN, of Easter Hillhead of Kirriemuir, sasine, 1768. [NRS.RS35.22.219]

TYRIE, THOMAS, in Nevay, born 1618, son of David Tyrie, husband of Janet Veilant, died 10 October 1651. [Nevay gravestone]

UDNY, ANDREW, a burgess of Brechin, husband of Elizabeth, parents of Elizabeth and Margaret, sasine, 1638. [NRS.RS35.S2.I.280]

UDNY, JAMES, a burgess of Brechin, husband of Isobel Livingstone, parents of Agnes, and Catharine, sasine, 1638. [NRS.RS35.S2.I.280]

UDNY, PATRICK, a glover in Brechin, husband of Isobel Cowy, sasine, 1669. [NRS.RS35.S3.IV.301]

URE, Provost JOHN, in Forfar, 1779, 1785. [NRS.GD137.1191; E326.3.19][AA.F5.181]

URE, WILLIAM, a baillie of Forfar, deeds, 1714, 1715. [NRS.RD4.115.470; RD2.105.537]

URE, Provost, in Forfar, 1791. [NRS.E326.1.169]

URE, WILLIAM, in Aberlemno, 1691. [NRS.E69.11.1]

VALENTINE, ALEXANDER, in Dunniken, Glamis, 1797. [NRS.E326.10.3.24]

VALENTINE, HENRY, and spouse Elizabeth Jamieson, in Meikle Carcary, Farnell, testament, 1601, Comm. Brechin. [NRS]

VALENTINE, JAMES, a tanner in Kirriemuir, 1791. [NRS.B19.3.27.243]

VALENTINE, JOHN, a merchant in Kirriemuir, deceased, father of Isobel and Margaret Valentine, assignation, 1737. [NRS.GD7.2.160]

VALLANCE, CHRISTIAN, spouse Andrew Bowak in Muirside, testament, 1605, Comm. St Andrews. [NRS]

VOLUM, ROBERT, in Kirriemuir, husband of Agnes Morris, a sasine,1653. [NRS.RS35.S2.IV.378, etc]

VOLUM, ROBERT, and his relict Margaret Hutcheon, a sasine,1698. [NRS.RS35.S3.X.60]

VOLUM, ROBERT, in Kirriemuir, relict Margaret Hutcheon, sasine, 1704. [NRS.RS35.11.70]

VOLUME, WILLIAM, a flesher in Forfar, 1742. [NRS.RH11.70.7]

WADDELL, ALEXANDER, senior, a burgess of Forfar, a witness in 1603. [RGS.VI.1404]

WADDELL, ALEXANDER, junior, a burgess of Forfar, a witness in 1603. [RGS.VI.1404]

WADDELL, ALEXANDER, in Forfar,1691. [NRS.E69.11.1]

WADDELL, JOHN, a tailor and councillor in Forfar, 1680s, 1684. [RBF#218] [AA.F1.1.2]

THE PEOPLE OF STRATHMORE, 1600-1799

WAITH, JOHN, in Dubton, parish of Brechin, testament, 1643, Comm. Brechin. [NRS]

WALKER, ALEXANDER, a burgess of Forfar, spouse Alison Hunter, sasine, 1646; 1660. [NRS.RS35.S2.II.534] [AA.F1.1.1], in Forfar,1691. [NRS.E69.11.1]

WALKER, ALEXANDER, a mason in Forfar, 1732. [NRS.GD18832.9]

WALKER, DAVID, a burgess of Kirriemuir, born 1591, died 1655, spouse Agnes Smith. [Kirriemuir gravestone]

WALKER, DAVID, in Maisondieu, parish of Brechin, and spouse Janet Gryme, testament, 1632, Comm. Brechin. [NRS]

WALKER, DAVID, and spouse Elspet Donaldson in Brechin, testament, 1642, Comm. Brechin. [NRS]

WALKER, DAVID, deacon of the Tailors of Forfar, 1656, 1658. [RBF#215]

WALKER, DAVID in Strathcathro, 1691. [NRS.E69.11.1]

WALKER, DAVID, a shoemaker in Kirriemuir, spouse of Helen Liddell, sasine, 1704; 1732. [NRS.RS35.11.17; GD7.2.151]

WALKER, DAVID, son of John Walker, son of David Walker a merchant in Kirriemuir, sasine, 1704. [NRS.RS35.10.425]

WALKER, ISABEL, daughter of David Walker, a shoemaker in Kirriemuir, and spouse of David Doig, church officer there, a sasine, 1718. [NRS.RS35.13.221]

WALKER, JAMES, a burgess of Brechin, father of Catharine, sasine, 1644. [NRS.RS35.S2.II.543]

WALKER, JAMES, a writer in Forfar, 1781. [NRS.NRAS.124/4/2/42]

WALKER, JOHN, in Rescobie, 1691. [NRS.E69.11.1]

WALKER, JOHN, in Methie Inverarity, 1691. [NRS.E69.11.1]

WALKER, JOHN, in Dykehead, in Rescobie, 1691. [NRS.E69.11.1]

WALKER, JOHN, son of David Walker, a merchant in Kirriemuir, sasine, 1704. [NRS.RS35.10.425]

WALKER, ROBERT, a brabiner burgess of Brechin, and spouse Bessie Fettous, testament, 1635, Comm. Brechin. [NRS]

WALLACE, ALEXANDER, in Dod, Rescobie, relict Isobel Pyott, testament, 1657, Comm. Brechin. [NRS]

WALLACE, JOHN, a merchant in Forfar, 1743. [NRS.RH11.70.7.7]

WALLACE, JOHN, in Forfar, 1759. [NRS.E326.1.169]

WALLACE, JOHN, versus Andrew Binny, Forfar Burgh Court, 22 September 1784, 6 November 1784, 29 December 1784. [AA.F1.8.1]

WALLACE, THOMAS, in Kirriemuir, 1746. [NRS.RH11.70.7]

WALLACE, WILLIAM, servant to Andrew, Bishop of Brechin, 1615. [RGS.VIII.17]

WALLACE, WILLIAM, versus .... Mitchell, Forfar Burgh Court, 30 November 1785. [AA.F1.8.1]

WALLACE, Mrs, in Forfar, 1791. [NRS.E326.1.169]

WALLS, DANIEL, in Glamis, 1691. [NRS.E69.11.1]

WALLS, DAVID, in Rescobie, 1691. [NRS.E69.11.1]

WALLS, DAVID, a flesher, in Forfar, 1691. [NRS.E69.11.1]

WALLS, DAVID, in Woodend, in Rescobie, 1691. [NRS.E69.11.1]

WALLS, JOHN, in Dunnichen, 1691. [NRS.E69.11.1]

WALLS, PATRICK, in Aberlemno, 1691. [NRS.E69.11.1]

WALLS, WILLIAM, in Forfar, 1691. [NRS.E69.11.1]

WALLUDINER, JOHN, in Forfar, 1691. [NRS.E69.11.1]

WARDROPER, JOHN, in Templeton, died November 1645, husband of Margaret Brown. [Nevay gravestone]

WARSALL, JAMES, in Tannadice, 1691. [NRS.E69.11.1]

WATCHMAN, ISOBEL, spouse of Patrick Mann in Pickerton, Guthrie, testament, 1614, Comm. Brechin. [NRS]

THE PEOPLE OF STRATHMORE, 1600-1799

WATERSTON, ALEXANDER, a shoemaker in Forfar, sasine, 1749. [NRS.RS35.17.13]

WATERSTON, ANDREW, in Forfar,1691. [NRS.E69.11.1]

WATERSTON, JAMES, in Forfar, 1691. [NRS.E69.11.1]

WATERSTON, JANET, spouse of Robert Adamson, a shoemaker in Kirriemuir, sasine, 1728. [NRS.RS35.14.372]

WATERSTON, JANET, in Forfar, 1759; a tack, 1760. [NRS.E326.1.169][AA.F5.73]

WATERSTONE, JOHN, a councillor of Forfar, 1690. [AA.F1.1.2], in Forfar, 1691. [NRS.E60.11.1]

WATERSTON, MARGARET, in Kirriemuir, 1745, 1746. [NRS.CH2.1302.245; RH11.70.7]

WATSON, ANDREW, a cordiner in Brechin, father of John, sasine, 1664. [NRS.RS35.S3.II.55]

WATSON, ANN, in Kirriemuir, 1786. [NRS.CH2.1302.2/123]

WATSON, CATHERINE, spouse of David Gordon, a cordiner in Kirriemuir, sasine, 1726. [NRS.RS35.14.138]

WATSON, DAVID, in Kirriemuir, husband of Helen Piggott, a sasine, 1653. [NRS.RS35.S2.IV.277]

WATSON, DAVID, a brewer in Kirriemuir, formerly in Dundee, sasine, 1704. [NRS.RS35.11.68]

WATSON, DAVID, in Glamis, 1797. [NRS.E326.10.3.24]

WATSON, JAMES, a glover in Brechin, husband of Margaret Livingstone, sasine,1692. [NRS.RS35.S3.IX.118]

WATSON, JAMES, in Kinnell, 1691. [NRS.E69.11.1]

WATSON, JAMES, in Herdhill, 1733. [NRS.CH2.1302.193]

WATSON, JAMES, versus David Mands jr., Forfar Burgh Court, 20 May 1785. [AA.F1.8.1]

WATSON, JOHN, a merchant in Brechin, 1656, relict Elspeth Syme. 1669; and a donor in 1660. [NRS.RS35.S3.IV.203, etc]

[Brechin Cathedral] [RGS.X.550]; a merchant burgess of Brechin, and spouse Elizabeth Sym, testament, 1669, Comm. Brechin. [NRS]

WATSON, JOHN, son of Andrew Watson, a cordiner in Brechin, husband of Janet Taylor, sasine,1675. [NRS.RS35.S3.VI.18]

WATSON, JOHN, son of James Watson, at the Meikle Mill of Brechin, testament, 1679, Comm. Brechin. [NRS]

WATSON, JOHN, in Forfar, 1691. [NRS.E60.11.1]

WATSON, JOHN, in Aberlemno, 1691. [NRS.E69.11.1]

WATSON, JOHN, in Oathlaw, 1691. [NRS.E69.11.1]

WATSON, JOHN, of Langbank, 1734, 1742, 1745. [NRS.CH2.1302.201; RH11.70.7]

WATSON, MARGARET, in Dunnichen, testament, 1723, Comm.Brechin. [NRS]

WATSON, MATILDA, born 1738, died 1778, wife of John Bennet in Seggieden. [Inverarity gravestone]

WATSON, PATRICK, a manufacturer in Kirriemuir, sasine, 1774. [NRS.RS35.24.432]

WATSON, THOMAS, a merchant citizen of Brechin, testament, 1635, Comm. Brechin. [NRS]

WATSON, THOMAS, a feuar in Kirriemuir, 1745. [NRS.RH11.70.7]

WATSON, THOMAS, a merchant in Kirriemuir, 1734, and spouse Jean Lindsay, 1745, sasine, 1751. [NRS.CH2.1302.211; RH11.70.7; RS35.17.307]

WATSON, THOMAS, a tanner in Kirriemuir, brother of John Watson of Longbank, sasine, 1736. [NRS.RS35.15.354]

WATSON, WILLIAM, servant to James Gardner a maltman burgess of Brechin, testament, 1612, Comm. Brechin. [NRS]

WATSON, WILLIAM, born 1590, died 12 May 1667, husband of Elspeth Smith, [Nevay gravestone]

THE PEOPLE OF STRATHMORE, 1600-1799

WATT, ADAM, a merchant citizen of Brechin, testament, 1628, Comm. Brechin. [NRS]

WATT, ALEXANDER, a burgess of Brechin, spouse Margaret Low, sasine, 1638, testament, 1661, Comm. Brechin. [NRS]; [NRS.RS35.S2.I.234]

WATT, ALEXANDER, a glover in Brechin, husband of Isobel Jamieson, parents of David, sasine, 1656.
[RGS.X.550][NRS.RS35.S3.II.83]

WATT, ALEXANDER, a glover in Brechin, spouse Isobel Jamieson, parents of David, a sasine, 1656.
[RGS.X.550][NRS.RS35.S3.II.83]

WATT, ALEXANDER, in Tannadice, 1691. [NRS.E69.11.1]

WATT, ALEXANDER, in Oathlaw, 1691. [NRS.E69.11.1]

WATT, ALEXANDER, a weaver in Ballinshoe, parish of Kirriemuir, testament, 1796, Comm. St Andrews. [NRS]

WATT, ANDREW, a merchant burgess of Brechin, spouse Euphame Liddell, testaments, 1612, 1630, Comm. Brechin. [NRS]

WATT, ANDREW, a glover in Brechin, spouse Margaret Cob, parents of Elizabeth, sasines, 1668. [NRS.RS35.S3.IV.194]

WATT, DAVID, a citizen of Brechin, husband of Elizabeth Gray, parents of Isobel, sasine, 1639. [NRS.RS35.S2.I.428, etc]

WATT, DAVID, a weaver and treasurer of Forfar, spouse Margaret Brandon, testament, 1681, Comm. St Andrews. [NRS] [AA.F1.1.2] , in Forfar,1691. [NRS.E69.11.1]

WATT, DAVID, a bailie of Forfar, and son of John Watt deacon of the weavers there, sasine, 1759, 1761, 1788; 1791.
[NRS.RS35.19.332; GD112; E326.1.169]

WATT, JAMES, a merchant burgess of Brechin, husband of Elspet Cant, parents of Agnes Watt, testament, 1624, Comm. Brechin. [NRS]

WATT, JAMES, reader in the church of Brechin, husband of Catherine Norrie, parents of John, a sasine, 1620, 1623.
[RGS.VIII.644][NRS.RS35.S2.I.192]

THE PEOPLE OF STRATHMORE, 1600-1799

WATT, JAMES, a wright in Brechin, spouse Isabel Baillie, daughter of James Baillie a burgess of Brechin, a sasine, 1675. [NRS.RS35.S3.VI.II]

WATT, JOHN, a maltman in Brechin, a sasine, 1649. [NRS.RS35.S2.III.280]

WATT, JOHN, a glover burgess of Brechin, testament, 1666, Comm. Brechin. [NRS]

WATT, JOHN, town clerk of Brechin, son of Alexander Watt a burgess there, husband of Helen Ramsay, a sasine, 1650. [NRS.RS35.S2.III.340]

WATT, JOHN, a wright, was admitted as a burgess and freeman of Forfar, 1690. [AA.F1.1.2], in Forfar,1691. [NRS.E69.11.1]

WATT, JOHN, a burgess of Forfar, sasine, 1738. [NRS.RS35.15.555]

WATT, JOHN, formerly Deacon of the Weavers Trade of Forfar, sasine, 1741. [NRS.RS35.16.65]

WATT, JOHN, in Forfar, 1759. [NRS.E326.1.169]

WATT, JOHN, versus Nicoll and Williamson, Forfar Burgh Court, 19 January 1785. [AA.F1.8.1]

WATT, JOHN, provost of Forfar, 1796. [AA.F5.154/155/157]

WATT, PATRICK, in Forfar, 1604. [RPCS.VII.564]

WATT, PATRICK, a flesher burgess of Forfar, deeds, 1688, son of Patrick Watt, 1680s/1690s. [NRS.RD3.69.322; RD4.73.1095] [AA.F1.1.2]

WATT, ROBERT, a maltman in Brechin, a bailie in 1643, spouse Eupham Gentleman, sasine, 1649. [AA.B1.10.13] [NRS.RS35.S1.VIII.257]

WATT, THOMAS, a surgeon in Cawnpore, India, son of .... Watt, a bailie of Forfar, 1791. [NRS.GD51.4.106]

WATT, WILLIAM, in Crosston of Aberlemno, testament, 1600, Comm. Brechin. [NRS]

THE PEOPLE OF STRATHMORE, 1600-1799

WATT, WILLIAM, a wheelwright in Brechin, spouse Elspeth Guthrie, sasine, 1675, testament, 1670, Comm. Brechin. [NRS] [NRS.RS35.S3.VI.44]

WATT, WILLIAM, a stonecutter in Brechin, sasine, 1684. [NRS.RS35.S3.VIII.174]

WATT, WILLIAM, the elder, a merchant in Forfar, deeds, 1690, 1692. [NRS.GD1.61.11; RD4.70.563] [AA.F1.1.2], in Forfar,1691. [NRS.E69.11.1]

WATT, WILLIAM, in Woodend, in Rescobie, 1691. [NRS.E69.11.1]

WATT, WILLIAM, son of Alexander Watt, a flesher in Forfar, a deed, 1693. [NRS.RD4.73.1095]

WATT, WILLIAM, versus David Hood, Forfar Burgh Court, 11 August 1784. [AA.F1.8.1]

WAUCH, ISABEL, spouse of David Hutcheon, a cordiner in Kirriemuir, sasine, 1719. [NRS.RS35.13.372]

WAUCH, JOHN, in Kirriemuir, husband of Elizabeth Easson, testament, 1626, Comm. St Andrews. [NRS]

WAUCH, JOHN, in Kirriemuir, husband of (1) Janet Hunter, and (2) Helen Lindsay, sasine, 1637. [NRS.RS35.S1.VIII.232]

WAUCH, JOHN, a baxter in Kirriemuir, son of John Wauch there, and husband of Margaret Millar, a sasine, 1653. [NRS.RS35.S2.IV.411, etc]

WAUCH, JOHN, a baxter in Kirriemuir, brother of Elizabeth, a sasine, 1669. [NRS.RS35.S3.IV.264]

WAUCHOPE, ROBERT, a burgess of Brechin, sasine, 1661. [NRS.RS35.S3.I.219, etc]

WEBSTER, ANDREW, in Brechin, sasine, 1669. [NRS.RS35.S3.IV.358]

WEBSTER, AGNES, spouse of Andrew Croll, sometime in Cremond Inch, Kirriemuir, testament, 1710, Comm. St Andrews. [NRS]

WEBSTER, CHARLES, a bailie of Forfar, 1753. [NRS.E326.1.169]

WEBSTER, Dr CHARLES, in Forfar, 1785. [NRS.E326.3.19]

WEBSTER, DAVID, a wright in Kirriemuir, deed, 1714. [NRS.RD4.89.1017]

WEBSTER, DAVID, a feuar in Kirriemuir, 1741. [NRS.RH11.70.7]

WEBSTER, DAVID, in Forfar, 1785, 1791. [NRS.E326.3.19]

WEBSTER, ELIZABETH, versus James Craik, Forfar Burgh Court, 22/25 September 1784. [AA.F1.8.1]

WEBSTER, ELIZABETH, in Kirriemuir,1787. [NRS.CH2.1302.2/125]

WEBSTER, GEORGE, a mason in Kirriemuir, sasine, 1780. [NRS.RS35.28.151]

WEBSTER, JAMES, a maltman and a donor in 1630. [Brechin Cathedral]

WEBSTER, JAMES, bailie of Forfar, 1660. [AA.F1.1.1]

WEBSTER, JAMES, son of John Webster a maltman, was admitted as a burgess and freeman of Forfar, 1686. [AA.F1.1.2]

WEBSTER, JAMES, in Aberlemno, 1691. [NRS.E69.11.1]

WEBSTER, JAMES, a merchant and treasurer in Forfar, 1680s, deeds, 1697, 1699. [NRS.RD4.84.411; RD4.80.239] [AA.F1.1.2], in Forfar,1691. [NRS.E69.11.1]

WEBSTER, JAMES, son of John Webster, a brabiner in Kirriemuir, a sasine, 1684. [NRS.RS35.S3.VIII.82]

WEBSTER, JAMES, son of David Webster, tenant of Careston, testament, 1714, Comm. Brechin. [NRS]

WEBSTER, JAMES, a spindlemaker in Hardhill, 1745. [NRS.RH11.70.7]

WEBSTER, JAMES, a writer in Forfar, 1777. [NRS.NRAS#124/4/1/78]

WEBSTER, JAMES, in Forfar, 1785. [NRS.E326.3.19; GD112.39.339.12]

THE PEOPLE OF STRATHMORE, 1600-1799

WEBSTER, JOHN, a brabiner burgess of Brechin, and spouse Isobel Walker, testament, 1659, Comm. Brechin. [NRS]

WEBSTER, JOHN, a brabiner in Kirriemuir, son of William Webster a brabiner in Forfar, and husband of Elizabeth or Euphame Stratton, a sasine,1666. [NRS.RS35.S3.III.96]

WEBSTER, JOHN, in Kirriemuir, formerly on Cramond Inch, husband of Isobel Webster, a sasine, 1684. [NRS.RS35.S3.VIII.82]

WEBSTER, JOHN, a wright in Brechin, husband of Isobel Wyld, sasine, 1685. [NRS.RS35.S3.VIII.248]

WEBSTER, JOHN, a webster in Kirriemuir, June 1686. [NRS.RH11.70.1/3]

WEBSTER, JOHN, a customer in Forfar, 1689. [AA.F1.1.2], in Forfar, 1691. [NRS.E60.11.1]

WEBSTER, JOHN, a mason in Forfar, 1717. [NRS.GD205.24.160]

WEBSTER, JOHN, a burgess of Forfar, sasine, 1734. [NRS.RS35.15.555]

WEBSTER, JOHN, jr., a mason in Kirriemuir, 1745. [NRS.RH11.70.7]

WEBSTER, JOHN, in Forfar, 1759. [NRS.E326.1.169]

WEBSTER, JOHN, a weaver, merchant, and bailie of Forfar, son and heir of Thomas Webster, weaver, 1762, 1777. [AA.F5.49] [NRS.NRAS#124/4/1/78]

WEBSTER, JOSEPH, in Drumshead, 1745. [NRS.RH11.70.7]

WEBSTER, RACHEL, in Kirriemuir,1786. [NRS.CH2.1302.2/123]

WEBSTER, THOMAS, in Brechin, testament, 1631, Comm. Brechin. [NRS]

WEBSTER, ROBERT, a merchant in Brechin, sasine, 1656. [NRS.RS35.S2.V.196, etc]

WEBSTER, THOMAS, tack of the wind and water mills of Forfar, 1662. [AA.F5.26; F1.1.1]

WEBSTER, THOMAS, born 1600, residing in Balingara, died on 12 April 1675, husband of Elizabeth Laing. [Kirriemuir gravestone]

WEBSTER, THOMAS, in Forfar, 1759. [NRS.E326.1.169]

WEBSTER, WILLIAM, a burgess, dead by 1660. [AA.F1.1.1]

WEBSTER, THOMAS, in Caldham, 1744. [NRS.RH11.70.7]

WEBSTER, WILLIAM, in Aberlemno, 1691. [NRS.E69.11.1]

WEBSTER, WILLIAM, in Kinnell, 1691. [NRS.E69.11.1]

WEBSTER, WILLIAM, versus John Robert, Forfar Burgh Court, 1 December 1784, in Forfar, 1791. [AA.F1.8.1][NRS.E326.1.169]

WEBSTER, Mrs, in Forfar, 1785. [NRS.E326.3.19]

WEIR, THOMAS, in Forfar, 1691. [NRS.E60.11.1]

WELCH, JAMES, a merchant in Forfar, sasine, 1766. [NRS.RS35.21.411]

WEMYSS, JOHN, indweller in Brechin, and spouse Margaret Laing, testament, 1650, Comm. Brechin. [NRS]

WHITE, ALEXANDER, a shoemaker burgess of Forfar, husband of Margaret ..., and heir to David White a shoemaker burgess of Forfar, his brother, 1716; sasine, 1720. [NRS.GD1.61.13/14]

WHYTE, DAVID, a skinner in Brechin, husband of Margaret Bowman, sasine, 1655. [NRS.RS35.S2.IV.385]

WHYTE, DAVID, a glover in Brechin, husband of Janet Watson, sasine, 1674. [NRS.RS35.S3.V.347]

WHYTE, DAVID, a smith or hammerman in Kirriemuir, 1716, 1738, 1744. [NRS.CH2.1302.1.103; CH2.1302.221; RH11.70.7]

WHITE, DAVID, a cordiner burgess of Forfar, and spouse Isobel Foular, in Forfar, 1678, 1687, [NRS.GD1.61.9/10] [AA.F1.1.2], in Forfar,1691. [NRS.E69.11.1]

THE PEOPLE OF STRATHMORE, 1600-1799

WHITE, DAVID, the elder, Deacon of the Shoemakers of Forfar, a deed, 1707; 1708. [NRS.RD4.100.463; NRAS.NA7365]

WHITE, DAVID, the younger, a shoemaker in Forfar, spouse Elizabeth Johnstone, testament, 1713, Comm. St Andrews. [NRS.NRAS.NA7365]

WHYT, JAMES, a tailor burgess of Forfar, was appointed as Deacon of the Tailors' Craft of Forfar, 1619. [RBF#214]

WHITE, JAMES, in Kinnell, 1691. [NRS.E69.11.1]

WHYTE, JAMES, versus his debtors, Forfar Burgh Court, 28 November 1785. [AA.F1.8.1]

WHYTE, JAMES, 1787. [NRS.CH2.1302.2/125]

WHYTE, JOHN, in Forfar,1691. [NRS.E69.11.1]

WHITE, JOHN, in Guthrie, 1691. [NRS.E69.11.1]

WHYTE, JOHN, a merchant in Kirriemuir, 1742, 1746; sasine, 1760; testament, 1774, Comm. St Andrews. [NRS.RH11.70.7; RS35.35.19.176]

WHITE, JOHN, a smith in Kirriemuir, spouse of Isobel Fender, sasine, 1777. [NRS.RS35.26.143]

WHYTE, JOHN, a weaver in Logy, 1745. [NRS.RH11.70.7]

WHITE, JOHN, late Deacon of the Shoemakers of Forfar, a sasine witness, 1748. [AA.F1.4.3/17]

WHYTE, RICHARD, a brabiner in Easter Drums, Brechin, spouse of Jean Connall, testament, 1630, Comm. Brechin. [NRS]

WHYTE, ROBERT, versus William Dildarg, Forfar Burgh Court, 2 June 1784. [AA.F1.8.1]

WHYTE, THOMAS, a pewterer in Brechin, son of John Whyte a pewterer there, and father of Janet, Margaret, sasine, 1664. [NRS.RS35.S3.II.182]

WHYTE, THOMAS, versus Donald and Butchart, Forfar Burgh Court, 29 December 1784, 7 January 1785; 16 November 1785. [AA.F1.8.1]

WHYTE, WILLIAM, a merchant in Kirriemuir, husband of Isobel Buchan, a sasine, 1648. [NRS.RS35.S2.III.180]

WHITE, WILLIAM, a merchant in Kirriemuir, spouse of Christian Steel, sasine, 1706. [NRS.RS35.11.335]

WHITEBURN, JOHN, in Hillside of Finavon, Oathlaw, testament, 1688, Comm. Brechin. [NRS]

WHITEBURN, ROBERT, versus .... Neave, Forfar Burgh Court, 20 April 1785. [AA.F1.8.1]

WHYTECROSS, ALEXANDER, a weaver in the Roods of Kirriemuir, grandson of John Whytecross a weaver there, sasine, 1755. [NRS.RS35.18.86/205]

WHITELAW, AGNES, grand-daughter of Alexander Whitelaw a shoemaker in Forfar, sasine, 1738. [NRS.RS35.15.580]

WHYTELAW, ALEXANDER, a cordiner in Forfar, ca.1645. [Forfar gravestone]

WHITELAW, ALEXANDER, a shoemaker in Forfar, sasine,1738. [NRS.RS35.15.580]

WHYTELAW, JOHN, a councillor in Forfar, 1690. [AA.F1.1.2] in Forfar,1691. [NRS.E69.11.1]

WHITTET, WILLIAM, in Glamis, 1691. [NRS.E69.11.1]

WHITTON, PATRICK, in Methie Inverarity, 1691. [NRS.E69.11.1]

WIGHTMAN, DAVID, born 1695, died 1760, wife Janet Sturrock, born 1691, died 1770. [Glamis gravestone]

WILKIE, ALEXANDER, in Kinnell, 1691. [NRS.E69.11.1]

WILKIE, ANN, in Clock Milne, 1730. [NRS.CH2.1302.179]

WILKIE, ANN, in Kirriemuir, 1736. [NRS.CH2.1302.211]

WILKIE, ARCHIBALD, in Hillside of Finavon, testament, 1623, Comm. Brechin. [NRS]

WILKIE, JAMES, a merchant in Kirriemuir, husband of Isobel Adamson, 1743, sasine 1750. [NRS.RH11.70.7; RS35.17.370]

WILKIE, JOHN, in Kirriemuir, June 1686. [NRS.RH11.70.1/3]

WILKIE, JOHN, in Tannadice, 1691. [NRS.E69.11.1]

THE PEOPLE OF STRATHMORE, 1600-1799

WILKIE, JOHN, in Kirriemuir, 1734. [NRS.CH2.1302.207]

WILKIE, PATRICK, schoolmaster in Airlie, Angus, 1690. [SHS.4.2]

WILKIE, THOMAS, in Muirhouses, Kirriemuir, husband of Isobel Smith, testament, 1641, Comm. St Andrews. [NRS]

WILKIE, ROBERT, 1766. [NRS.CH2.1302.2/25]

WILKIE, THOMAS, in Aberlemno, 1691. [NRS.E69.11.1]

WILKIE, THOMAS, versus James Thom, Forfar Burgh Court, 22 October 1784; versus John Tindal, Forfar Burgh Court, 17 November 1784. [AA.F1.8.1]

WILKIE, THOMAS. 1786. [NRS.CH2.1302.2/121]

WILL, DAVID, in Over Tenements of Caldhame, a burgess of Brechin, husband of Margaret Black, sasine, 1684. [NRS.RS35.S3.VIII.84]

WILL, JAMES, in Oathlaw, 1691. [NRS.E69.11.1]

WILL, JEAN, spouse John Dirow, in Adicat, Strathcathro, testament, 1661, Comm. Brechin. [NRS]

WILL, JOHN, a cordiner citizen of Brechin, 1621, husband of Elizabeth Smith, sasine, 1639; testament, 1646, Comm. Brechin. [NRS.RS35.S2.I.547][RPCS.XII.427]

WILLIAMSON, DAVID, in Holmylne, parish of Brechin, testament, 1634, Comm. Brechin. [NRS]

WILLIAMSON, ISABEL, in Kirriemuir, 1725. [NRS.CH2.1302.149]

WILLIAMSON, JAMES, in Forfar,1691. [NRS.E69.11.1]

WILLIAMSON, LUDOVIC, a weaver in Kirriemuir, spouse of Elspeth Marshall, sasine, 1704. [NRS.RS35.10.424]

WILLIAMSON, MARGARET, relict of William Russell sometime gardener in Kirriemuir, 1744. [NRS.RH11.70.7]

WILLIAMSON, THOMAS, a wheelwright in Brechin, husband of Janet Gibson, sasine, 1662. [NRS.RS35.S3.I.316, etc]

WILSON, ALEXANDER, in Tannadice, 1691. [NRS.E69.11.1]

WILSON, CHARLES, tenant in Bastard Brae, parish of Kirriemuir, testament, 1786, Comm. St Andrews. [NRS]

WILSON, DAVID, and spouse Elspet Medden in Kincraig, Brechin, testament, 1636, Comm. Brechin. [NRS]

WILSON, DAVID, in Forfar,1691. [NRS.E69.11.1]

WILSON, DAVID, versus ....Butchart, Forfar Burgh Court, 25 June 1784. [AA.F1.8.1]

WILSON, ISOBELL, spouse to Alexander Beanie (or Binny) a burgess of Forfar, died in 1651. [Forfar gravestone]

WILSON, ISABEL, spouse of Andrew Ballentyne, a merchant in Kirriemuir, a sasine, 1750. [NRS.RS35.17.177]

WILSON, JAMES, a bailie of Forfar, 1660. [AA.F1.1.1]

WILSON, JAMES, a maltman in Forfar, a tack, 1669.[NRS.RD3.22.248]

WILSON, JAMES, miller at Balgonie mylne, 1690. [AA.F1.1.2]

WILSON, JAMES, in Oathlaw, 1691. [NRS.E69.11.1]

WILSON, JOHN, in Kirriemuir, husband of Isabel Mearns, a sasine, 1620. [NRS.RS35.S1.I.120]

WILSON, JOHN, grieve at the Mains of Kinnordie, 1742. [NRS.RH11.70.7]

WILSON, KATHERINE, an indweller of Brechin, testament, 1611, Comm. Edinburgh. [NRS]

WILSON, MARY, in Glamis, 1681. [NRS.E69.11.1]

WILSON, P., versus William Potter, Forfar Burgh Court, 4 February 1785. [AA.F1.8.1]

WILSON, ROBERT, in Dollinch, Kirriemuir, testament, 1617, Comm. St Andrews. [NRS]

WILSON, SYLVESTER, 1745. [NRS.RH11.70.7]

WILSON, THOMAS, son of the late James Wilson maltman, was admitted as a burgess and freeman of Forfar, 1686. [AA.F1.1.2]

THE PEOPLE OF STRATHMORE, 1600-1799

WILSON, WILLIAM, burgess of Brechin, husband of Catharine Barclay, sasine, 1638. [NRS.RS35.S2.I.275]

WILSON, WILLIAM, servant to David Brown, 1737. [NRS.CH2.1302.215]

WILSON, WILLIAM, in Standheugh, 1746. [NRS.RH11.70.7]

WILSON, WILLIAM, versus Cooper and Mitchell, Forfar Burgh Court, 1 September 1784. [AA.F1.8.1]

WINDRAM, DAVID, sr., in Little Carcary, Farnell, testament, 1629, Comm. Brechin. [NRS]

WINDRAM, DAVID, merchant in Idvie, testament, 1737, Comm. St Andrews. [NRS]

WINRAM, JOHN, born 1583, died 1 February 1619, husband of Margaret Watt. [non extant Brechin gravestone]

WINDRAM, THOMAS, son of the laird of Newton, was admitted as a burgess of Forfar, 1661. [AA.F1.1.1]

WINTER, GEORGE, in Hudhill, Kirriemuir, husband of Isobel Watson, testament, 1620, Comm. St Andrews. [NRS]

WINTER, ROBERT, servant to William Lyon an advocate, 1742. [NRS.RH11.70.7]

WINTER, WILLIAM, in Tannadice, 1691. [NRS.E69.11.1]

WINTON, ELIZABETH, relict of Peter Oliphant of Turing, testament, 1647, Comm. Brechin. [NRS]

WISHART, ALEXANDER, a glover burgess of Brechin, and spouse Jean Longsandie, testament, 1683, Comm. Brechin. [NRS]

WISHART, ANDREW, and spouse Lucress Beaton, in Murton, Strathcathro, testament, 1623, Comm. Brechin. [NRS]

WISHART, ANDREW, a tailor in Brechin, 1632. [RGS.VIII.1938]

WISHART, CATHERINE, daughter of the late Thomas Wishart, in Balnadarg, Kirriemuir, testament, 1616, Comm. St Andrews. [NRS]

WISHART, DAVID, in Rescobie, 1691. [NRS.E69.11.1]

THE PEOPLE OF STRATHMORE, 1600-1799

WISHART, GEORGE, in Ballindarg, Kirriemuir, testament,1601, Comm. Edinburgh. [NRS]

WISHART, GILBERT, late minister of Dunnichen, testament, 1688, Comm. Brechin. [NRS]

WISHART, JOHN, son of Alexander Wishart, a glover in Brechin, sasine, 1686. [NRS.RS35.S3.VIII.526]

WISHART, THOMAS, in Ballindarg, Kirriemuir, father of Marion, testament, 1605, Comm. Edinburgh. [NRS]

WOOD, ALEXANDER, and spouse Margaret Adam, in Brockhollow, Oathlaw, testament, 1667, Comm. Brechin. [NRS] shoemaker burgess of Forfar, born 1588, died 1666, wife Margaret Adam, born 1594, died 1668. [Kirriemuir gravestone]

WOOD, ALEXANDER, in Forfar, spouse Margaret Guthrie, sasine, 1680. [NRS.RS35.S3.VII.252]

WOOD, ALEXANDER, versus Baxter and Smith, Forfar Burgh Court, 5 November 1784. [AA.F1.8.1]

WOOD, ANDREW, born 1624, a cordiner in Kirriemuir, died 1679. [Kirriemuir gravestone] [NRS.RS35.S3.VII.22]

WOOD, DAVID, born 1569, eldest son of James Wood a cordiner burgess, died on 1647, spouse of Eupham Cuthbert. [Forfar gravestone]

WOOD, DAVID, a mason, was admitted as a burgess and freeman of Forfar, 1690. [AA.F1.1.2]

WOOD, DAVID, a bailie of Forfar, wife Margaret Stevenson, 1690; a deed, 1693, a sasine, 1695. [NRS.GD1.61.11; RD4.72.417/1250] [AA.F5.92; F1.1.2] , in Forfar,1691. [NRS.E69.11.1]

WOOD, GEORGE, burgess of Forfar, 1611, died in February 1642. [RPCS.VII.19] [Forfar gravestone]

WOOD, GEORGE, a bailie of Forfar, relict Elizabeth Piggot, sasine, 1655; receipt, 1659; bond, 1669; deeds, 1687, 1689. [NRS.GD1.64.3; RD4.23.119; RD3.66.481; RD3.70.160] [AA.F5.32] , in Forfar,1691. [NRS.E69.11.1]

WOOD, GEORGE, a cordiner in Kirriemuir, husband of Margaret Smyth, sasines,1669. [NRS.RS35.S3.IV.305]

THE PEOPLE OF STRATHMORE, 1600-1799

WOOD, GEORGE, a burgess of Forfar, spouse of Mary Mathie, testament, 1681, Comm. St Andrews. [NRS] [AA.F1.1.2]

WOOD, GEORGE, in Kirriemuir, husband of Isobel Mackie, sasines, 1686. [NRS.RS35.S3.VIII.218]

WOOD, GEORGE, a councillor and treasurer in Forfar, 1680s, 1690; a bailie of Forfar, deed, 1696.
[AA.F1.1.2][NRS.RD3.86.108]

WOOD, GEORGE, a cordiner in Kirriemuir, sasine, 1730. [NRS.RS35.14.601]

WOOD, GRIZEL, in Forfar, 1655. [NRS.GD1.64.3]

WOOD, HARRY, a merchant burgess of Forfar, a bond, 1669; testament, 1674. [NRS.RD4.25.464; NRAS#1750, bundle 20]

WOOD, HELEN, in Forfar,1691. [NRS.E69.11.1]

WOOD, HENRY, a shoemaker in Brechin, husband of Janet Fenton, parents of Katherine, sasine,1672. [NRS.RS35.S3.V.266]

WOOD, HENRY, a merchant in Forfar, sasine, 1704. [NRS.RS35.10.458]

WOOD, ISABEL, a petition, Forfar Burgh Court, 16 June 1784. [AA.F1.8.1]

WOOD, JAMES, a cordiner and burgess of Forfar, died in 1607. [Forfar gravestone]

WOOD, JAMES, son of Andrew Wood, a cordiner in Kirriemuir, sasines,1679, 1686. [NRS.RS35.S3.VII.22; RH11.70.1/2]

WOOD, JANET, in Forfar, 1655. [NRS.GD1.64.3]

WOOD, JOHN, a cordiner in Brechin, sasine,1691, husband of Janet Fawnes. [RPCS.XVI.605] [NRS.RS35.S3.VII.155]

WOOD, JOHN, a vintner in Forfar, a deed, 1702. [NRS.RD3.99.1.141]

WOOD, JOHN, a writer in Forfar, a deed, 1702. [NRS.RD3.99.1.41]

WOOD, JOHN, in Forfar, witness, 1744. [AA.F1.4.3/12]

WOOD, MARGARET, relict of Alexander Beg in Kirkhill of Farnell, testament, 1625, Comm. Brechin. [NRS]

WOOD, MARGARET, daughter of the late Andrew Wood sometime a cordiner in Kirriemuir, testament, 1683, Comm. St Andrews. [NRS]

WOOD, MARGARET, relict of David Taylor late tenant of Chapel of Auldbar, testament, 1776, Comm. Brechin. [NRS]

WOOD, PATRICK, a cordiner in Brechin, 1621. [RPCS.XII.427]

WOOD, PATRICK, of Hillhead, 1742, 1745. [NRS.RH11.70.7]

WOOD, RODGER, 1660. [AA.F1.1.1]

WOOD, WILLIAM, in Oathlaw, 1691. [NRS.E69.11.1]

WOOD, WILLIAM, son of Henry Wood, a merchant in Forfar, a sasine, 1704. [NRS.RS35.X.458]

WRIGHT, ALEXANDER, in Kirriemuir, a sasine, 1766. [NRS.RS35.21.360]

WRIGHT, DAVID, in Farnell, 1691. [NRS.E69.11.1]

WRIGHT, GEORGE, a notary burgess of Brechin, 1609, testament, 1623, Comm. Brechin. [NRS][RPCS.VIII.704]

WRIGHT, JAMES, in Dunnichen, 1691. [NRS.E69.11.1]

WRIGHT, JOHN, foreman of the jury at a witch-trial in Forfar, 1662. [AA.F5.35]

WYLD, JAMES, a wright burgess of Brechin, testament, 1645; spouse Christian Laing, testament, 1640, Comm. Brechin. [NRS]

WYLD, JAMES, in South Muir of Forfar, tacks, 1708, 1716. [AA.F5/23]

WYLLIE, ANDREW, versus Masterton and Mitchell, 9 June 1784; versus Mundy and Husband, Forfar Burgh Court, 25 August 1784. [AA.F1.8.1]

WYLLIE, DAVID, in Glamis, 1681. [NRS.E69.11.1]

WYLLIE, JAMES, a writer in Forfar, 1777, 1791. [NRS.NRAS#124/4/1/78, 80; E326.1.169]

THE PEOPLE OF STRATHMORE, 1600-1799

WYLLIE, JAMES, versus Duncan and Mands, Forfar Burgh Court, 23 February 1785, 20 April 1785. [AA.F1.8.1]

WYLLIE, JANET, spouse to David Palmer, merchant at Wardend of Keithock, testament, 1750, Comm. Brechin.[NRS]

WYLLIE, JOHN, spouse Isobel Forsyth, in Careston, testament, 1626, Comm. Brechin. [NRS]

WYLLIE, THOMAS, in Kinnell, 1691. [NRS.E69.11.1]

YEAMAN, AGNES, 1742. [NRS.RH11.70.7]

YEAMAN, JAMES, in Forfar, 1691. [NRS.E69.11.1]

YEAMAN, WILLIAM, was admitted as a burgess of Forfar, 1661. [AA.F1.1.1]

YOUNG, AGNES, spouse of Andrew Key a tanner in Kirriemuir, a sasine, 1620. [NRS.RS33.S1.110]

YOUNG, ALEXANDER, merchant in Brechin, husband of Agnes Baillie, 1686; late bailie of Brechin, 1691. [NRS.RS35.S3.VIII.269, etc][RPCS.XVI.605]

YOUNG, ALEXANDER, in Oathlaw, 1691. [NRS.E69.11.1]

YOUNG, ANDREW, in Oathlaw, 1691. [NRS.E69.11.1]

YOUNG, ANDREW, in Wardend of Finavon, testament, 1702, Comm. Brechin. [NRS]

YOUNG, CATHERINE, spouse of David Ellis, a brewer and wright in Kirriemuir, a sasine, 1704. [NRS.RS35.10.523]

YOUNG, DAVID, in Barhill, parish of Brechin, testament, 1649, Comm. Brechin. [NRS]

YOUNG, DAVID, a flesher in Kirriemuir, husband of Janet Key, a sasine,1644. [NRS.RS35.S2.II.375]

YOUNG, DAVID, a baxter in Kirriemuir, sasine, 1694. [NRS.RS35.S3.IX.433]

YOUNG, DAVID, a baxter in Kirriemuir, a sasine, 1718. [NRS.RS35.13.206]

YOUNG, DAVID, a merchant in Kirriemuir, 1742, 1745, a sasine,1769. [NRS.RH11.70.7; RS35.22.383]

THE PEOPLE OF STRATHMORE, 1600-1799

YOUNG, DAVID, in the Backmuir of Glaswell, 1745. [NRS.RH11.70.7]

YOUNG, DONALD, in Forfar, 1691. [NRS.E69.11.1]

YOUNG, EUPHAME, mother of David Ogilvie of Clova, a sasine, 1643. [NRS.RS33.S2.II.113]

YOUNG, ISABEL, spouse of David Cadger in Kirriemuir, a sasine, 1704. [NRS.RS35.10.423]

YOUNG, JAMES, in Balmakathy, 1736. [NRS.CH2.1302.211]

YOUNG, JAMES, versus ... Soutar, Forfar Burgh Court, 29 December 1784. [AA.F1.8.1]

YOUNG, JOHN, in Auchquiroche, Kingoldrum, testament, 1610, Comm. Brechin. [NRS]

YOUNG, JOHN, in Beanstie, Kirriemuir, testament,1685, Comm. St Andrews. [NRS]

YOUNG, JOHN, in Kinnell, 1691. [NRS.E69.11.1]

YOUNG, JOHN, in Caldham, 1745. [NRS.RH11.70.7]

YOUNG, JOHN, a writer in Forfar, a sasine, 1771. [NRS.RS35.23.195]

YOUNG, MARGARET, spouse to James Daw in Carcary, Farnell, 1638, Comm. Brechin. [NRS]

YOUNG, MARGARET, daughter of David Young, a baxter in Kirriemuir, and spouse of Andrew Murdoch a baxter there, a sasine, 1718. [NRS.RS35.13.206]

YOUNG, PATRICK, a mason in Kirriemuir, a sasine, 1779. [NRS.RS35.27.230]

YOUNG, ROBERT, of Auldbar in Aberlemno, 1691. [NRS.E69.11.1]

YOUNG, ROBERT, in Forfar, 1785, 1791; versus Peter Jack, Forfar Burgh Court, 17 November 1784, 23 February 1785. [AA.F1.8.1] [NRS.E326.3.19]

YOUNG, THOMAS, a cordiner in Kirriemuir, sasine 1639. [NRS.RS35.S2.I.456]

THE PEOPLE OF STRATHMORE, 1600-1799

YOUNG, THOMAS, servant to Alexander Whyte in Ballochs, 1745. [NRS.RH11.70.7]

YOUNG, THOMAS, a merchant in Kirriemuir, husband of Margaret Martin, sasine, 1775. [NRS.RS35.25.250]

YOUNG, WILLIAM, a writer in Forfar, 1777. [NRS.NRAS#124/4/1/78]

YOUNG, WILLIAM, a merchant in Forfar, versus .... Robertson, Forfar Burgh Court, 5 October 1784; 1787. [AA.F1.8.1; F5.153] in Forfar, 1791. [NRS.E326.1.169]

REFERENCES

AA = Angus Archives, Restenneth

F = Fastii Ecclesiae Scoticanae

Imm. NE= Immigrants to New England

JA = Jacobites of Angus, 1689-1746

NRAS = National Register of Archives, Scotland

NEHGS = New England Historic Genealogical Society

NRS = National Records of Scotland, Edinburgh

RBF = The Royal Burgh of Forfar,[Forfar, 1902]

RGS = Register of the Great Seal of Scotland, series

RPCS = Register of the Privy Council of Scotland, series

WCB =The Compt Buik of David Wedderburne. [Edinburgh, 1898]

www.ingramcontent.com/pod-product-compliance
Lightning Source LLC
Chambersburg PA
CBHW070257230426
43664CB00014B/2564